WALKING & CLIMBING
IN THE ALPS
A GUIDE TO THE FINEST ROUTES

SWAN·HILL
PRESS

WALKING & CLIMBING IN THE ALPS
A GUIDE TO THE FINEST ROUTES

Contents

Author
Stefano Ardito

Illustrations of the routes
Mina Carpi

Three-dimensional maps
Luigi Siclari

Editors
Valeria Manferto De Fabianis
Laura Accomazzo

Graphic layout
Patrizia Balocco Lovisetti

Translation
Antony Shugaar

The author and the publisher would like to thank the following persons for their invaluable assistance:
Furio Chiaretta, Michael Pause,
Jean Pierre Nicollet.

1 A walker admires the spires of the Piccole Dolomiti from the "Strada delle Gallerie", one of the most spectacular routes built during the First World War. Photograph by Stefano Ardito

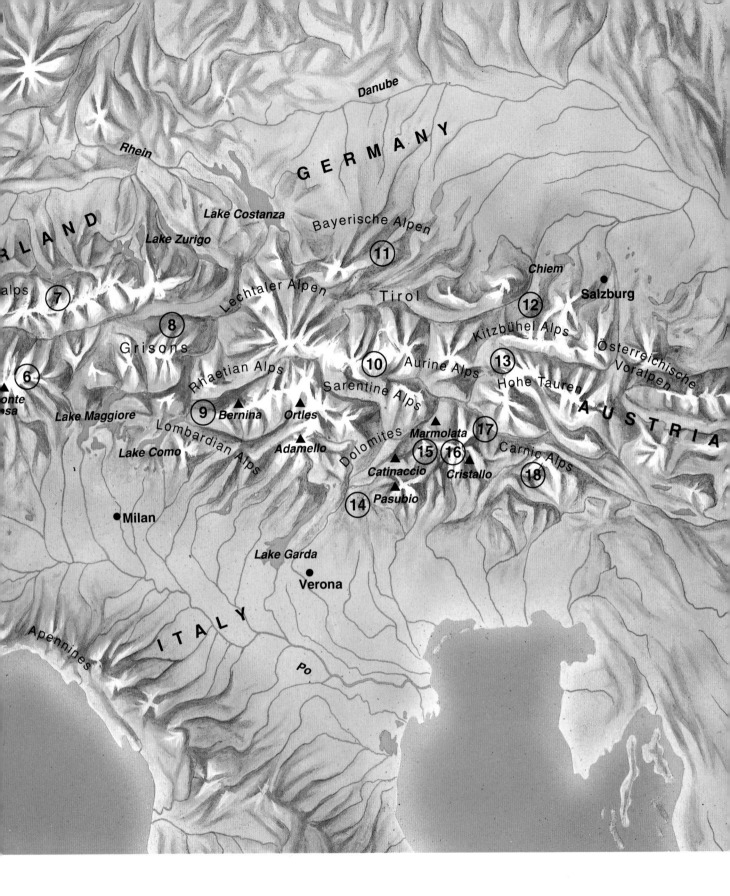

First Published in the UK in 1995 by Swan Hill
Press, an imprint of Airlife Publishing Ltd.

British Library
Cataloguing in Publication Data
A catalogue record for this book is available from
the British Library

ISBN 1 85310 579 1

Printed in Italy by Grafedit Bergamo, Italy.
Colour separations by La Cromografica,
Ghemme (Novara), Italy.

SWAN HILL PRESS
an imprint of AirlifePublishing Ltd.
101 Longden Road,
Shrewsbury SY3 9EB, England

INTRODUCTION

"What moves you, o humanity, to abandon your homes in the city, to leave your relatives and friends, and to go to rural settings, in mountains and valleys — what moves you, if not the beauty of the world?" Quoting these words in order to place Leonardo da Vinci among the forerunners of those who trek through the Himalayas or the Alps would be going too far, even for the most enthusiastic walker or author. However, the yearning for knowledge and desire to test oneself, and the exploratory urge expressed by the great Tuscan man of letters and art, are all remarkably similar to the impulses that drive people to trek, at the dawn of the third millennium. "Thousands of tired, hypercivilized people are beginning to discover that going to the mountains means going home, and that unspoiled nature is a basic human need. And that parks and nature reserves are not only sources of lumber and water for irrigation, but also sources of life."

John Muir, founder of the *Sierra Club* and the father of the great parks of the American West, was truly an enthusiastic walker. He had no knowledge of the techniques of alpinism, but Muir was gifted with indomitable energy, and he walked from east to west and from north to south across the mountains and valleys of California, Oregon, Alaska, and Maine. Through personal meetings, speeches, lectures, and books, his passion was communicated to politicians, government officials, and the mass of American citizens. On the one hand, he made possible the creation of national parks such as Yosemite, Sequoia, King's Canyon, and the Grand

Canyon. On the other, John Muir helped to lay the foundations for the modern fashion of walking. *Trek* is a South African word, formed in Afrikaans from the Dutch word *walken* meaning "to travel." The *voortrekkers* are still considered by the South Africans of Dutch descent to be the forefathers and inspirational figures of the fatherland. For the entire nineteenth century, leaving the Cape colony in the hands of the British, the *voortrekkers* crossed with their carts the plains, deserts, and mountains of the inland, heading for the Orange Free State, the Transvaal, and Natal. The first one to use the word "walking" to describe a trek in the mountains was Jimmy Roberts,

a Briton and former officer of the Gurkha Regiment, stationed in Kathmandu, the capital of Nepal. After organizing teams of native porters and sherpas for the earliest mountain climbing expeditions admitted into Nepal after 1950, Roberts had the idea of helping visiting walkers to go walking along the ancient and spectacular trails leading to Annapurna, Everest, and Makalu. The idea was immediately successful. Hiking has been a leisure activity in the Alps for more than a century. Mountain climbers and "active pedestrians," as the mostly British walkers called themselves, were the target reader for the guides written by

Edward Whymper and John Ball; they travelled through the great mountain chain on their summer holidays, or as part of long or even exceedingly long travels — the much vaunted Grand Tour — across continental Europe. For those who were in better shape, as we see from the books and journals of Edward Whymper, walking across one pass after another, from Chamonix to Zermatt, or from Courmayeur to La Grave, was certainly not tiring, but rather a way of relaxing from the true trials of climbing rock faces and making one's way across icy slopes. Walking, at the very most, was considered to be a reasonable way of getting into shape. As early as 1871, however,

Leslie Stephen, an honored member of the Alpine Club and the climber of many important new rates on major peaks (as well as being the father of the writer Virginia Woolf) set forth the concept of the Alps as the "Playground of Europe," where an entire continent might come to restore itself in health-giving exercise. Between the two world wars, the type of play practiced in this "playground" — whether it was alpinism or mere walking — became the pastime of the masses, as the playground of the Alps could be reached easily by many of the inhabitants of the cities of Vienna, Milan, Lyon, and Munich. Then came cars and skiing, and for most Europeans the Alps came to take on an entirely new meaning. The peaks, the great climbs, the trails remained where they had been for decades. For many, however,

hotels on the valley, instead of being merely base camps, became the main attractions. Over the last twenty years, the picture has changed radically once again. Prompted by the stories brought back by climbers of walks among forests, waterfalls, and ibex, and encouraged by tales from Roberts and the numerous followers that have imitated his work, millions of Europeans have begun to trek once again. Some of those European walkers have begun to look further afield, heading off for the Himalayas and the Karakorum, Kilimanjaro, the Andes. For most Europeans, however, there was nothing but the Alps. Year after year, the *Alte Vie* of Italy, the *Grandes Randonnées* of France, the *Fernwanderwegen* of Bavaria and Austria have once again begun to teem with walkers. Perhaps

6 top The massifs that stand between Italy, France, and Switzerland offer the most dramatic glacial landscapes in the Alps. This is the northern slope of the Barre des Ecrins (4,104 metres) in the heart of the French massif of the Oisans.
Photograph by
Jean Pierre Nicollet

6 centre An ancient Roman quarry at an altitude of sixteen hundred metres on the Vercors plateau indicates the degree to which human civilization had reached the high mountains even in early times.
Photograph by
Stefano Ardito

6 bottom No walker is immune to the charm of the edelweiss: these blooms were photographed among the rocks of the Italian Dente del Pasubio.
Photograph by
Stefano Ardito

certain French studies overstate things when they say that there are now more people walking in the mountains every summer than sunning on the beaches. Yet, without a doubt, many of the old trails, once used only by mountaineers and soldiers, pilgrims and merchants, now receive heavy traffic.
And deservedly so. To anyone who observes them from a distance, the Alps may seem all alike: an endless procession of forests and glaciers, chamoises and marmots, romantic wooden sheepherders' huts and modern ski facilities. This is not the case, however: the great arc of mountains that link Vienna and Mitteleuropa with Nice and the Mediterranean is extremely rich in variety, and abounds in surprises. Facing southward, the peaks and valleys of Provence, the Cuneese and

the Italian Prealps offer the visitor a rich array of rocky, sun-drenched, high valleys and uplands that are reminiscent of Anatolia, scattered patches of Mediterranean vegetation. On the slopes that face north — the Tarvisiano and the forests of Carinthia and the Tyrol, the Engadine and the Berchetsgaden Alps — the endless fir-tree forests that teem with herds of deer, under the watchful hovering eye of the eagle and the wood-grouse are more reminiscent of Scandinavia or Canada. The glaciers like the Mer de Glace, the Aletsch, the Pasterze,
and the Gorner offer a tour through space and time, reaching north to the Arctic and backward in time to the era when great sheets of ice covered much of what we now call Europe. Nature and wildland in the Alps, however, are capable of confusing the accepted categories.

In the limestone massifs in particular — the Vercors, Triglav, the Wilder Kaiser, and many corners and high points of the Dolomites — typically Nordic features mix abundantly and charmingly with southern, patently Mediterranean aspects. In these places and in many others, it is precisely this close alternation of forests and rock walls, of waterfalls, mountain torrents, and Karst highlands that drives the basic experience. It is no accident that the the Dolomite High Route No 1 — the very trail that offers most of this sort of contrast — should be the most popular and the most crowded in the entire range. Alongside the variety of the landscapes, one cannot help but noting the rich variety of nature and the abundant array of human culture. Over the last several decades, both humans and wildland here have been through much. Hunters, subjected to almost no restraints whatsoever, have pushed many of the most precious species to the brink of extinction. A model of economic development based chiefly on summer and winter tourism has created a common way of life for the Langue d'Oc people, the "Alps of the Sun," and the Tyroleans and Carinthians, likening the men born at the foot of Mont Blanc and the Matterhorn to those who live at the base of the limestone peaks to the east. Not everything has been lost, of course, as those who frequently trek on Alpine trails are well aware. The tireless labour and dedication of a

7 top The village of Chiappera, at the head of the Val Maira, in the shadow of the Torre Castello, is one of the most distinctive little towns in the Piedmontese Alps. Photograph by A. Gogna/K3

7 centre The slender, pointed bell tower of Elva, an ancient village overlooking the Gorge of Elva, is one of the most distinctive little towns in the valleys of the province of Cuneo. Photograph by Stefano Ardito

7 bottom In the northeastern corner of Italy, on the border with Slovenia and Austria, the forest around Tarvisio is one of the loveliest stretches of woods in the Alps. Here we see a view of the sides of the high valley of Rio Bianco, at the easternmost tip of the Carnic Alps. Photograph by Gianluca Boetti

small number of humans has led to the rescue of the ibex, the reintroduction of the bearded vulture and protection for the eagle and the wood-grouse. Other animals have rescued themselves, by occupying spaces believed lost. The wolf that returns from Abruzzi to the peaks and high valleys of France, the bear and the lynx that have spread out from the fastnesses of the east, scattering into the most remote corners and crannies of Trentino and Friuli — all these instances are so many demonstrations that nature is deeply vigorous and vital, and are so many more reasons to walk, trek, and climb these mountains. And the same encouraging news can be

reported concerning the human beings of these mountains, too. What seemed like just moments before ski lifts, four-wheel-drive vehicles, and rainbow-coloured ski outfits flooded the entire chain, reducing it one huge theme park, the pride of the ethnic minorities — Langue d'Oc people, Walser, Ladins, Cimbers and so on — brought about a rebirth of traditional literature, music, traditions, and architecture. Once again, the wealth of history and of the stories of individual men is another of the chief attractions to those who keep their eyes open as they move through the Alps. On the trails that run across the great mountain chain, linking Italy to the heart of Europe, marks and signs have been left, by Roman legions marching millennia ago toward Gaul, by Saracen armies marching from the Cote d'Azur to the Val Pesio, by the soldiers of Napoleon and those of Hannibal, not to mention the writers and painters — Goethe, Ruskin, Sargent, and Carducci — who have rendered famous peaks and villages that were once completely unknown. Ancient fortresses, medieval castles, Renaissance palaces overlook the roads, mule-tracks, and high passes in their thousands. Almost everywhere, in the trails described in this book, one can find ancient cobble-roads and trails carved into the rock, arched bridges, so-called "of the Devil" and little churches perched on crags. Some of the trails that are described in this book are modern inventions. Many of them, however, follow very ancient routes: the roads that the Walser used in their migrations, the Roman roads running around Mont Blanc, the thousand-year-old salt routes. For many, that leaves one question, the most important of all. "Can I do it myself?" Answering "everyone can do it" is charming but deceptive. It is more accurate to say that a great many can do it: if, of course, they are well equipped, in good shape, and perhaps accompanied by a guide or a more experienced friend. In the pages that follow, the reader will find a number of practical suggestions, and then an array of routes through every corner of the great mountain chain. Some of these are quite easy, while others involve climbs over glaciers, easy rock scrambling, iron ladders or fixed ropes. Some of the routes are quite brief, with stages that allow one to look around and smell a flower or two. Others — or at least some of the stages — demand great effort and commitment in physical terms. Fortunately, alpine walking from hut to hut has little in common with American rucksacking, in terms of the size of the rucksack. Almost everywhere there are "short cuts". Roads, cable cars, rack railways, allow one to shorten the stages if one is tired or if the weather turns foul. The huts are all quite comfortable. The granite towers, the forests, the waterfalls, and the glaciers, the castles and the dolomite spires are still there. And the same is true of the ibex, eagles, the traditions, and the panoramic vistas. In the Alps, everyone can find an adventure all their own. Bon voyage.

8 top A colourful stand of arnica softens the harsh granite landscape of the rock faces of the Ligoncio and the Sfinge, in the mountains between the Italian Val Masino and the Swiss Val Bregaglia. Photograph by Gianluca Boetti

8 centre top A colorful explosion of yellow anemones enlivens a meadow in the Western Alps, in the heart of the alpine spring (May to June). Photograph by Gianluca Boetti

8 centre bottom In the Alps, the history of mountain climbing is evident at every point. In this picture, the director of the Alpine Museum of Grindelwald displays an old hemp rope used in rescue operations on the north face of the Eiger. Photograph by Stefano Ardito

8 bottom Fine traditional food is another attraction that brings tourists to the valleys of the Alps. A shepherd from Beaufort, in the Vanoise, checks the aging of wheels of "toma" cheese in his aging-house. Photograph by Gianluca Boetti

WHO CAN GO WALKING

This activity is open to one and all — adolescents and the elderly, athletes and armchair sportsfans.

Walking brings one into contact with nature and clean air, but remains an athletic activity, and it requires a minimum of physical preparation. We shall discuss the best ways in the following section. For beginners, we would emphasize in all seriousness that there is a certain psychological commitment required for those who wish to trek in the mountains.

The lovely views at dawn and sunset, the pleasant memories of evenings spent around the fireplace or pot-bellied stove, or of spectacular vistas enjoyed from atop cols and peaks — all of these happy memories in our mind's eye (and those of our friends) conceal other, less pleasant memories, reluctant to come to the fore but equally real. These are memories of climbing endlessly, as the rucksack sags, becoming miraculously more heavy at each step as the sun hammers down mercilessly. Memories of making one's way painfully down through the pelting rain as the village or hut seems to draw ever further away. Memories of finally reaching a hut full to bursting, and having to spend the night on the floor, sometimes despite a perfectly valid reservation. It has been said that mountains and walking are schools of life. We would say simply that the willingness to deal with delays, unforeseen obstacles and problems, uncomfortable situations of all sorts — this is an essential mindset for those who wish to walk the high trails.

HOW TO PREPARE

Those who regularly engage in walking, climbing, or any other of the "endurance" sports, such as jogging or cross-country skiing, will have absolutely no difficulty in adapting to the physical demands of walking. For those who are not exactly spring-chickens, and who lead a fairly sedentary lifestyle, it would be useful to get into shape, perhaps preceded by a medical examination. Even the city park offers excellent opportunities to get into training by taking long and pleasurable walks, making them gradually longer and longer, during the spring, readying

oneself for the more tiring and demanding Alpine treks in the summer. Those who regularly run or walk on flat ground are advised to modify their routes so that they are working on considerable slopes: the muscles and the lungs work differently on a slope than they do on the level. The question of the level of technical difficulty of many of the routes described in this volume, presents itself, as well as that of many others in the various regions of the Alps. The trails described here that include stretches over glaciers or on equipped trails or "via ferrata", although they may be quite easy from the point of view of an alpinist, require some familiarity with the use of an ice axe,

9 *The standard route of the Monch (4,099 metres), in the Bernese Oberland, is an example of how alpine routes between three and four thousand metres require clothing and equipment suited to the high-mountain environment.* Photograph by Stefano Ardito

crampons, harness and rope. This familiarity cannot be conjured up on the spot: it is possible to prepare oneself by attending a course in mountain climbing (organized by climbing clubs and by alpine guides), or one may choose to go on a guided trek, with professional accompaniment.

WHAT ROUTE TO CHOOSE

Altitude, environment, considerations of geography, the degree of technical and physical difficulty — all these factors must enter into one's choice of route. Some walkers prefer the dramatic settings and the high elevations of the Western Alps, while others love

the meadows and scree of the Dolomites or the French, Austrian, or Italian Prealps. There are those who love the wilderness and there are those who love to trek in mountain summer meadows, mountain retreats, and ancient villages; some seek out the most spectacular trails, others avoid the very well known ones, which are inevitabily crowded. There are some who seek out undemanding trails, while others want glaciers and rock scrambling. Of course, personal experience plays some role in the choice: those who have already walked in the Dauphiné and in Piedmont may well feel more interested in the Dolomites and the Wilder Kaiser, while those who are familiar with the Bavarian Pre-alps may feel more drawn toward the sunny limestones of the Lessinia and Garda. Lastly, the estimated expense must affect the decision-making process: as we write, for example, Switzerland, and Germany are more expensive, while France, Italy and the Tyrol remain quite affordable. Therefore, the individual will have to make his own choice. In the introduction to each in the routes in this book, we have attempted to provide the greatest amount of information, to make it easier to make a choice.

ALONE OR IN A GROUP?

The Alps are closer than the Himalayas for some of our readers: therefore, walking with a small group of friends does not place very onerous organizational burdens upon one, nor does travelling with a group make for much of a saving in terms of airfare, hiring sherpas, or renting beasts of burden. Travelling with friends does have certain clear advantages, of course: one is with trusted, familiar people, small groups mesh nicely with the system of huts, it is relatively easy to come to a quick agreement on detours and variant trails. Going with a group tour does have certain advantages however. One gets to know new travelling companions, somebody else bothers with the reservations and the logistics, and if the group is organized by a mountain guide or a mountaineering association, even the least experienced can venture out on equipped trails and glaciers with confidence and in total safety.
The addresses of the local alpine club or of local guides can be found easily in the phone book or in the specialty press. Only in a few areas of Italy and in a few other countries (foremost among them, France) can one still find guides for walking in mid-elevation mountains which is to say, professionals to accompany private clients and groups through the world of woods, scree, and mountain summer meadows. In Italy especially, one should be quite cautious of illegal, not professional guides, who may prove to be hazardous to the safety of their hapless clients.

HUTS, HOTELS, OR TENTS?

More than a hundred and fifty years have passed since the English mountain climber Leslie Stephen

10 top Overnight stays in a tent tend to bring one closer to nature, but they are not always possible in the crowded massifs of the Alps. Here we see a camping site facing the glacier of Trient (Mont Blanc). Photograph by M. Lanfranchi/ Overseas

10 bottom Long ago a hunting lodge belonging to the royal family of the Savoy, the Vittorio Sella hut on the Lauson, which stands at an altitude of 2,584 metres in the heart of the massif of the Gran Paradiso, is a handsome example of wood-and-stone construction. Photograph by F. Raiser/K3

described the Alps as the "Playground of Europe." Nowadays, without a doubt, the Alps are the heartland of the Old World for the tourists of the world, and they are visited every year by millions of walkers, summer climbers, skiers, and tourists of all sorts. It goes without saying that the experience of walking in any of the areas of the Alpine chain is far different from the experience of rucksacking as it is normally practised on the major trails in the United States, Scandinavia, Canada, New Zealand, and South Africa, where a walker must carry in his rucksack everything that he is likely to need over one or more weeks' time.
The treks described in this guide — and dozens more — all offer overnight stays in huts, hotels, bed-and-breakfasts or other facilities for overnight accommodations of all sorts (usually these are huts in the valley, with private rooms, or else large dormitories), so that a walker is only obliged to carry a "day-pack," containing a windbreaker, a camera, whatever technical material is required, and a little food. It is necessary to remember that during the summer, making a reservation is recommended everywhere and is most important in the most crowded huts and hotels. We should point out

that membership of the Italian Alpine Club or any foreign alpine club will lead to considerable savings on overnight stays in huts. Despite all these considerations, a number of walkers still make their way through the Alps with a tent on their backs.
This solution is cheaper, but that is not the only consideration. A tent gives far greater privacy than an overcrowded hut, and it allows a trekr to feel closer to nature. Those who choose to carry and use a tent must take into account that it will probably take longer to travel all of the distances involved (the times given for the routes in this book are estimated for walkers that are not too loaded down). Above all, it should be kept in mind that those who plan to camp out are not exactly welcome in the Alps. There are restrictions in the valley, as well as in the parks and in the many reserves. Other problems may be created by the rocky terrain. For every route, the section entitled "If you want to camp out" gives some helpful information.

CLOTHING AND EQUIPMENT

Until a few years ago, walkers and climbers dressed in the same way. A wool pullover and shirt, breeches, and relatively heavy walking boots. Nowadays, on the classic routes of the

Alps and the other great ranges of Europe, one can run into walkers, walkers, and climbers dressed in a wide range of styles. Some have remained faithful to tradition. Others prefer to wear jeans, while yet others look to the modern technology of *fleece* and *Gore-tex*. Lightness and comfort are of course the most important qualities to be considered in preparing clothing for walking. In order to trek at the average elevations of the Alps (which means in a range of fifteen hundred to three thousand metres, for many of the routes shown here), the best combination is to wear a pair of cotton trousers (if possible, looser and more comfortable than jeans), which can be replaced with a pair of shorts during the hottest hours of the day, and with *fleece* trousers for the colder moments of the day. The classic breeches are still quite comfortable, and can be worn with thermal underwear tights when it gets really cold. For the upper body, a

It is best to choose a model of medium capacity (from fifty to seventy liters), without the cumbersome external frame that often gets tangled in low-hanging vegetation or gets bumped in narrow passages. This rucksack should ideally be equipped with a small rigid inner frame, without external pockets. The truly crucial issue for a walker, of course, is the foot-wear: a mistaken choice here can truly ruin a mountain holiday. It is important that one's walking boots have been thoroughly worn in and tested during the months prior to the trip. Today, walking boots in synthetic material are used by one and all, and they are indeed the best gear for many of the routes indicated here. Only for long treks at high elevation (such as the routes we describe in the Ötztal Alps) is it a good idea to replace them with the plastic boots used generally for climbing on ice and snow. For the many routes that involve stretches of snow, the best solution may be simply to go back to the classic style, meaning

a pair of leather walking boots. It is extremely useful to include in one's rucksack a pair of light footwear in order to give your feet a rest (sandals, jogging shoes which can be worn in the hut or in town).

MAPS, COMPASSES, ORIENTATION

Many of the walking routes in the Alps are marked by painted trail-markers or by signposts, or else by the old-fashioned, amiable, little cairns. On the snow-covered stretches of the classic trails, the tracks of walkers that have gone before are usually quite evident. In most cases, therefore, topographical maps are useful chiefly in "reading" the landscape, rather than for truly finding one's way. Should there be fog, low clouds, or in particularly wild landscape, maps can be true life-savers. Besides a map, it is wise to have a compass and an altimetre: it is of course a good idea to practice using these instruments before one has

wool or *fleece* jumper can be worn over a classic woolen shirt or a more modern sweater made of synthetic material. One absolutely must have complete rain gear (a jacket and trousers) made of *Gore-tex* or some similar material. The list is completed by a wool cap or a cotton hat against the sun, a pair of wool or *fleece* gloves, and a pair of sunglasses. Among the various accessories, one must have a canteen or water-bottle, spare laces for one's walking boots, and a multipurpose penknife (a Swiss Army knife). It is also fundamental to carry a torch, best if it is a headlamp. The rucksack is another fundamental element of the required equipment.

11 In the summer, on a clear day, one can walk in shorts and a sweater along the alpine meadows. The massif of Mont Blanc serves as a backdrop to the meadows of the upper Val Ferret. Photograph by Marco Milani/K3

a chance to test one's skills in a real emergency. Let us mention, moreover, that maps drawn to a scale of 1:25,000, if they are available and well made, are far better than maps drawn to a scale of 1:50,000, like those used by most walkers. The quality of reproduction of the terrain is one important criterion; another is how well the map has been updated. Roads, trails, tracks, huts, and ski resorts pop up with remarkable speed all over the Alps.

CLIMBERS EQUIPMENT

Until the end of the Second World War, climbers almost always used the same equipment, whether they were scaling a great peak in the Western Alps or a rock face in the Dolomites, whether they were venturing out to traverse glaciers or setting out on a Himalayan expedition. The last twenty or thirty

years, however, have led to considerable development of materials and equipment, and an increasingly sharp division between those who practice the various types of mountaineering — divisions that are at once cultural and technical. For even the most demanding walking, one need not bring the sophisticated equipment that is used by top-level rock climbers.

The routes described in this book that require one to cross glaciers or climb peaks rising to four thousand metres or so, demand a number of things: adequate cloth, crampons, an ice axe, harness, rope and karabiners. On the equipped trails, standard equipment, on the other hand, includes harness, a short but strong piece of rope (best if it is 10 or 11 mm), two screw gate karabiners, and in some cases, the very useful abseil device, and a helmet.

An ice axe and crampons can be very useful in the Dolomites at the beginning of the season for crossing short but treacherous stretches of late snow.

A twenty- or thirty-metre length of 9-mm rope can be useful for securing the less experienced.

IN CASE OF TROUBLE

Walking and easy climbing are not activities for daredevils. And yet, according to statistics provided by the mountain rescue operations of all the countries, in Europe the vast majority of accidents in the mountains (80 per cent) take place on easy terrain. Often, the accidents are the result of careless: we would recommend the greatest caution on steep grassy slopes, scree, and snow fields. In case of doubts about one's skill or the conditions in the mountains, one should choose to turn back. In case of an accident of any sort, the most important thing is to remain calm. The group member or group members who set off to call for help must leave injured person or

persons with all the extra clothing and food that they have, establish as closely as possible the exact status of the victim, and the type of assistance that is needed, and mark on a map — if possible — the exact location of the victim. If there are at least three persons, then it is necessary that one member of the group stay with the victim: loneliness and fear can have quite serious consequences.

The injured person or persons should be made comfortable in a place that offers shelter from wind and from rain, though the victim should not be moved at all if there are any

indications of damage to the spinal cord. The victim's boots can be removed only if there is no damage to the feet or ankles.

In the Alps, all of the huts and high-elevation hotels are also equipped to call for the Rescue. In isolated areas, one can make use of the international distress signal.

In order to make a distress signal, one must make a loud noise or visual signal of any type, repeating it six times a minute (once every ten seconds), stop for a minute, and then start over again.

To send a response, one makes a signal as described above three times a minute (once every twenty seconds). Stop for a minute, and then begin again. In the Alps, if the weather allows it, rescues are almost always made by helicopter. It is best to indicate one's location to the crew (all that is needed is an isolated individual with arms upraised and outspread), and after the rescuers arrive, one must obey their every instruction: there will be plenty of time to discuss matters, if that is necessary, down in the valley.

12 left High-elevation hiking in the Austrian mountains requires one to cross a great many high glacier passes. This photograph shows part of the climb up to the Gross Venediger, in the Hohe Tauern. Photograph by Stefano Ardito

12 right Stopping to check one's map is always a good idea: this photograph was taken near the Entre-Deux-Eaux hut, in the Vanoise National Park. Photograph by Gianluca Boetti

PHOTOGRAPHIC EQUIPMENT

Sunsets and animals, panoramic vistas and ancient huts and chapels, glaciers and mountain flowers in bloom. There are an endless array of photographs to be taken in the Alps and on the walking routes that criss-cross that great mountain range. For the tekking photographer, however, there is an extra problem, as opposed to those who travel by car or cable car. And that problem, of course, concerns weight. The fundamental choice for the walker — a choice that will make a difference of a kilogram or two in the weight of the rucksack — is between a lightweight 35 mm non-reflex camera, capable of immortalizing the most magnificent views and moments in the trek, despite its weight of a few grams, and a 35 mm reflex camera with two or three lenses, with which one can truly undertake a photographic essay. If one opts for the second type, then one must be careful to choose the appropriate lenses: a 28 mm wide angle, a 35 mm or a 50 mm lens, and a 105 or 135 mm telephoto lens (or a 70 mm to150 mm zoom) are probably going to be the most useful. The filters are fundamental (skylight or UV polarizer filter) and one needs a small tripod, which is so important in capturing on film the "magic moments" of sunset and dawn. Among the reversible films, the best ones are low-sensitivity, or slow films, with an ASA rating from 25 to100.

IN FAVOUR OF THE SLIGHTEST POSSIBLE IMPACT

"Even the excessive noise you might make around the campfire at night, even the bright colours of your clothing can restrict the enjoyment of the wilderness experienced by others who are walking the same trail." This, and other, more technical considerations, is the advice given to walkers by the official guide to walking the Grand Canyon: one of the largest and most impressive wilderness areas in the world. "Nothing can make a landscape look more inhabited than a group of highly visible tents... the advantage of mingling with the landscape will always prevail." With these words, John Hart, author of *Walking Softly in the Wilderness*, a walking guide published by the *Sierra Club*, exhorts his readers to blend in with the landscape. Of course, the Alps are not the Grand Canyon, and the crowded trails of the Dolomites are hardly a "natural, uncontaminated landscape." Still, the great mountain chain that joins bits of France, Italy, Switzerland, Austria, Germany, and Slovenia remains the largest reserve of uncontaminate wildland in all of Europe, and should be adequately safeguarded. All those who walk or climb on summits, high valleys, glaciers, and trails must behave appropriately. And the same applies to the administrations of nations, regions, provinces, and townships. In particular, those administrations are responsible for extending and adequately protecting the natural areas (parks, reserves, oases), and they should limit construction at high altitudes (be they ski facilities, roads, huts or secured trails), and should place strict controls on access to the high mountains by four-wheel-drive vehicles, trail bikes, motor sledges, and helicopters, as well as restricting hunting. The alpine clubs — in coordination with the government agencies — are responsible for resisting any useless increase in the number of huts, to prevent signage from becoming a form of pollution, and to promote environmental education. The behaviour of those who walk and climb in the mountains is important as well. In particular, aside from the general recommendation not to go overboard with colours, noise, or voices, one should also avoid leaving rubbish or waste behind one (and one should actively gather that left behind by others), one should reduce to the greatest possible extent the impact one has on the land when camping, and one should tolerantly accept the official restrictions (restrictions of access and limited numbers) imposed by the agencies that administer parks and reserves. Often ignored but extremely important are the recommendations concerning plant and animal life: plants and flowers can be picked and gathered only in certain cases, established by law (and it is just best as a matter of policy to bring nothing back from the trip), and animals must be left alone no matter how much you love them. Photographers who get too close to animals, alpine skiers who disturb animals in the most delicate phase of the year, and rock climbers who disturb bird's nests can be doing very serious harm.

13 An unexpected day of bad weather may make even the gentlest and friendliest of landscape grim and foreboding: an instance of this is seen on this meadow blanketed with a summer snowfall on the Monte Baldo, within sight of Lake Garda. Photograph by Gianluca Boetti

AMONG THE ROCKS AND
THE FORESTS OF THE VERCORS

A week of hiking toward Mont
Aiguille, in the wildest limestone
massif of the French Prealps

*14-15 The massive
silhouette of Mont
Aiguille (2,097 metres)
and the valley of
Trièves are depicted*
here, as seen from the
eastern edge of the
plateau of Vercors.
Photograph by
Philippe Bonhème

A splendid limestone tower in the heart of the Dauphiné, and at the same time, a monument to the first adventure of humans in the world of the vertical. Spectacular and needle thin, Mont Aiguille is the best known and the most impressive peak in the Vercors. Very familiar to and popular with walkers and climbers in the Dauphiné, it caught the public eye in 1992, on the occasion of the fifth centennial of the climb made by Antoine de Ville and his party to the

2,086-metre peak, which marked the "official" birth of mountain climbing. The Vercors, however, is not only Mont Aiguille. At just a short distance from the well known peak, other elegant limestone peaks, such as the Deux-Soeurs, the Rochers du Parquet, and the Grand Veymont tower above Gresse, the Clelles, Chichilianne, and the other villages of the Trièves. Stretching behind these rock faces, the entire southeastern sector of the massif is occupied by a majestic and dramatic limestone plateau riddled with grottoes, natural wells, and dolinas. One of the most enchanting and unspoilt spots in the Prealps, one can get a taste of the Mediterranean's sunny harshness. "A blend of the Dolomites, Sardinia, and Greece," is how Gian Piero Motti, a climber and author from Turin described this area in 1978. To the north, toward Grenoble and the great bend in the River Isère, the massif shows a face that is at once gentler and more Nordic. Around the villages of Lans-en-Vercors and Autrans, in the zone of the Quatre Montagnes, great majestic forests of fir trees offer wonderful opportunities for winter cross-country skiers and those in search of relaxed summer walks, excursions on horseback or by mountain bike. On this side, too, however, the massif is well fortified with steep forests and rock faces. There are more great forests to the south, around Lente, La-Chapelle-en-Vercors, and other towns and villages made famous by the partisan fighting that took place here in 1943 and 1944. And there are more rocks and oddities of the limestone further west, where the waters of the Vernaison and the Bourne make their way downhill through wild and daunting canyons such as the Petits Goulets

and the Grands Goulets. Everywhere in the massif, there are numerous grottoes and caverns. Ranging from the smaller caves, where humans once lived, all the way up to the huge caverns of Chorance, great tourist attractions located not far from Pont-en-Royans and the walls of Presles, one passes on to the sheer verticality and daunting challenges of the Gouffre Berger, the first cave in the world in which cavers ventured below one thousand metres, and which nowadays has been explored to 1,140 metres. As early as 1777, observations were made of the various caves by the geologist Déodat de Dolomieu, who gave his name to the most spectacular limestone mountain chain in Europe and in the world.

The forests and meadows of the Vercors have always been intensely exploited and grazed by humans, and they are famous everywhere in France. In 1492, King Charles VIII commanded Antoine de Ville to attempt to climb Mont Aiguille. In 1689, a royal edict prohibited the locals from cutting the great beech trees found on the massif, as the beechwood was to be set aside for the construction of royal galleys. Alpine tourism here has deep and very venerable roots. Not far from Grenoble, the true "capital" of the French Alps, easier to reach than the great Alps for those who are travelling from Paris, Lyon, or from the Midi, the Vercors has been the site ever since the turn of the century of a feverish activity among walkers and climbers, who were soon joined by cavers and skiers. On the walls of Mont Aiguille and the Deux-Soeurs, and on the cliffs of Glandasse and Presles, over the years, great names of French mountain climbing such as

15 Boulders, meadows, and firs make up the landscape of the plateau of Vercors: in the background one can see the mountains of Belledonne. Photograph by Philippe Bonhème

Serge Coupé, Georges Livanos, and Patrick Cordier have left their marks. Sports caving, too, has one of its most important centres here in the Vercors. In the winter, aside from the ski slopes, the great woods around Autrans feature lengthy and splendid circuits for cross-country skiing. Further south, between the Col du Rousset and Villard-de-Lans, one can cross the Hauts-Plateaux on cross-country skis, a forty kilometres way across one of the most interesting and unspoilt areas of its kind in the French Alps. There is an almost infinite range of possibilities for walkers. Aside from the hundreds of local and shorter trails, the Vercors boasts a great many marked hiking trails, such as the GR9 and its variant trails, the GR91, GR93, and

GR95, the Tour du Trièves, the Tour du Glandasse, and the Sentier Central. It is possible to combine these routes in accordance with the season, one's personal preferences, the amount of time available, and one's own knowledge of the massif. More than elsewhere, the route that we describe across the Vercors is only one of the great many possible combinations. We would recommend a week's walk from the gates of Grenoble to the foot of Mont Aiguille, in a setting that is increasingly wild and unspoilt. Forests, rocks, karst fields, and monuments built by man make this a route that one will not easily forget, within the boundaries of one of the largest natural parks in France.

16 A group of walkers working its way up the trail that runs around the base of Mont Aiguille, the ascent of which in 1492 marked the birth of alpinism.
Photograph by Gianluca Boetti

USEFUL INFORMATION

Duration: 7 days.
Elevations: ranging from the 215 metres of Pont-en-Royans to the 2,341 metres of the Grand Veymont.
Season: from late May to late October.
Signage: red and white for the GR 9, 95, 91 and for the local trails, yellow-and-red for the Sentier Central.
Degree of difficulty: minimal.
How demanding: average, considerable in the heart of the summer, because of the low elevations.
Equipment: walking gear. Sleeping bag and padding necessary for the last overnight stay at the Jasse du Play.
Peaks: the Grand Veymont (2,341 metres), the highest peak of the Vercors, is part of the route. The walk has a worthy ending with the climb up Mont Aiguille (2,086 metres): this is however an alpinistic route with stretches of second and third degree. Guide recommended.
How to get there: Grenoble can be reached from Italy by train or by car through the Valle di Susa or the Fréjus

(by train, one must change at Chambéry) and it is well served from Lyon, Paris, and Geneva. From Grenoble, there are frequent scheduled buses for St.-Nizier-de-Moucherotte. From Chichilianne and Clelles, one can return to Grenoble by bus or train.
How to get around: buses from Autrans, Rencurel, Chorance, Pont-en-Royans, Lente, and St. Agnan; the railroad station of St.-Nazaire is just a few kilometres from Pont-en-Royans.
Overnight accomodations: privately owned huts and hotels. The last night is spent in a non-equipped hut.
If you want to camp out: you may be able to do so; in some areas you must receive permission from the park administration.
Weather Forecasts: call (33) 36680238.
Mountain Rescue: CRS Grenoble (33) 76214444, PGHM Grenoble (33) 76404440, Summer rescue (33) 76795100.
Information Offices: Bureau of Tourism of Autrans (33) 76953070,

Rencurel (33) 76389729, Pont-en-Royans (33) 76360910, and St.-Agnan (33) 75482784.
Useful phone numbers: Parc du Vercors (33) 76954033, Maison de la Randonnée St.-Nizier-du-Moucherotte (33) 76534178, Gite d'étape de la Sure (33) 76953068, Refuge de Romeyère Rencurel (33)76389690, Refuge du Breuil Pont-en-Royans (33) 76360189, Hotel Faravelon Col de la Machine (33) 74455767, Maison du Parc Chichilianne (33) 76344495.
Maps: the best maps are the 1:25,000 by IGN. As an alternative, the 1:50,000 maps by Didier-Richard and the IGN.
Guide Books: the best one is *Tours dans le Vercors*, by the *Fédération française de la Randonnée Pédestre*, including the GR9, 91, 93, 95 and the Séntier Central
Readings: *La guide du Vercors* by Maguy Dupont (La manufacture, 1987) rich in detail about the wildland and history of the massif.

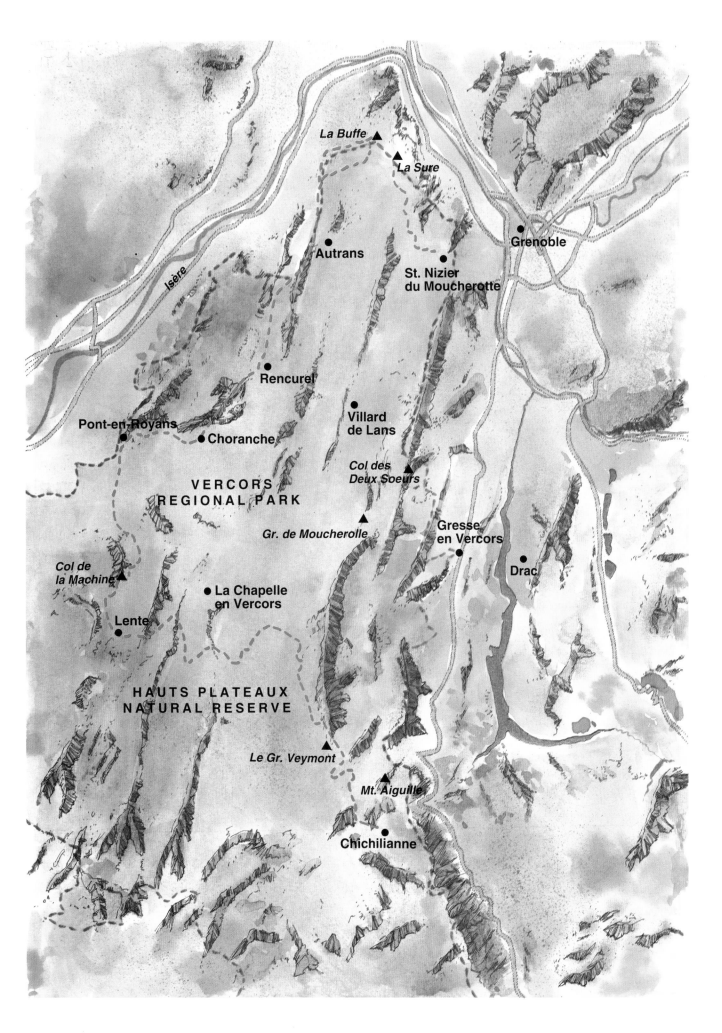

La Buffe ▲

La Sure ▲

Grenoble ●

Autrans ●

St. Nizier
du Moucherotte ●

Isère

Rencurel ●

Villard
de Lans ●

Pont-en-Royans ●

Choranche ●

Col des
Deux Soeurs ▲

VERCORS
REGIONAL PARK

Gr. de Moucherolle ▲

Gresse
en Vercors ●

Col de
la Machine ▲

Drac ●

La Chapelle
en Vercors ●

Lente ●

HAUTS PLATEAUX
NATURAL RESERVE

Le Gr. Veymont ▲

Mt. Aiguille ▲

Chichilianne ●

FIRST DAY

*from St-Nizier-du-Moucherotte
to Refuge de Gève
distance climbed: 850 metres
distance descended: 730 metres
Time: 6 hours*

This day of the trek leads to the Plateau
de Sornin and to the peaks of La Sure
and Pyramide de la Buffe, a vantage-

SECOND DAY

*from the Refuge de Gève to Rencurel
distance climbed: 700 metres
distance descended: 1,170 metres
time: 5 hours*

Another day largely running through
the forest. After a number of splendid
panoramic vistas in all different
directions, one passes quite close to

THIRD DAY

*from Rencurel to Pont-en-Royans
distance climbed: 700 metres
distance descended: 1,290 metres
time: 6 hours*

This stay is devoted to the walk down to
the base of the western slope of the
Vercors, where one should pay special
attention to the cavern of Chorance

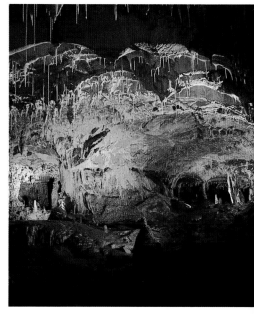

point overlooking Grenoble and the Alps;
from here, one descends into the Nordic
domaine skiable of the Vercors. One
begins in the village of St.-Nizier (1,162
metres), following the GR 9, which runs
down to Engins (939 metres) and then
climbs back up through woods and
gullies toward the Plateau du Sornin
(1,380 metres), where it is possible to
detour to the right, toward the mouth of
the Gouffre Berger. One walks through
Karst fields to the peak of La Sure
(1,643 metres), from the top of which
one can gaze out over the Isère valley.
Along the crest that seals off the Vercors
to the north, one can reach the Pyramide
de la Buffe (1,623 metres), and then one
descends to the Pas de la Clé (1,509
metres), continuing down through the
woods to Refuge de Gève (1,286 metres).

Autrans, one of the most important
tourist resorts in the Vercors. One
begins by returning to the ridge in the
area around Signal de Nave (1,609
metres), and from there one can pass
back over the Col de la Clé and climb
over the Bec de l'Orient (1,568 metres).
The trail continues southward,
keeping lower than the ridge, and
then comes to a fork (1,070 metres)
a short distance from Autrans. From
here, one climbs up to the Pas de
Pertuson (1,435 metres), descending
into the woods and then continuing
along the slope, without reaching the
Col de Romeyère, and one continues
along, passing by various farms, all
the way to Rencurel (807 metres).

and the lovely little town of Pont-en-
Royans. The first part of the stay runs
through the handsome forest of the
district of Coulmes. The trail climbs up
to the houses of Glénats (930 metres)
and Les Ailes (1,023 metres), and then
continues climbing among the larches
all the way to the hut of the Serre du
Satre (1,350 metres). Here, the trail
turns to the right, and continues with a
great deal of climbing and descending
through the magnificent forest as far as
the hut of the Grande Goulandière
(1,065 metres) and the Pas du Ranc
(1,040 metres); from there it descends
along very steep terrain, becoming less
steep as one gets nearer to the road (this
is a recommended detour, one hour
round trip, plus the time to look around)
leading to the cavern of Chorance. After
a very steep descent to the village of
Chorance (270 metres), one continues
obliquely along the slope all the way to
Pont-en-Royans (215 metres), the
western entrance to the Vercors.

*18 The dolomitic
silhouette of Mont
Aiguille looms over
the meadows of
Chichilianne. These
rock faces have*

*long posed a
challenge, and men
first accepted the
challenge in 1492.
Photograph by
Gianluca Boetti*

*19 left During the
first scree, the trail
runs by the rocks of
the Pas de la Clé, at
the northern edge of
the Vercors.
Photograph by
Philippe Bonhème*

*19 right The Chorance
cave, a Karstic grotto
more than 13
kilometres in length,
cuts into the western
slope of the Vercors.
Photograph by
Ernst Höhne*

FOURTH DAY
From Pont-en-Royans to Lente
distance climbed: 1,050 metres
distance descended: 170 metres
time: 6 hours

The climb up to the plateau, really a very warm undertaking during the summer (it may be a good idea to take a bus, so as to shorten the trek by a day), leads one from the gentle, populated hills of the Royans to the heart of the Vercors, where one walks through the forests of the district of La Sapine-Cotebelle and Lente. The GR9 runs to S.te-Eulalie-en-Royans, and then runs obliquely along the slope above St.-Laurent-en-Royans, entering the wild high valley of Laval, climbing steeply from there to the easy rocks of the Pas du Pas (980 metres).

One continues, not far from the road, all the way to the Col de la Machine,

the ruins of Miroflée (1,080 metres), and to a fork in the road. Toward the left, along the GR95, one continues through the woods as far as Lente (1,075 metres).

FIFTH DAY
From Lente to St.-Agnan
distance climbed: 300 metres
distance descended: 590 metres
time: 4 hours

This is a fairly short stay with a great deal of climbing and descending, which runs deep through the historic heart of the Vercors, passing nearby La-Chapelle, and ending in the quite little village of St.-Agnan. One begins in the open ground to the south of the town, and then one climbs on the left along the trail markers of the Sentier Central, which cuts across a number of forest roads, finally reaching the Col de Carri (1,202 metres).

One descends beyond this col into the Combe de l'Osc, one crosses a crest, descending to the houses of Les Griffes and Les Reveilles (possible detour via La-Chapelle-en Vercors), and then one continues to climb up into the solitary Combe Libouse. After crossing the Col du Souillet (1,150 metres) one descends quickly to St.-Agnan-en-Vercors (784 metres). It is certainly worthwhile reaching the Grotte de la Luire (five kilometres, by road to the south, bus line in operation), a spectacular natural cavity used by the French Resistance from 1943 to 1944 as a hospital.

SIXTH DAY
From St-Agnan to Jasse du Play
distance climbed: 900 metres
distance descended: 50 metres
time: 4 hours

This is another stay that is fairly short, and it runs from the villages of the historic section of the Vercors to the more pristine and wild parts of the massif, the Hauts-Plateaux which lie in the looming shadow of the jagged ridge line of the Grand Veymont, dotted with mountain summer meadows and picturesque huts. The hut of the Jasse du Play can accommodate about fifteen people, and has no attendant: one must bring a sleeping bag and sufficient provisions. One sets out again along the trail-markers of the Sentier Central, which climbs until it reaches a forest road and the edge (1,308 metres) of the plateau. One continues along a gentle slope, across the Karst highland of Tiolache, until one reaches the GR91, which climbs off to the right of the Jasse du Play (1,610 metres). Red signs indicate the presence of a spring, which is about a quarter of an hour's walk away.

SEVENTH DAY
From Jasse du Play to Chichilianne
distance climbed: 900 metres
distance descended: 1,550 metres
time: 6 hours 30 minutes

The final day of walking features some of the most spectacular views of the massif, and spans two radically different worlds. From majestic Karst highlands, in fact, one passes on to the remarkable vista seen from the peak of the Grand-Veymont, and from there on to the astounding bulk of Mont Aiguille, at the base of which the route comes to an end. A less tiring alternative, which we would highly recommend on days when the weather is dicey, involves continuing along the GR91 as far as Pré Peyret, and climbing up to the Pas de la Selle, stopping by the Roman quarries of the Plaine de la Queyrie, where partially excavated

20 *The limestone face of Presles, which looms over the deep valley of the Bourne, is the most popular with rock climbers in the entire massif.* Photograph by Stefano Ardito

21 left *The Grand Veymont, which is the highest peak on the massif, rising to an elevation of 2,341 metres, dominates the plateau of the Vercors.* Photograph by Philippe Bonhème

21 right top *The southern face of Mont Aiguille is illuminated by the early morning light. A group of walkers is shown watching it from the lush clearings of Chichilianne.* Photograph by Gianluca Boetti

columns still await completion and transport to Die. One begins on the fairly level GR91, and one continues all the way to the Jasse de la Chau (1,614 metres); from there, the Sentier Central climbs steeply up to the Pas de la Ville (1,925 metres). An easy ridge takes one to the peak of the Grand Veymont (2,341 metres), which one crosses, climbing down then to the Pas des Bachassons and on to the Pas de la Selle (1,895 metres). One descends beyond along a lovely trail that crosses some scre and then runs off south toward the Col de l'Aupet (1,627 metres); from here one can detour as far as the foot of the rocks of Mont Aiguille. A steep descent through the woods brings one to Chichilianne (995 metres).

21 right bottom *The luxuriant evergreen forest of the Col de l'Aupet extends to the base of Mont Aiguille, before dropping away sharply in the direction of Chichilianne.* Photograph by Stefano Ardito

FROM THE QUEYRAS TO THE OISANS

Through the most unspoilt and
spectacular massifs in the French Alps

"This region contains the highest mountains in France, with the exception of Mont Blanc, as well as some of the loveliest landscapes. It may not boast the same beauty as Switzerland, but it does possess its own charm and allure: the sheer crags, the rushing mountain streams, the ravines — all are unrivalled. The deep savage valleys offer a scenery of such grandeur as to touch the level of the sublime. In no other place on earth do the mountains take on such daring shapes. The numerous valleys rival each other in the singularity of their nature and the variety of their climates." These words were written by Edward Whymper. The famed climber of the Jorasses and the Matterhorn, the Verte and the Dolent spent a considerable amount of time in the Dauphiné. In 1861, he climbed the Pelvoux, and three years later he made extensive explorations around the base of the Meije, and scaled the Barre des Ecrins, which is both the highest peak in the Oisans and the southernmost "four-thousand metre peak" in the Alps. From the 4,101-metre height of the peak, Whymper admired a view "as vast as all England." Today, as fifty years ago, the lofty summit ridge of the Barre is one of the most popular

who made Mont Blanc his home, the guide and teacher of all of us who wrote books like this one. "Here the environment always prevails over technique... long and unspoilt high valleys, marvelous wildernesses of stone, where nature is intact as it was on the first day of creation." Sensations such as these are not limited to climbers: walkers too, in increasing numbers, flow toward the spectacular massif, which has been the largest and most unspoilt of all the French Alpine Parks since 1973 (though the first efforts to protect this area date from 1913). With its rocks and ice, however, the heart of the massif is not easy to reach for those who walk only on trails. It is no accident, therefore, that two of the most popular and major trails of France make a circuit around the massif, at different distances. These two trails are the GR 54, or the "Tour de l'Oisans," and the GR 50, or the "Tour du Haut Dauphiné." To the east, toward the Italian border, within sight of the Ecrins and the Meije, stands a profoundly different massif. This is the highland of the Queyras, which has been a protected area since 1977, in the shadow of the French slope of the Monte Viso but marked by elevations that are fairly low and unspoilt, like the Grand Queyras (3,114 metres), the Pic d'Asti (3,220 metres), and the Pic de Rochebrune (3,320 metres). If the massif of the Ecrins is a kingdom of adventure, the Queyras is ideal for cross-country skiing — there are over a hundred kilometres of tracks — and for summer walks along the GR 58 "Tour du Queyras," its many variations, and the numerous local trails. The high valleys at the foot of the Meije have always resisted the encroachments of humans. Beyond the Durance, instead, the architecture of the villages and the wooden houses, the cheeses such as the "Tomme du Guil" and the "Bleu du Queyras," and

22 A flock of sheep grazing in a meadow in the high valley of the Romanche. In the background, one can see the impressive walls of the Meije and the Rateau.
Photograph by
Jean Pierre Nicollet

23 The spectacular northern face of the Meije, the most dramatic and difficult peak in the Oisans, overlooks La Grave and the Romanche valley.
Photograph by
Pascal Tournaire

destinations in the Alps. The same is true of the Meije, the daunting rocky peak first scaled in 1877 by a guide from La Grave named Pierre Gaspard, and of the Olan, the Agneaux, the Pelvoux, and the other major peaks of the mountain group. Ever since the age of heroic mountain climbs, the Oisans have inspired other devoted climbers, almost all of them of French birth. Of them all, we will mention just one: Gaston Rébuffat from Marseilles,

the exceedingly fine woodcarving have always been signs of a deep-set bond between the land and the people. At an altitude of 2,040 metres, St.-Véran is the highest village in the Alps and in all of Europe. Now renowned among connoisseurs in search of relaxed holidays, the Queyras is still unknown to the public at large. This is another factor that makes it one of the most reserved and tranquil places in the Alps. An authentic pilgrimage toward the Meije and the Ecrins, but running largely through the Queyras, the route we present here is a combination of several *grandes randonnées*, as the French mountain trails are called. In fact, we follow the GR 58 through forests and highlands to the south of

the valley of Guil, and then the GR 541 in the steep descent toward the Durance at St.-Crépin, and the subsequent climb back up to Freissinières and through the stark high valley of Fournel. The trail continues between Vallouise and the Col de l'Eychauda, Monetier-les-Bains and the Col d'Arsine, and in the final descent to the base of the Meije one has an opportunity to appreciate the spectacular and wild atmosphere of the tallest peaks of the Dauphiné. Whoever wishes to have a better understanding of the wild valleys of the Queyras can begin at Abriès and reach St-Véran via the Refuge de l'Agnel. The same hut can also be reached from the Val Varaita in Italy.

Duration: 8 days.
Elevations: ranging from the 904 metres of St.-Crépin to the 2,806 metres of the Col Vieux.
Season: from July to September.
Signage: red and white for the GR 58, 58A, 541, and 54.
Degree of difficulty: minimal.
How demanding: average, but with a few particularly lengthy stages.
Peaks: just a short distance from the route are such vantage-points as the Pain de Sucre Rocher de l'Yret (2,830 metres).
Equipment: walking gear.
How to get there: a genuine doorway to Queyras, Guillestre is on the railroad line running from Gap to Briançon. The quickest way to get here from Italy is via

the Colle dell'Agnello, otherwise one can take the Monginevro or the Colle della Maddalena. From Guillestre one can ride up by bus to St.-Véran. La Grave is linked by regularly scheduled bus with Grenoble, Modane, and Briançon.
How to get around: regularly scheduled buses and trains (to Briançon and Gap) at St.-Crépin, as well as buses at Ceillac, Vallouise, and Monetier-les-Bains.
Overnight accommodations: huts, rest points and privately owned bed-and-breakfast.
If you want to camp out: you should be able to, even though there are some restrictions in the two parks of the Queyras and the Ecrins against camping out freely.
Alpine Guides: in all major towns, just

contact the tourist bureau.
Weather Forecasts: Météo Briançon (33) 36680205, Météo Grenoble (33) 76511111.
Mountain Rescue: PGHM Isère (33) 76404440, PGHM Hautes-Alpes (33) 92213436, PGHM Grenoble (33) 76404440.
Information Offices: Bureau of Tourism of St.-Véran (33) 92458221, Bureau of Tourism of Ceillac (33) 92450574, Bureau of Tourism of La Grave (33) 76799005
Useful phone numbers: Parc du Queyras Guillestre (33) 92450623, Parc des Ecrins Gap (33) 92514071, Parc des Ecrins Briançon (33) 92210849, Parc des Ecrins Vallouise (33) 92233231, overnight information at Le Chant de l'Alpe St.-Véran (33) 92458219, overnight information at Les Gabelous St.-Véran (33) 92458219, overnight information at Les Baladins Ceillac (33) 92450023, overnight information at Le Riou Vert Bramousse (33) 92467161, Refuge de Furfande (33) 92467473, overnight information at Eygliers (33) 92451229, overnight information Chez Sandrine Pallon (33) 92209442, overnight information at Maison de la Vallée Freissinières (33) 92209409, overnight information at Edelweiss Vallouise (33) 92233001, overnight information at Le Baouti Vallouise (33) 92233354, overnight information at La Bergerie Monetier-les-Bains (33) 92244120, overnight information at La Breche Villar-d'Arène (33) 76799206, overnight information at Edelweiss La Grave (33) 76799093, overnight information at Le Refuge La Grave (33) 76799139.
Maps: adequate are the Didier & Richard 1:50,000 n. 10 *Queyras et Haute-Ubaye* and n. 6 *Massif et Parc des Ecrins*, more detailed are the IGN 1:25,000 n. 3637 *Ouest Aiguilles*, 3537 *Est Ceillac Château-Queyras*, 3536 *Briançon*, and 3435 *La Grave*.
Guide books: *Walking the Alpine Parks of France & Northwest Italy* by Marcia Lieberman (The Mountaineers) - walking in the Mercantour, Queyras, Ecrins, Vanoise and Gran Paradiso; *Tour of the Oisans* by Andrew Harper (Cicerone Press) - Gr54, out of print; *Tour de l'Oisans* - GR54, *Tour du Haut-Dauphiné* - GR50 and *Tour du Queyras* - GR58, all are of the: Fédération française de la Randonnée Pédestre.

25 A close encounter with a chamois always constitutes an exciting moment, which intensifies one's contact with nature in the parks of the Queyras and the Oisans.
Photograph by Gianluca Boetti

FIRST DAY

From St.-Véran to Ceillac
Distance climbed: 800 metres
Distance descended: 1,150 metres
Time: 5 hours 30 minutes

The first stage in this trek links the two loveliest villages in the Queyras. St.-Véran, the highest-elevation district capital in the Alps, lies on a slope with southern exposure, while Ceillac stands on a plateau of the Vallée du Cristillian. This stage is pretty exhausting, but the views are remarkable. From St.-Véran (2,008 metres) one climbs down to Le Raux and to the Pont du Moulin (1,849 metres), and from there one begins climbing up the stark high valley of the Rif de Lamaron, which leads to the Col des Estronques (2,651 metres). From here, it is worth taking a detour

to the nearby, Tête de la Jacquette (2,757 metres). One climbs down along a winding trail among the meadows, and one continues on a nearly level path all the way to Le Villard (there is a handsome wooden church) and on to Ceillac (1,650 metres).

SECOND DAY

from Ceillac to Bramousse
distance climbed: 600 metres
distance descended: 1,150 metres
time: 4 hours 30 minutes

This day is almost pure relaxation, and is more "Mediterranean" than the previous day's walk, featuring the splendid Bois de Cheyet and the gentle slopes around the pass. After passing through the old town of Ceillac,

one reaches the Gothic church of S.te-Cécile, and then continues climbing up to the mountain huts of L'Ochette. After going past a number of rocky towers, one enters the woods, emerging after a while into the meadows just before the Col de Bramousse (2,251 metres). One descends on the other side until reaching a handsome larch grove. From the Chalets de Bramousse (1,848 metres), one follows a dirt road that winds down to Bramousse (1,400 metres), with its very nice overnight accommodation, some of the most modern and comfortable in the mountains of France.

THIRD DAY

from Bramousse
to the Refuge de Furfande
distance climbed: 760-1,090 metres
distance descended: 180-400 metres
time: 3-5 hours

This stage is interesting towards the end, but we would highly recommend that one make every effort to get a ride from Bramousse to Les Escoyères, an ancient settlement along the Roman road that led to the Queyras; an ancient Roman marker stone is preserved in the little church of S.te-Marie Madeleine. The descent from Bramousse to the valley of the Guil (1,183 metres), and the subsequent climb back up to Les Escoyères (1,532 metres) run along road. One continues along the classic route of the GR58, which runs along the road as far as Le Chalelard, and then continues through the wild

26 top   The wooden buildings of the Queyras are among the most charming in all the Alps. In this photograph, a group of buildings at St.-Véran is shown; at 2040 metres, this is the highest village in the Alps.
Photograph by
Furio Chiaretta

*26 bottom
The ancient village of Le Queyron overlooks the fog-shrouded gorges of the Guil. In the background, one can see the impressive peaks of the Oisans.*
Photograph by
Furio Chiaretta

and unspoilt Vallon de la Lauze, after which the gentle meadows of Furfande run up to the hut with the same name (2,283 metres).

FOURTH DAY
from Refuge de Furfande to St.-Crépin
distance climbed: 150 metres
distance descended: 1,380 metres
time: 5 hours

This lengthy and interesting descent, largely through the forest, takes one to the valley of the Durance and on to the pleasant little village of St.-Crépin. One begins by passing the Lac de la Valette on one's right, climbing to the Col Garnier (2,279 metres). Then one continues down along the slope until one reaches the edge of the larch forest, continuing downhill through the trees until one reaches the ruins of the malgas of Les Girards (1,670 metres).
An oblique trail along the slope leads to a bridge and to the cart-road that descends to the sheepherders' huts of Gros (1,385 metres). A long stretch along a paved road brings one to the hut of Guillermin (1,260 metres), after which one descends sharply all the way to St.-Crépin (905 metres). It is possible to stay overnight in a hotel in the village, or else one can continue on to the overnight accommodations of Les Eygliers (1,027 metres a half-hour longer).

FIFTH DAY
from St.-Crépin to Freissinières
distance climbed: 350 metres
distance descended: 50 metres
time: 3 hours

This is a short stage, coming just before the longest and most tiring of all the stages in this trek, running up from the valley of the Durance to the woods and meadows of Freissinières, a farming village that has changed very little over time. After passing over the bridge over the Durance, one begins to climb, passing the houses of Champcella and Chambon, beyond which a detour leads to the remarkable gorges of Gourfouran. A bit further along, one emerges among the houses of Pallon (1,127 metres) and from here one continues on to the nearby Freissinières (1,200 metres).

27 top A chamois, easy to spot in both of the parks through which the trail runs, surveys the valley from high atop a jutting crag of gneiss.
Photograph by Gianluca Boetti

27 centre Light and shadows play along the steep walls that so distinguish the massif of the Écrins.
Photograph by L. Ramires/ White Star

SIXTH DAY
via the Col du Bal
from Freissinières to Vallouise
distance climbed: 1,900 metres
distance descended: 1,940 metres
time: 9 hours

This is a tiring stage, long and rough, and it takes the walker from the Durance valley up to the foot of the massif of the Ecrins. Vallouise, site of the "Maison du Parc des Ecrins" is worthing stopping off to see. It may be a good idea to stay an extra day in this area, so as to have time to tour Ailefroide and to push along toward the Pré de Madame Carle and the Glacier Blanc. It is possible to shorten the distance, cutting the amount of time and climbing involved almost in half. We shall explain how shortly, with the variant trail via the Col de la Pousterle. One begins by climbing through the

27 bottom This photograph displays the spectacular beauty of the massif of the Écrins near Vallouise, where the "Maison du Parc des Écrins" is located.
Photograph by L. Ramires/ White Star

woods all the way up to the Col des Lauzes (1,837 metres); from here one climbs down to the Pont du Fournel (1,326 metres), in the high valley of the same name. One climbs along this valley as far as the Cabane de la Balme (2,006 metres), and from there one begins the steep final climb up to the Col du Bal (2,601 metres). A long descent to the solitary Combe de Nerreyroux takes one to a number of handsome waterfalls, and then on to Puy-St-Vincent (1,400 metres) and to Vallouise (1,166 metres).

of the Col de la Pousterle (1,763 metres). A little later, one leaves the GR 50, and one descends to the left to Prey d'Amont (1,629 metres), Prey d'Aval (1,513 metres), Les Prés (1,408 metres), and Puy-St.-Vincent (1,400 metres).

28 left The village of Vallouise lies peacefully beneath the still snow-covered spurs of the Oisans.
Photograph by L. Ramires/ White Star

28 right A group of walkers walks along a variation of the seventh stage of the trek, through the larch forests of the Oisans. In the background, one can see the elegant rocky spires of the Ténailles de Montbrison.
Photograph by Gianluca Boetti

SIXTH DAY
via the Col de la Pousterle
from Freissinières to Vallouise
distance climbed: 980 metres
distance descended: 1,020 metres
time: 5 hours

The easiest way of reaching Vallouise involves a route around the crest that separates it from the Vallon du Fournel toward the Col de la Pousterle and the villages of Les Prés. The landscape, in the last stretch, is in poor shape: this is a large *domaine skiable*. After reaching the Pont du Fournel (1,326 metres), one follows the forest road (trail-marker of the GR 50) that runs up to the plateau

SEVENTH DAY
from Vallouise to Monetier-les-Bains
distance climbed: 1,270 metres
distance descended: 960 metres
time: 6 hours 30 minutes

This is a fairly easy stage, and it can be shortened considerably at the beginning by taking a bus, from which one can enjoy the harsh high-mountain landscape during the climb to the Col de l'Eychauda and to the two nearby vantage-points — both of which we recommend — of the Rocher de l'Yret and the Cucumelle. The climb down to Monetier-les-Bains is somewhat tainted by the

*29 top The summit ridge of the Agneaux, a splendid peak that rises to an elevation of 3,664 metres serves as a backdrop to the trail that runs across the meadows and the stony fields the Col d'Arsine.
Photograph by Jean Pierre Nicollet*

*29 centre This picture portrays the glaciers of the northern face of the Meije. This peak, which was first scaled in 1877, was the site of one of the greatest feats of mountaineering in the Oisans.
Photograph by Pascal Tournaire*

presence of a great many ski slopes and facilities. One begins on the road that leads to Le Sarret (there is also a walking trail on the far bank of the Gyr), and from there one begins to climb, crossing a secondary road a number of times. After entering the Vallon de Chambran, over which looms the Pic Gardiner, the Pic de Séguret, and other nearby peaks, the environment becomes quite interesting. One walks past the chalets of Chambran (1,719 metres), turns right at a fork in the path, and climbs at considerable length all the way up to the Col de l'Eychauda (2,425 metres). One descends from there into an area that is contaminated by ski slopes and ski lifts, and then one enters a larch forest, descending until one crosses the Guisane, reaching Monetier-les-Bains (1,490 metres) through more pleasant walking territory.

EIGHTH DAY

*from Monetier-les-Bains to La Grave
distance climbed: 1,020 metres
distance descended: 1,030 metres
time: 7 hours 30 minutes*

The last day of this trek is also quite exhausting, perfectly in tune with the daunting walls of the Meije.
One begins on a level, walking as far as Le Casset (1,512 metres), and then one immediately begins to climb steeply up, to the seracs of the Glacier de Casset. In the steep valley of the Petit Tabuc one reaches the Col d'Arsine (2,348 metres), within sight of the northern slope of the Agneaux and of the Pic de Neige Cordier. Slightly gentler is the descent that takes one down to the Lac de l'Etoile (2,224 metres) and then on to the Chalets de l'Alpe de Villar d'Arène (2,096 metres), where the high valleys of the Clot des Cavales and the Plate des Agneaux converge, from westward.
One continues on among meadows and rocks, at the foot of the eastern slope of the Meije, all the way to Villar-d'Arène (1,650 metres).
A final descent among the larch trees takes one to La Grave (1,474 metres), where this trek comes to an end.

*29 bottom
The north face of the Rateau overlooks La Grave and the deep valley in which the Romanche flows.
Photograph by Pascal Tournaire*

FROM ARGENTERA TO MONTE VISO

Through the majestic valleys of the
Cuneese, along the Great Crossing
of the Alps, which links the two
giants of the southern Alps

*30-31 At dawn, the
classic view of
Monte Viso (3,841
metres) from the
Pian del Re near
where the River Po
rises spreads out
before the walkers
heading for the
Quintino Sella hut
and the Lago
Grande.*
Photograph by
Gianluca Boetti

*31 The ibex is quite
common and is
easy to spot in the
Park of Argentera,
the most extensive
and protected wild
area in the entire
Piedmont region.*
Photograph by
Marcello Bertinetti/
White Star

At the edge of the woods, the house
of the Bèla Rosìn makes for a fairly
poor first impression. Subjected for
more than a century to the harshness
of the elements, then transformed
into an annex of a hotel, it gives only
the faded memory of its glorious past,
and of the year — 1856 — in which
the sovereign of Piedmont and the
future king of Italy gave it to his
favorite mistress. All around, the
evergreen forests of the high Gesso
Valley are still lush and spectacular.
Four hundred metres of climbing and
an hour-and-a-half of walking brings
one to the royal hunting lodge of Pian
del Valasco, likewise in fairly bad
shape. Huge cracks zigzag through the
walls of one of the most unusual
structures built for the hunting
expeditions of Victor Emanuel II, the
"hunter king" of nineteenth-century
Italy. Despite the fact that the entire
massif is a protected territory, weeds
and rubbish cover much of the interior
of the old lodge. Restoration is
scheduled, but it may come too late.
It is impossible, however, to talk about
the mountains of Cuneo, the Italian
slope of what the French call the
"Alpes du Soleil," without thinking of
the house of Savoy. Just as in the
Gran Paradiso, and perhaps to an even
greater degree, Victor Emanuel II loved
to ride up among the high valleys of
Argentera to hunt chamois and ibex.
Here he established his hunting
preserve, here he built a chalet for this
favorite mistress. And here he came
often, until his death in 1878. Beloved
and much visited by Ligurians and
Piedmontese, the Cottian and the
Maritime Alps do not receive the
attention that they deserve from the
rest of Europe. "The Maritime Alps,
distant, far down in the west, were
truly maritime in my youthful
imagination, that is, none too tall,
and when tall, gentle and easy to
climb... with the soft breezes that

bore Mediterranean aromas, just like
in Provence and Liguria. These
Maritime Alps are true mountains,
however! And the people that live
in them are true mountaineers!"
The surprise of the great Trentino-
born author, Mario Rigoni Stern,
recorded years ago in the Italian
daily, *La Stampa*, is indicative of a
common set of beliefs. When walking
from the base of the Argentera and
its walls toward Monte Viso, the
wealth and spectacular beauty of the
mountains of the *Provincia Granda*,
as the Cuneese is familiarly called,
appear at every step. In a harsh and,
in many ways, Mediterranean
landscape — enlivened however by
splendid forests, like that of Swiss
pine of Alevé — the limestone walls
of the Barricate and of Mount Oronaye
loom overhead, as do the dramatic
gneiss towers of the Castello-
Provenzale massif, and many walls and
ridges of lesser peaks. And there are
more than just peaks here. Chamois,
ibex, marmots, eagles, and lovely
blooms all make the Park of Argentera
and the adjacent French Park of
Mercantour one of the most fascinating
wildlife areas of the Alps. There are
myriad and multiform traces of human
presence: the straw roofs of San
Bernolfo recall an ancient and nearly
extinct tradition, the impressive
fortresses built at the orders of
Mussolini are evidence of Fascist
expansionism and the attack on France
in 1940. Other forts — including the
daunting structure of Vinadio, just off
this trail — are reminders that these
valleys have always been points of
passage and of clashes between
France and Piedmont. But history here
is not made only of rock. The Cuneese
valleys are home to some of the
most active surviving areas of the
culture of Langue-d'Oc in Italy, while
the *Bahio* festival of Sampeyre, which
commemorates the expulsion of the

Saracens from these valleys, is one of the most interesting traditional celebrations in Italy. In many valleys, cooperative groups of young people, with Langue-d'Oc names such as *Lou Baus* ("the rock") and *Lou Viol* ("the trail") have for many years helped to maintain the protected areas, providing great assistance to visitors to the region. Among the many recent projects, we should of course mention the GTA, or *Grande Traversata delle Alpi,* — Great Crossing of the Alps — developed in the Seventies in imitation of the French project developed by an association with the same name, and with the assistance of local agencies and organizations. The trail, which connects the Ossola with the Ligurian Alps, is pretty harsh

and tiring in this stretch, with steep climbs and descents, through often arid and sun-beaten high valleys. It is however precisely this harsh and wild character that makes these mountains so alluring. At the base of Monte Viso, the Oronaye, the Torre Castello and the Rocca Provenzale, it is easy to understand that the Alps of the Sun are one of the most remarkable places along the entire mountain chain. We hope that greater effort and attention from local government can help to bring the GTA out of the doldrums of recent years.

USEFUL INFORMATION

Duration: 11 days.
Elevations: ranging from the 1,281 metres of Strepeis to the 2,950 metres of the Colle delle Traversette.
Season: from July to September.
Signage: red and white for the GTA and the local trails.
Degree of difficulty: there are no climbing or equipped trails. At the beginning of the season, it is possible to encounter some fairly steep snow fields.

32 During the first stage, one passes by the lakes of the Head of the High Valley of Valasco, in whose waters are reflected the mountains of Argentera. This picture shows the lake of Claus, near the Questa hut. Photograph by Gianluca Boetti

How demanding: average.
Equipment: walking gear, ice axe useful at the beginning of the season.
Peaks: many peaks along the route are accessible to the tekker, beginning with the Argentera (3,297 metres). Monte Viso (3,841 metres), the peak that looms in clear view during the last stretch of the walk, has a standard route (stretches of second degree, steep snow fields) which is accessible to walkers accompanied by a guide.
How to get there: the Valdieri and Crissolo hot springs are linked by regular buses running from Cuneo.
Overnight accommodations: huts of the CAI (Italian Alpine Club) and privately owned rest points.
If you want to camp out: there are no restrictions against it, but you will feel the extra weight on certain particularly fatiguing stages.
Alpine Guides: Cooperativa Guida Alpine at Cuneo (39) (171) 65955 or else the Associazione accompagnatori (39) (171) 682390.
Weather Forecasts: contact the tourist bureaus or the regional government (39) (11) 3185555.
Mountain Rescue: dial 118 - Piemonte Elisoccorso.
Information Offices: Association GTA Torino (39) (171) 978388, Park of the Argentera Valdieri (39) (171) 97397, Bureau of Tourism of Dronero (39) (171) 917080, Local bureau of turism of the Saluzzo area (39) (175) 46710.
Useful phone numbers: La Grange hut (33) (93) 231463, overnight accommodations at Sant'Anna di Vinadio (39) (171) 959125, Hotel Strepeis (39) (171) 95831, Migliorero hut (39) (171) 95802, Chamber of Agritourism of the Gardetta (39) (171) 998119, overnight information and campgrounds of the Base Camp of Chiappera (39) (171) 98068, overnight information at Pelvo Bellino (39) (175) 95194, overnight information at the Furest Pontechianale (39) (175) 950161, Vallanta hut (39) (175) 95183, Refuge du Mont Viso (33) (92) 467566, Quintino Sella hut (39) (175) 94943, Hotel Pian del Re (39) (175) 94967, overnight information at Pian Melzé (39) (175) 94944.
Maps: the easiest solution is given by the IGC 1:50,000, n. 8 *Ligurian and Maritime Alps*, n. 7 *Valli Maira, Grana, and Stura* and n. 6 *Monviso*.

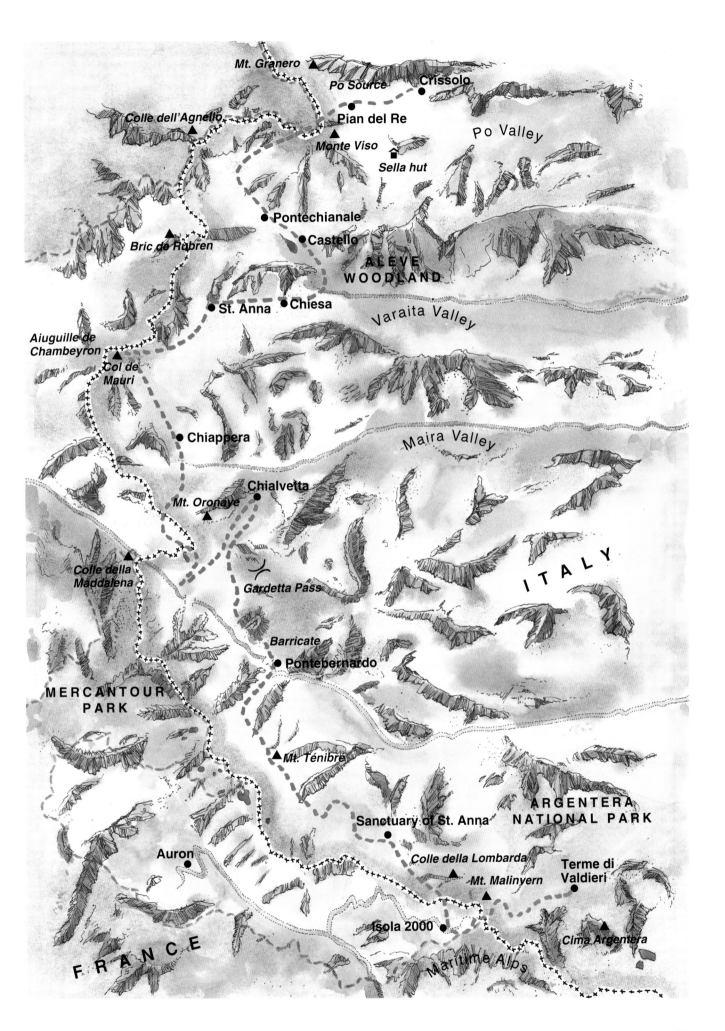

Mt. Granero ▲
Po Source
Crissolo ●
Po Valley
Colle dell'Agnello ▲
Pian del Re ▲
Monte Viso ▲
Sella hut
Pontechianale ●
Castello ●
Bric de Rubren ▲
ALEVE WOODLAND
St. Anna ● Chiesa ●
Varaita Valley
Aiuguille de Chambeyron ▲
Col de Mauri
Chiappera ●
Maira Valley
Chialvetta ●
Mt. Oronaye ▲
ITALY
Colle della Maddalena ▲
Gardetta Pass
Barricate
Pontebernardo ●
MERCANTOUR PARK
Mt. Ténibre ▲
ARGENTERA NATIONAL PARK
Sanctuary of St. Anna ●
Auron ●
Colle della Lombarda
Terme di Valdieri ●
Mt. Malinvern ▲
Isola 2000 ●
Cima Argentera ▲
FRANCE
Maritime Alps

FIRST DAY

From Terme di Valdieri to Isola 2000
Distance climbed: 1,240 metres
Distance descended: 390 metres
Time: 6 hours

The first stage of this walk allows one to review many of the most classic and spectacular sites of the park of Argentera. Worthy of note are the royal mule-tracks and the battlemented hunting lodge of Valasco, while the lakes of Valscura are also lovely. From the Terme, or hot springs (1,368 metres), one follows a dirt road — shortcuts are possible and highly recommended along the old mule-track — that runs up to the Pian del Valasco (1,762 metres) and the hunting lodge. A steep climb among the larch trees and a stretch running obliquely along the slope bring one to the lower lake of Valscura (2,274 metres). In a somewhat starker setting, one climbs up to the upper Valscura Lake (2,471 metres) and to the pass of the Bassa del Druos (2,628 metres) between the peaks of the Malinvern and Tavels.
At this point on French territory (and in the park of Mercantour) one descends toward Isola 2000 and the Refuge de La Grange (2,234 metres), an oasis of tranquillity in an area that has been badly torn up to make ski slopes.

SECOND DAY

from Isola 2000 to Strepeis
distance climbed: 600 metres
distance descended: 1,750 metres
time: 7 hours

This is a very long stage, and it can be broken into two parts by spending the night at the accommodations of the GTA at S. Anna di Vinadio. There are splendid views from the Colle della Lombarda, from the border ridge, and from the pass of Bravaria, while the final descent is very steep. One begins by climbing up among ski slopes and ski lifts to the Colle della Lombarda (2,351 metres),
and just beyond that point one reaches and turns off onto the border ridge. From the area around the Cima Moravacciera (2,378 metres) begins the climb down toward the sanctuary of S. Anna di Vinadio (2,010 metres). A long stretch running obliquely along the slope on ground that is at times marshy, followed by a climb, takes one to the pass of Bravaria (2,311 metres).
A long descent among mountain meadows, and then through woods, leads to Strepeis (1,281 metres).

34 bottom
The battlemented hunting lodge built at the orders of Victor Emanuel II looms over the meadows of the Piano del Valasco, one of the most celebrated places in Argentera. Used nowadays as a seasonal sheep-fold, the building bears a plaque dating from 1888. Photograph by Stefano Ardito

35 The Piano del Valasco is one of the most verdant and pleasant spots in the Maritime Alps. From this broad clearing, crossed by a melodious brook, one can climb up a steep trail leading to the lakes of Valscura. Photograph by Gianluca Boetti

THIRD DAY
from Strepeis to the Migliorero hut
distance climbed: 1,200 metres
distance descended: 370 metres
time: 5 hours

This is a fairly short stage, mostly a transition; at the beginning the straw roofs of the little village of San Bernolfo are interesting.
This stay can be shortened by climbing up to the hut through the high valley of Ischiator and continuing from there to the Talarico hut, or else hitchhiking all the way to San Bernolfo.
The route follows the road — which runs along an ancient route of the salt caravans — to Callieri and San Bernolfo (1,702 metres), where there is emergency overnight accommodation in a hayloft.
Then one climbs up to the pass of Laroussa (2,471 metres) and from there one descends through extensive scree to the Migliorero hut (2,100 metres).

FOURTH DAY
from the Migliorero hut to the Talarico hut
distance climbed: 620 metres
distance descended: 1,000 metres time:
4 hours 30 minutes

This is a fairly undemanding stage, through dramatic settings, and along this route it is likely that one will see marmots and chamois.
On the meadows of the high valley (Prati del Vallone), it is worthwhile stopping to tour a small botanical garden and some juniper growings.
One begins by passing a bunker, and climbing fairly steeply all the way to the pass of Rostagno (2,536 metres). One descends, running past the Zanotti hut (2,200 metres usually closed), one descends until reaching a dirt road (2,042 metres), and then one continues to climb up to the pass of Scolettas (2,223 metres), where there are other fortifications dating from the 1930s.
A long series of switchbacks takes one up to the Prati del Vallone and to the Talarico hut (1,712 metres).

FIFTH DAY
from the Talarico hut to Pontebernardo
distance climbed: 1,150 metres
distance descended: 1,550 metres
time: 6 hours 30 minutes

This is an interesting stage, fairly lengthy but easy because of the good mule-tracks that served the bunkers. The high-point of the day is the tour of the amazing fortifications of the Becchi Rossi, with galleries that can be entered, with considerable caution.
One begins with a long climb running up into the high valley of Stau and leading to the Colle di Stau (2,500 metres). One begins to descend into the high valley of Forneris, crossing the meadows of the Comba del Pilone and the Rio Forneris (1,888 metres).
Then one climbs back up to the Colle dei Becchi Rossi (2,235 metres), alongside which stand the bunker and little forts. A long series of switchbacks through lovely stands of larch brings one to the meadows of Murenz (1,567 metres) and then on to Pontebernardo (1,322 metres), in one of the most Dolomitic spots of the Piedmontese mountains.

SIXTH DAY
from Pontebernardo to Chialvetta
distance climbed: 1,200 metres
distance descended: 950 metres
time: 7 hours

Another long and tiring stage, which leads to the Val Maira through solitary and wild settings. Right at the beginning, the gorge are limestone walls of the Barricate very impressive, and can be seen clearly from the village.

The silhouette of Monte Oronaye is also quite distinctive. One begins at the foot of a rock wall, where there are some of the toughest rock-climbing routes in all of Piedmont, then one climbs up to the houses of Serre (1,496 metres) and then on to the lake of Oserot (2,320 metres). After crossing over the pass of Gardetta (2,437 metres), one descends to the base of the wall of Monte Oronaye and toward the handsome villages of the high valley of Unerzio. The rest point is at Chialvetta (1,494 metres).

SEVENTH DAY
from Chialvetta to Chiappera
distance climbed: 850 metres
distance descended: 700 metres
time: 4 hours 30 minutes

This is a short stage. It is possible to skip it entirely by following the valley, or else one can take a detour that is wilder and more difficult through the high valley of Enchiausa. The first part runs along the mule-track to Pratorotondo and Grange (1,784 metres), and from there one takes an old military dirt road, climbing up to the Colle Ciarbonet (2,206 metres). From there one descends among stands of larch and meadows, one climbs back up among huge boulders, and then one descends to the source of the river Maira (1,645 metres). Climbing and descending, one continues on to Chiappera (1,661 metres), at the base of the group Castello-Provenzale.

EIGHTH DAY
from Chiappera to Chiesa di Bellino
distance climbed: 1,150 metres
distance descended: 1,350 metres
time: 7 hours

This is a long and greatly varied stage through the meadows of the Alta Val Maira, and then descending through the various villages of Bellino — Blins in Langue-d'Oc — which are some of the best preserved examples of the traditional architecture of these valleys. From the Colle di Bellino, one finally sees the pyramid of Monte Viso growing closer. One begins along a somewhat boring dirt road, but within sight of the waterfall of Stroppia and the walls of the Rocca Provenzale. After passing a number of huts, one reaches the fork between the trail of Col Maurin and the trail of Colle di Bellino. On the right, one reaches the Colle di Bellino (2,804 metres). One descends into the wild high valley of Bellino, one passes the gorge of the Barricate, one crosses the grassy Pian Ceiol, and then one passes the villages of S. Anna (1,882 metres), Chianale (1,705 metres), Préfauchier (1,700 metres), and Pleyne (1,576 metres). At Chiesa (1,480 metres) one will find overnight accommodation.

36 left
The limestone walls of the Monte Oronaye, an elegant peak that rises to an elevation of 3,100 metres, separate the Valle Stura from the Val Maira, and loom high above the trail of the Grand Tour of the Alps in the stretch between Pontebernardo and Chialvetta.
Photograph by Stefano Ardito

36 right The massif formed by the Torre Castello (2,448 metres) and the Rocca Provenzale (2,402 metres) looms over the head of the Val Maira with its rock faces and its jutting points, all made of very sound rock and therefore very popular with Piedmontese climbers.
Photograph by A. Gogna/K3

NINTH DAY

*from Chiesa di Bellino
to Pontechianale
distance climbed: 800 metres
distance descended: 870 metres
time: 4 hours 30 minutes*

This is a brief, very panoramic stage, which runs past a number of mountain summer meadows which are still well used. The trail runs up to the Granges dell'Alpe (1,703 metres) and to the Granges di Esperià (1,924 metres), then it follows the old military road up to the Grangia Forest (1,998 metres). The Colletto della Battagliola (2,260 metres) offers a remarkable view of Monte Viso. After crossing through a forest of alder, one climbs over a shoulder with a remarkable view, and then descends across from the dense forest of Alevé to Pontechianale. Overnight accommodation available in the village of Forest (1,614 metres).

*37 top The Monte Viso (3,841 metres) and the Visolotto (3,348 metres) are reflected in the waters of lake Chiaretto, which is surrounded by a splendid stand of blooming rhododendrons in the early summer.
Photograph by Gianluca Boetti*

*37 bottom The Upper Lake of Viso, at an altitude of 2,313 metres, is one of the most enchanting lakes in the Cottian Alps, and can be reached via a brief and spectacular variant of the walk.
Photograph by Stefano Ardito*

TENTH DAY

*from Pontechianale
to the Monte Viso hut
distance climbed: 1,200 metres
distance descended: 350 metres
time: 6 hours 30 minutes*

This is a final long and tiring climb up the wild high valley of Vallanta, over which looms the western slope of Monte Viso and its satellite peaks, chief among them the Punta Caprera and the Visolotto. The forest of the Alevé, the largest stand of Swiss pines in Italy, is particularly lovely. Otherwise, one can climb up from Chianale to the hut through the high valley of Soustra. One begins by reaching the houses of Castello (1,603 metres), and there a trail begins that runs up the high valley of Vallanta. At the grange of Gheit (1,912 metres) one passes on the right — a possible variation — the trail that leads up to the pass of San Chiaffredo and the Sella hut, and then one continues along the high valley, which becomes progressively wilder and more unspoilt, until one reaches the new Vallanta hut (2,450 metres) and the old Gagliardone hut. A last steep climb takes one up to the pass of Vallanta (2,811 metres), and from there one descends into the upper Vallée de la Guil until one reaches the Monte Viso hut (2,460 metres).

ELEVENTH DAY

*from the Monte Viso hut to Crissolo
distance climbed: 520-590 metres
distance descended: 1,580-1,650 metres
time: 6 hours*

The final stage in this walk completes the tour of Monte Viso, taking one back into Italy, past the Colle delle Traversette and the "Buco di Viso," the first Alpine tunnel in history, some seventy-five metres in length, built between 1475 and 1480 at the orders of the Marquis Ludovico II of Saluzzo. From the hut, a short descent and a very tough climb take one up to the Colle (2,950 metres), just beneath which (2,882 metres) is the entrance to the tunnel, which is sometimes blocked by snow, and which requires a torch. A good mule-track leads down to the Pian Mait di Viso (2,711 metres), to the Pian Armoine (2,410 metres), and then on to the Pian del Re (2,020 metres), where there is a comfortable hut, and the source of the river Po. Partly by road and partly by an old mule-track, one descends to the Pian Melzé (1,714 metres), and then on to Crissolo (1,317 metres)

FROM THE GRAN PARADISO
TO THE VANOISE

"Walking among the ibex" in the
great national parks along the border
between France and Italy

*38 A party of
mountaineers
following the track
that leads up to the
4,061-metre
elevation of the
summit of the Gran
Paradiso, one of the
easiest and most
popular "four-
thousands" in the
Alps. Here, every
summer, thousands
of people enjoy the
views and thrills of
high altitudes.*
Photograph by
Stefano Ardito

"The best interest of the natural
sciences, and, in particular, of the
zoological sciences, demands that
we take every precaution imaginable
to protect the species of those
animals that are reduced to only a
few individuals, thus running the risk
of total extinction. One such an
animal, indeed, in the royal domains,
is the ibex, known in Italian as
stambecco and in French as the
Bouquetin des Alpes, called by
naturalists the Capra ibex, and by the
inhabitants of the Val d'Aosta the
Bouc-castagn. It is therefore, based
on our certain knowledge, and
availing ourselves of our power as
royal highness, conferred upon us,
that we order as follows: First, that
from this moment forth it is forbidden
to hunt and kill the ibex in any part of
our royal kingdom." These words,
written long-ago in 1821, are the first
declaration of what was to become
known as the *Regie Patenti*, the
documents, drawn up over the
signature of the knight Thaon de
Revel, that lay the foundation stone of
the structure that led to the salvation
of one of the most remarkable animals
in Europe. As early as the beginning
of the eighteenth century, in fact, the
ibex had become extinct in Austria,
and over the course of the nineteenth
century, the last ibexes were
slaughtered in Switzerland and in the
Dauphiné. In the Kingdom of Sardinia,
from that year forward, the last few
hundred surviving ibex became *de
facto* personal property of the
monarchs. Thus, Victor Emanuel II
(the "Hunter King" of Sardinia, and the
first king of Italy) and his descendents
arrogated to themselves alone the
right to hunt the ibex, in their hunting
preserves of the Maritime Alps and the
Gran Paradiso. The royal hunting was
not enough to wipe out the species,
and in 1922, when many of the royal
hunting grounds were turned over to

the Italian state, the new-born
National Park of Gran Paradiso
proved to possess the last surviving
ibex in Europe. More than seventy
years of effort, combatting problems
of every sort and poachers that have
never entirely given up their prey,
has led to a successful reestablishment
of the species. From the Gran
Paradiso core groups, ibex have been
reintroduced into many areas of the
Alps, from the region near Tarvisio to
the Marmarole, from the massif of
the Monte Rosa to the Stelvio. All on
their own, step by step, one by one,
these magnificent animals have
returned to many places in the Valle
d'Aosta and, just over the border, in
the magnificent French National Park

*39 The impressive
pyramidal shape of
the Grande Casse
(3,855 metres) as it
appears from the
bridge of Moncroévie,
in the heart of the
massif of the Vanoise.*
Photograph by
Gianluca Boetti

of the Vanoise, which was established in 1963. Besides the ibex, of which there are now thousands of individuals, this great protected area is inhabited by chamois, golden eagles, ermine, alpine hares and marmots. There are also splendid flowers, and forests of evergreens on both slopes. Among the walkers and naturalists of Europe, the two twin parks have joined the list of places not to miss. At the heart of the protected areas are some of the highest and most unspoiled massifs of the Western Alps. In the Gran Paradiso, aside from the peak of the same name (which towers 4,061 metres above sea level and is one of the most popular four-thousand metre peaks in the Alps), one should take special note of the savage rock pyramid of the Grivola (3,969 metres), the Gran San Pietro (3,692 metres), and the proud Herbetet (3,778 metres). On the boundary dividing the two parks and the two nations stand the Levanne (3,619 metres) and the Punta di Galisia (3,346 metres). Among the many peaks in the Vanoise, we should mention the pristine Mont Pourri (3,779 metres), the anything-but-trivial Grande Casse (3,852 metres), the Grande Motte (3,626 metres) — sadly defaced by the ski resorts of Val d'Isère — and the Dent Parrachée (3,684 metres).
Both of the parks are particularly suited to summer mountain-climbing, at levels of average or slight difficulty, cross-country skiing and alpine skiing, especially in the springtime. Also, as in all the parks, walking is the activity that brings one closest to the wildlife of the mid-elevation and high-elevation mountains. Here, for those who like to walk, there is almost no end to the possibilities. From each of the main villages in the two parks (Cogne, Rhême-Notre-Dame, Valsavaranche, and Ceresole Reale in Italy, Val d'Isère, Lanslebourg-Mont-Cenis, Pralognan-la-Vanoise, and Bonneval-sur-Arc in France) there are dozens of stays of all lengths and degrees of difficulty. The harsh Vallon de la Rocheure and the green and wooded Valnontey, the meadowlands of the Nivolet and of the Col de la Vanoise, the panoramic views of the Money or of the lake of Djuan are renowned among alpine walkers everywhere. The Sentier Balcon of the valley of

the Arc, which largely runs along the border of the Park of the Vanoise, is one of the loveliest trails of its sort in all of the Alps. Also worthy of note are the traditional wooden buildings found in the Valle di Cogne, the "hunting lodges" built at the orders of Victor Emanuel II — one of them has been transformed into the Sella hut — as well as the old stone houses of Bessans, the little capital of the Haute Maurienne. For those who are interested in longer routes, three

of the most important walking routes in the area come exceedingly close here, without ever touching: the French GR 5 (also known as the Grande Traversée des Alpes), the Piedmontese Grande Traversata delle Alpi , and the High Route No 2 of the Valle d'Aosta. While the French route (with its variants, the GR 5E and the GR 55) includes a great many splendid walks. Both of the Italian routes are quite difficult, because of the long and tiring climbs and

40 The Grande Casse, the highest summit in the massif, looms over one of the handsome grassy hollows of the Vanoise. This flock at pasture was photographed nearby the Entre-Deux-Eaux hut. Photograph by Gianluca Boetti

descents. What we are describing here is a completely new route, which we feel incorporates the best of each of the two parks. This is a route that includes more than one tough climb (in particular, a steep climb up to the Col Lauson), running past a number of magnificent vantage-points; there are a number of fine variations on the theme, with this route, and at many points along the way, one is likely to be treated to the spectacle of chamois and ibex leaping and climbing high above. In a few years, when the Park of Mont Blanc is joined — as we fervently hope — with the two existing parks, this route will allow one to explore the historical centre of the largest protected areas in the Alps.

41 top The ibex, which has now been reintroduced on many of the massifs of the Alps, owes its survival to the creation of the Park of the Gran Paradiso in 1922. Photograph by Marcello Bertinetti/ White Star

41 center A party of mountaineers is hard at work climbing the standard route on the Gran Paradiso, one of the most spectacular of the many high-altitude trails in the park. Photograph by Marcello Bertinetti/ White Star

41 bottom A walker crosses the Erfaulet bridge (1,850 metres), along the classic trail that runs uphill through woods, mountain summer meadows, and rocky slabs to Valnontey. In the background are the imposing seracs of the glacier of the Tribolazione. Photograph by Stefano Ardito

Duration: 8 days.

Elevations: ranging from the 1,418 metres of Pralognan-la-Vanoise to the 3,296 metres of the Col Lauson.

Season: from July to September.

Signage: yellow triangles of the Alta Via number 2 of the Valle d'Aosta, red and white trailmarkers of the GR, local trailmarkers are yellow and red-and-white.

Degree of difficulty: minimal technical difficulties, aside from the snow fields that one may encoùnter at the beginning of the season.

How demanding: average, but with a few stages (in particular, the stage of the Col Lauson) that are quite fatiguing and demanding.

The average elevation is considerable.

Equipment: normal mountain gear, ice axe needed for the Col Lauson and the Colle del Carro until the end of July.

Peaks: from the Sella hut it is traditional to climb up to the Gran Serra (or Grand Sertz, 3,552 metres), while from the Nivolet, it is possible to climb up to the Punta Fourà (3,411 metres) or the Punta Basei (3,338 metres), and from the Col de la Vanoise begins the none-too-easy (AD) standard route of the Grande Casse (3,855 metres). The climb that is most recommended along the route is that of the Gran Paradiso (4,061 metres), in two days from Pont, with an overnight stay at the Vittorio Emanuele II or Chabod huts.

How to get there: Cogne can be reached by bus from Aosta, which can in turn be reached from Milan and Turin by train (very slow) or by bus, and from Geneva by bus. From Pralognan-la-Vanoise one can take a bus to Moutiers, continuing by train to Chambéry, along the railroad line Lyon-Turin. If one stops one's walk at Plan du Lac, one can climb down to Termignon and one can reach the railroad at Modane.

How to get around: buses from Eaux-Rousses and Dégioz to Aosta, and from Bonneval-sur-Arc, Bessans, and Termignon to Modane.

Overnight accommodations: huts of the CAI (Italian Alpine Club), of the CAF (French Alpine Club) and of the National Park of the Vanoise; hotels and privately owned hotels and rest points.

If you want to camp out: camping is forbidden in the park of the Gran Paradiso and is only permitted alongside certain huts in the park of the Vanoise.

Alpine Guides: contact bureaus of tourism or else the Cooperativa Interguide at Aosta (39) (165) 40939.

Weather Forecasts: Météo Savoie (33) 36650273 - Valle D'Aosta (39) (165) 44113.

Mountain Rescue: in Italy, contact the headquarters in Aosta (39) (165) 238222, in France, the PGM of Bourg St. Maurice (33) 50531689, the PGM of Modane (33) 79051188 or the CRS of Pralognan (33) 79087115.

Information Offices: Chamber of Tourism of Cogne (39) (165) 74040, Tourist Bureau of Valsavaranche (39) (165) 95055, Tourist Bureau of Ceresole Reale (39) (124) 953121, Syndicat d'initiative di Bonneval-sur-Arc (33) 79059595, Syndicat d'initiative di Bessans (33) 79059652, Syndicat d'initiative di Lanslebourg (33) 79052366, Syndicat d'initiative di Termignon (33) 79050367, Syndicat d'initiative di Pralognan-la-Vanoise (33) 79087168.

Useful phone numbers: main office of the national park of Gran Paradiso (39) (11) 8171187, national park of Gran

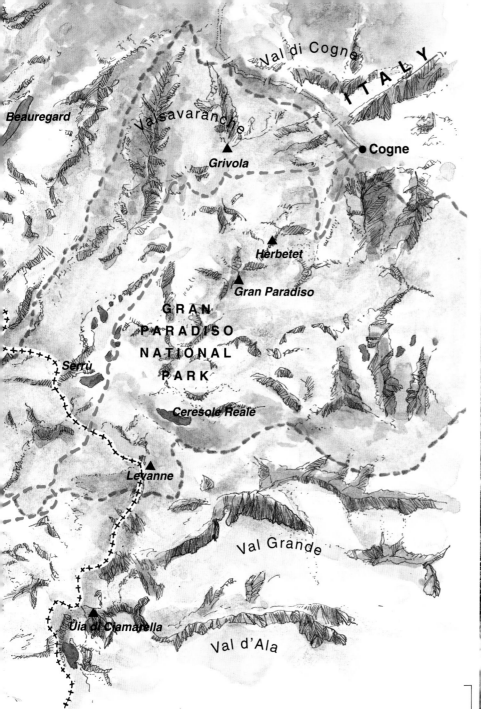

Paradiso Cogne (39) (165) 96116, national park of the Vanoise (33) 79623054, Sella hut (39) (165) 74310, Città di Chivasso hut (39) (124) 953150, Carro hut (33) 79059579, Vallonbrun hut (33) 79059393, Porte de Plan du Lac hut (33) 79205085, Entre-Deux-Eaux hut (33) 79205167, Félix-Faure hut (33) 79082523.

Maps: for the Italian slope, the Kompass n. 86 *Gran Paradiso-Valle d'Aosta* and the IGC n. 3 *Parco Nazionale del Gran Paradiso* (both to a scale of 1:50,000). In France one can choose between the Didier et Richard 1:50,000 n. 11 *Parc National de la Vanoise* or the more detailed IGN to a scale of 1:25,000.

Guide books: *Walking in the*

Tarentaise and Beaufortain Alps by J.W. Akitt (cicerone Press) - includes Vanoise National Park; *Walking the French Alps* by Martin Collins (Cicerone Press) - GR5 out of print; *Walking the Alpine Parks of France & Northwest Italy* by Marcia Lleberman (The Mountaineers) - walking in the Mercantour, Queyras, Ecrins, Vanoise and Gran Paradiso; *La Vanoise Parc National GR5-55* by the Fédération Française de la Randonée Pédestre and *Le valli del Moncenisio* (The Valleys of Moncenisio) by Gruppo Ricerche Cultura Montana (CDA 1992).

43 Ibex in great numbers appear in the high section of the Lauson, not far from the Sella hut, and at the fork where the trails to the Col Lauson and the Colle della Rossa intersect. Photograph by F. Reiser/K3

FIRST DAY

from Cogne to the Sella hut
distance climbed: 920-1,000 metres
distance descended: 0-80 metres
time: 2 hours 30 minutes-4 hours
30 minutes

Set at the heart of a green hollow, enclosed between the massifs of Grivola and Gran Serra (or Grand Sertz), the Sella hut at Lauson receives more visitors than any other hut in the park of Gran Paradiso, and it is the best location for observing ibex. It is possible to climb directly up to the hut along the sunny mule-track from Valnontey, but it is a much nicer walk if one goes up through the Valnontey, passing the Herbetet huts, a remarkable vantage-point of the massif. From Cogne (1,534 metres) one can reach Valnontey (1,666 metres) by bus; one can walk the distance in roughly an hour. The mule-track leading up to the hut begins at the alpine garden Paradisia, climbing through hairpin turns in the woods, and then obliquely along the slope through the high valley of Lauson all the way up to the hut (2,584 metres). Otherwise, one can continue along the valley, walking past the mountain hut of Valmiana (1,729 metres) and the Erfaulet bridge (1,830 metres). A steep climb through hairpin turns takes one up to the mountain hut of Herbetet (2,435 metres), a remarkable vantage-point of the seracs of the glacier of Tribolazione, the largest in the entire massif. A handsome trail, with a few exposed stretches, traverses obliquely along the slope lengthwise in a northerly direction, running right by the Laghetto del Lauson (2,656 metres) and then dropping down to the hut. At dusk, it is not a bad idea to climb another twenty minutes up the high valley over the hut, all the way up to the area where ibex are more common.

SECOND DAY

from Sella hut to Eaux-Rousses
distance climbed: 710 metres
distance descended: 1,630 metres
time: 6 hours

The stage that is devoted to crossing the Col Lauson is a long and tiring one, and it follows an ancient mule-track that runs between Val di Cogne and Valsavaranche. The landscape is the fitting reward to the effort expended. The old royal mule-track has collapsed here and there, and at the beginning of the season, one might well make profitable use of an ice axe and crampons. One starts out along the trail that runs up the high valley, and then passes on the right (2,844 metres) the fork with the path running out to the Colle della Rossa, and then one climbs sharply up to the foot of the spurs of the Grivola. A slightly more exposed stretch (fixed ropes) leads to the Col Lauson (3,296 metres). One climbs past there, with a number of switchbacks, up into a very wild high valley dominated by the shapes of the Grivola and the Herbetet; at the end of this high valley, one crosses a little bridge, and one reaches the mountain summer meadows of Lower Leviona (2,303 metres).
A large mule-track runs obliquely along the slope through the woods, and then drops down sharply to Eaux-Rousses (1,666 metres).

THIRD DAY

from Eaux-Rousses to Colle del Nivolet
distance climbed: 1,100 metres
distance descended: 200 metres
time: 6 hours

A fairly long but not tiring climb up to the lake of Djuan, followed by a lengthy traverse across to the pastures of the Nivolet, split this stage sharply into two parts. After the forest of the first section, one walks over open ground, facing out over an unbelievable view of the mountain range that runs from the Gran Paradiso to the Grivola. The area surrounding Lake Djuan has long been threatened by plans for the construction of skilifts, which would clash greatly with the true nature of the Park. One starts out along a steep trail that runs into the woods, becoming gentler and then leading on to the ruins of the hunting lodge of Orvieille (2,164 metres), which may be the most splendid of all the hunting lodges built by Italy's king, Victor Emanuel II, in the late nineteenth century. Set upon open ground, the trail climbs obliquely along the slope all the way up to the mountain summer meadows of Djuan (2,230 metres) and to the Lake Djuan (2,515 metres), a remarkable vantage-point. Leaving the High Route No 2, one follows the trail that runs over Costa le Manteau, crossing the high valley of the Meyes, runs around the Costa Aouillé, leading finally to Pian Borgno and Piano del Nivolet. One climbs up this trail all the way to Savoia (2,532 metres) and Città di Chivasso huts (2,604 metres).

FOURTH DAY

from the Colle del Nivolet
to the Refuge du Carro
distance climbed: 1,200 metres
distance descended: 940 metres
time: 6 hours 30 minutes

Another tiring stage, which runs over the border crest between the Aiguille Rousse and the massif of the Levanne along a trail repaired between 1992 and 1993 in commemoration of the seventieth anniversary of the foundation of the park of Gran Paradiso. Along the first part of this trail, the road is quite distracting, while in the second half, wilderness once again becomes the prevailing presence. Hitchhiking during the first half can save one a bit more than an hour. After crossing the Colle del Nivolet (2,612 metres), one follows the road (shortcuts are

possible) that runs down to the lakes of Agnel (2,295 metres) and Serrù (2,275 metres). After a number of switchbacks, a trail leading off to the right leads up to the mountain summer meadows of Prato Rotondo (2,166 metres) and Sansoero (1,919 metres) and to the bottom of the high valley of the Carro. One climbs for a considerable time along this valley, in an increasingly unspoilt setting, dominated by the Aiguille Rousse and the Punta dell'Uja. After reaching the Colle del Carro (3,109 metres) one descends quickly to the Lakes Noir and Blanc and to the Refuge du Carro (2,759 metres).

FIFTH DAY

from Refuge du Carro to Bessans
distance climbed: 320 metres
distance descended: 1,120 metres
time: 7 hours

A restful stage, at first downhill and then along level ground, which leads to the Arc valley and to the pleasant Bessans. The final section of this trail, which runs along the GR5, is called the Balcon de Maurienne, and features a handsome vista of the massifs of the Albaron de Savoie, the Ciamarella,

44 top The trail that links the isolated cottages of the Herbetet with the little lake of the Lauson and the Sella hut offers a splendid view of the peaks and the woods of the Valnontey.
Photograph by Gianluca Boetti

44 bottom The shepherds' huts of the Herbetet, at an altitude of 2,424 metres, are a classic destination for day-trips from Cogne, as well as providing a spectacular vantage-point over the glacier of the Tribolazione and the Gran Paradiso.
Photograph by Marcello Bertinetti/ White Star

45 top The trail of the Costa della Civetta, a brief and solitary variant in the area around the Colle del Nivolet and its huts, allows one to observe the long climb that leads up to the Colle del Carro.
Photograph by Gianluca Boetti

45 bottom From the Colle del Nivolet, a spectacular panorama opens out over the peaks that form the head of the Valle dell'Orco. From left to right, one can see Punta Basei (3,338 metres), Grande Aiguille Rousse (3,483 metres), Colle del Carro, and Levanne (3,619 metres).
Photograph by Gianluca Boetti

and the Charbonnel. A slightly shorter route passes through L'Ecot and Bonneval-sur-Arc. One begins on the trail that leads up to the hut, which traverses at length, running past the Lac du Pys, and then one descends as far as a fork in the trail (2,611 metres). Here one takes a right, going past the small lakes of Plan des Eaux and then, in the Vallon de la Lenta, one runs into the road toward the Col de l'Iseran. Beyond this road, on the GR 5, one reaches the meadows of Les Roches (2,453 metres) and Le Vallon (2,240 metres), followed by the Refuge du Mollard (2,230 metres) in the French National Park of Vanoise, winding up in the lovely village of Bessans (1,705 metres), which deserves a thorough exploration.

SIXTH DAY
from Bessans to the Refuge du Cuchet
distance climbed: 700 metres
distance descended: 240 metres
time: 4 hours 30 minutes

This is a fairly undemanding stage, continuing on the Sentier Balcon, with a fine view of the massifs that straddle the border between France and Italy. One walks along for quite a way along the boundary of the park, amid pleasant meadows. There is only one brief stretch that is sharply steep and tiring.
One begins along a plain trail on the right bank of the Arc, and then, from the Col de la Madeleine (1,752 metres) one climbs steeply away up to the Chalets du Mollard (2,130 metres), followed by the houses of La Fesse-d'en-Haut (2,290 metres), and on to Refuge de Vallonbrun (2,272 metres). From here, it is possible to detour toward the prehistoric site of Pierre-aux-Pieds (2,730 metres, 2 hours 30 minutes, round trip, extra), made up of about eighty cupels, and about as many engravings. This marks the beginning of the long walk across the foot of the arid slopes of the Grand Roc Noir and the other nearby peaks, which leads to the stream of Nay and to Refuge du Cuchet (2,160 metres), equipped but without attendant. Those walkers who might prefer to stay overnight in a hotel can climb down (700 metres, of descent, and an extra hour-and-a-half) to Lanslebourg-Mont-Cenis (1,400 metres).

SEVENTH DAY
from the Refuge du Cuchet
to the Refuge d'Entre-deux-Eaux
distance climbed: 680 metres
distance descended: 720 metres
time: 4 hours 30 minutes

After completing the high-line route, one enters with this stage into the broad high valley carved out by the Doron de Termigon, which is called at higher elevations the Vallon de la Rocheure.
Here, at the foot of the rocks of the Grande Casse and the Grande Motte, and within sight of the glaciers of the Dôme de Chasseforet, is the heart of the National Park of the Vanoise.
One begins descending slightly as far down as the fork of Pré Vaillant (1,917 metres), where those who climbed down to Lanslebourg can return to the main trail.
A further climb brings one up to the chalets de la Turra de Termignon (2,290 metres) and then one climbs further obliquely along the slope until reaching the chalets of La Femma (2,473 metres), after which one descends to the parking area of Bellecombe (2,307 metres).
Along a road that has been closed to traffic, or along a trail that runs parallel to this one, one reaches the "gate of the Park" on the Plan du Lac (2,364 metres): one would be well advised to make a brief detour right up to the rim of the canyon of Doron de Termignon.
A trail drops down to the mountain stream of Vallon de la Rocheure (2,053 metres), where one leaves the GR 5, and one climbs up to the Refuge d'Entre-Deux-Eaux (2,120 metres).

47 top
The prehistoric petroglyphs of the Pierre-aux-Pieds give some indication of just how ancient is the presence of humans on the slopes of the Vanoise, among the meadows and the moraines above an altitude of twenty-five hundred metres. The detour that runs up here is of particular interest.
Photograph by Furio Chiaretta

EIGHTH DAY

from Refuge d'Entre-Deux-Eaux
to Pralognan-la-Vanoise
distance climbed: 420 metres
distance descended: 1,120 metres
time: 4 hours 30 minutes

The final day of walking, long and pleasant, leads one up to the broad grassy saddle of the Col de la Vanoise, shaped by ancient glaciers, now dotted with numerous lakes. One begins by descending obliquely along the slope, crossing the Leisse over the Pont de Croé-Vie (2,099 metres), and then one climbs steeply back up to the edge of the broad plateau that leads to the Col de la Vanoise and to the Félix-Faure hut (2,517 metres), between the Lac Rond and the Lac Long. The trail continues northward, to the base of the steep Glacier des Grands Couloirs, which is crossed by the difficult standard route of Grande Casse, then it runs to the left, descends to the Lac des Vaches (2,319 metres), and then continues along the bottom of the Vallon de la Glière, partly cluttered with ski facilities. After passing by the Refuge des Barmettes (2,010 metres) one climbs down to the shepherds' huts of Fontanettes and to Pralognan-la-Vanoise (1,418 metres).

47 centre A narrow little waterfall enlivens the rocks that were sculpted long ago by ancient glaciers, tumbling down from the Grande Casse, at the foot of the Col de la Vanoise.
Photograph by Gianluca Boetti

47 bottom In the comfortable Entre-Deux-Eaux hut, it is possible to enjoy moments of rest and relaxation, while admiring the dramatic bulk of the Grande Casse.
Photograph by Gianluca Boetti

46 The lake of Serrù is one of the most remarkable in all the mountains of the Piedmont region. It lies at an altitude of 2275 metres along the road that runs down from the Colle del Nivolet toward the Valle dell'Orco, before climbing back up toward the Colle del Carro.
Photograph by R. Carnovalini

TOUR OF MONT BLANC

Around the most spectacular
mountain in Europe

*48-49 In the summer,
at dawn, the snowy
Bosses ridge is
always crowded
with alpinists. It is
not easy to find
seclusion and
solitude on Mont*
*Blanc's standard
route, where as
many as three
hundred persons
might pass by in
just a few hours.*
Photograph by
Gianluca Boetti

*49 From the
Bosses ridge, one
can survey the
Vallot hut and the
broad glacial
slopes of the Col
du Dôme and the
Dôme du Gouter*
*(4,304 metres). In
this setting, in the
late eighteenth
century, man first
climbed to high
altitudes.*
Photograph by
Gianluca Boetti

Mountain meadows and the occasional grazing cow, delicate little waterfalls, small rocky outcroppings.

The distinctive features found while climbing up from the Vallée des Glaciers to the Col de la Seigne are not among the most exciting. Once one reaches the high pass, however, things change radically. This pass has been used ever since ancient times. The view is spectacular. Spread out before one is the marshy plateau of Combal, in the shadow of the jagged Pyramides Calcaires, while at the far end of the Val Vény one can glimpse the Grandes Jorasses, the Dente del Gigante, and the grim and distant Grand Combin. Closer in appears the remarkable jumble of boulders, ice, and unbridled nature of Mont Blanc. It is a breathtaking view. Here, at the Col de la Seigne, one may well take a halt to rest and to read the comments of travellers of the past.

"The remarkable series of the Lex Blanche, the Val Vény, and the Val Ferret is like a Wagnerian opera," wrote Samivel, the most romantic French author to write about the mountains. "The pyramid of the Aiguille Noire soars straight up beyond belief, while to the westward, the gaze is captured by the majestic group of the Aiguilles des Glaciers and of Trélatète," according to the *Guida delle Alpi Graie*, by Bobba and Vaccarone (1896). "An active pedestrian can cross from Chamonix to Courmayeur along this route in two days' time... the landscape makes this part of the route always very interesting for true nature-lovers," wrote John Ball, the first president of the Alpine Club, in 1863. Ball was the author of the first guidebook to the Western Alps, where the Mont Blanc massif was mentioned for the first time. Huge, evocative, solemn landscapes, like those which can be seen from the Col de la Seigne, are quite common fare when one travels entirely around Mont Blanc on foot. The Col de Balme, for example, is another: here, after making the difficult climb up from Trient, one can admire the great glacial flows of the massif, as well as the jagged silhouettes of the Chamonix Aiguilles. Another spectacular feature worth mentioning is the meadows of Bellevue, at the foot of the ice face of the Aiguille de Bionnassay, the bulwark of the massif overlooking the Vallée de Montjoie and Sallanches. On the Swiss slopes, an exhausting walk through the Vallon d'Arpette leads one to look out upon the imposing and crooked séracs and huge crevasses and to listen awe-struck to the silence broken only by the sinister creaking and thumps of the Glacier du Trient, the easternmost glacier of Mont Blanc.

50-51 A phase in the easy climb up to the Col Ferret, amidst gentle meadows in which very thormy alpine plants called cirsium *stand out. In the background, one can see the Pré de Bar glacier and the massif of Mont Dolent (3,819 metres).*
Photograph by
M. Lanfranchi/Overseas

50 bottom The pointy, jagged Aiguille Noire de Peuterey, a remarkable rocky summit rising 3774 metres looms over the evergreen forests of the Val Vény. The south ridge, which can only be seen in part in this photograph, is one of the classic climbs in the Alps.
Photograph by
Stefano Ardito

51 bottom To the north of Chamonix, the massif of the Aiguilles Rouges offers remarkable views of Mont Blanc. Here we see the classic panorama of the mount, seen from the granite slabs around Lac Blanc.
Photograph by
Pascal Tournaire

From the pleasant hut of Pré, overlooking Courmayeur as if from a high balcony, an easy and lovely grassy ridge leads one gradually up to the Mont de la Saxe, to the Testa della Tronche, and to the Col Sapin. Directly across the way, the Grandes Jorasses seem to become increasingly jagged and sharp. Alongside them, the Aiguille de Leschaux, the massif of Gruetta, and Mont Dolent appear increasingly elegant. On the French side, still, the Tour of Mont Blanc includes the best known and most spectacular trail in the Alps: the one that runs from Montroc and from the fir-tree forests, at the foot of the looming Aiguillette d'Argentière, on past the Lac Blanc, the Flégère, Planpraz, and the summit of the Brévent that travellers and climbers have praised as an

excellent vantage point ever since the early nineteenth century.

As a sequence of panoramic outlooks and dizzying terraces, the Tour of Mont Blanc is unrivalled throughout the Alps, and perhaps this can be extended to all of the world's mountains. In the eleven days of walking that are required to complete this circuit — just seven, if one "cheats" here and there with cable cars and bus lines — one sees the great peaks so beloved by climbers from a number of different vantage points. Grandes Jorasses, one of the rough, steep, and jagged south face that drops down to the Italian Val Ferret, and - a few days later - one can see in the distance the terrifying sheer wall of the North Face, which was the site during the Thirties of the greatest feats of climbing in the Western Alps. Mont Blanc itself — the ceiling of Europe, at 4,810 metres — looms over the Val Vény with its séracs and granite pillars, then drops away toward Chamonix with a series of glaciers sufficiently impressive to merit comparison with the Himalayas, particularly magnificent if viewed from the Flégère or the Brévent. One by one, all of the other great peaks of the massif make their appearances: the elegant Aiguille Verte and the obelisk of the Dent de Géant, the dizzying, soaring structures of the Dru, and the solemn and sorrowful atmosphere of the peaks of Trélatète, reminiscent of the Gran Paradiso and the Oisans.

I have walked the Grand Tour around Mont Blanc twice, with different states of mind that were, however, basically

52-53 A view of the Aiguille Verte and the Dru seen from Lac Blanc, after a sudden summer snowfall has made the landscape more dramatic. Photograph by Didier Givois

related. Once at the age of eighteen, when the massif was still unknown territory to me. Looking out over the glaciers, the granite towers, and the razor-sharp ridges of snow, I dreamed of adventures and climbs that were later to become reality. I came back to the same route later, after more than a decade's worth of climbing. And, at the slower pace of walking, savouring the pleasure of observation from a distance, at my own rate, watching the passing procession of chalets and pastures, I discovered a more tranquil form of communication with the mountains, with the fond memories of past climbs. In all of the Western Alps, there could be no better walking routes for

beginners, for those who come from far away, for those with little experience of the high mountains. The easy terrain, the reasonable length of the stages, the broad array of possible variants and detours, make this Tour — by definition — the natural choice for those who have just begun to feel their way through the mountains. The same can be said for mountain climbers who wish to take a little time for meditation, for those who do not wish to climb — or who want to take a break from climbing — for those who wish to relive their adventures or else dream of new adventures. Summits, ridges, and glaciers appear from different points of view every day. And they are all

always equally stunning. There is more than just the spectacular view. By walking outside of the massif proper, one has an opportunity to become familiar with a different sort of nature, a more serene state of being than is found in the jumbled chaos of boulders and glaciers that lies within one's view. The trails that lie at the foot of the jagged Aiguilles Rouges merge into the great marshy upland of the Combal, which then gives way to the grassy ridges that close off the Italian Val Ferret and the great fir woods that surround the Lake of Champex. In August and September, many of the mountain slopes become vast meadowlands of bilberry. More

Blanc Tunnel, there are long lines of long tractor-trailers, chugging away, producing noxious gases that are harmful to forests and humans alike. There is the proliferation of ski lifts at Chécrouit, Flégère, Planpraz, and the "Cable Car of the Glaciers" that connects the Aiguille du Midi with the Torino hut. A new equilibrium has yet to be established. For some time now, the environmentalists of all three nations that claim territorial rights to the massif — France, Italy, and Switzerland — have been considering establishing a park around Mont Blanc and other nearby massifs. An international park is under consideration, but there have been no solid results as of yet. Only the French department of Haute-Savoie has succeeded in establishing protection for part of the territory in question, with seven nature reserves, among which we should single out for mention the reserves of Passy, of the Aiguilles Rouges, and of Les Contamines-Montjoie. We certainly hope that, in a not too distant future, this trail can become the highest and most spectacular "Park tour" in Europe.

54-55 The northwest face of the Aiguille de Bionnassay (4,051 metres) is one of the most spectacular in the group. It was climbed for the first time in 1865, considered at the time to be a great exploit. It is shown here from the Tête Rousse hut, along the standard route up Mont Blanc. Photograph by Gianluca Boetti

55 bottom The remarkable granite obelisk of the Dru (3,793 metres), looms over the Mer de Glace and Chamonix. The peak that can be seen behind Dru is Aiguille Verte, one of the most challenging "4,000-metres" in the Alps. Photograph by Marc Twight

numerous with every passing year, chamois, ibex, and marmots can be sighted fairly easily. There is also the human side of Mont Blanc. The history of these valleys can be found most clearly in the places least touched by tourism: the Swiss Val Ferret, with its wooden shepherds' huts, the Vallée des Glaciers, where herding is still the chief economic activity. In Chamonix, Courmayeur, Les Houches, Argentière, Les Contamines, and Champex, high-volume tourism has clearly established itself. In many places, the human presence has inflicted cruel wounds over the past few decades upon the massif. There are the highways that run from France and from Italy up to the Mont

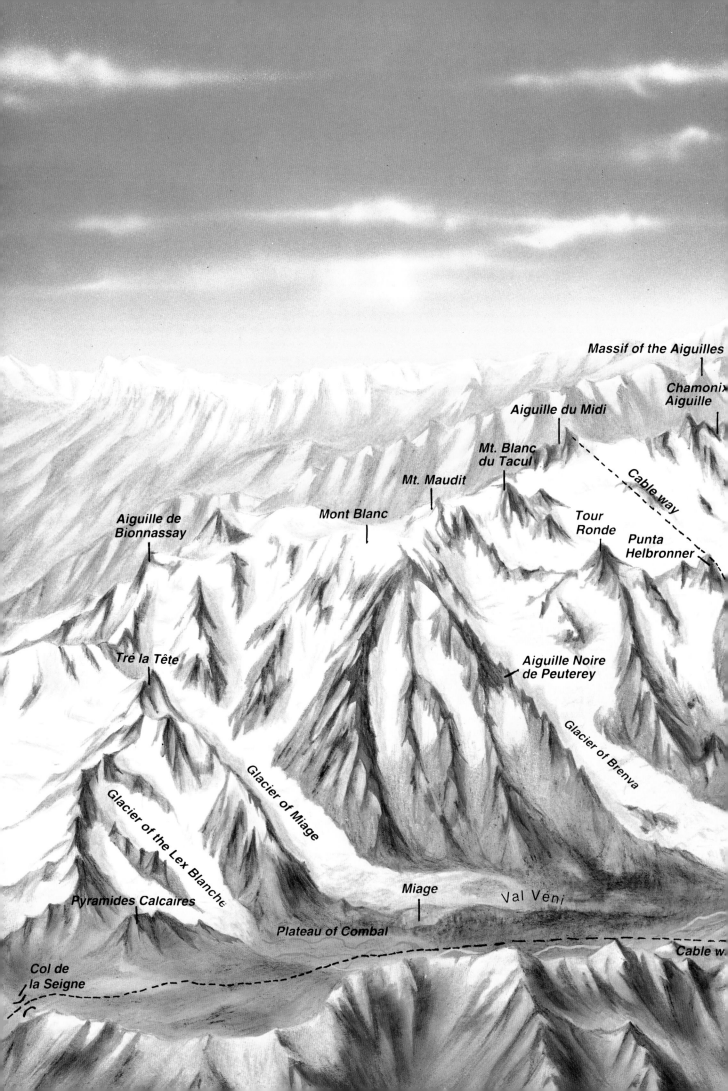

Massif of the Aiguilles

Chamonix Aiguille

Aiguille du Midi

Mt. Blanc du Tacul

Mt. Maudit

Cable way

Mont Blanc

Tour Ronde

Aiguille de Bionnassay

Punta Helbronner

Aiguille Noire de Peuterey

Tré la Tête

Glacier of Brenva

Glacier of Miage

Glacier of the Lex Blanche

Pyramides Calcaires

Miage

Val Véni

Plateau of Combal

Cable w.

Col de la Seigne

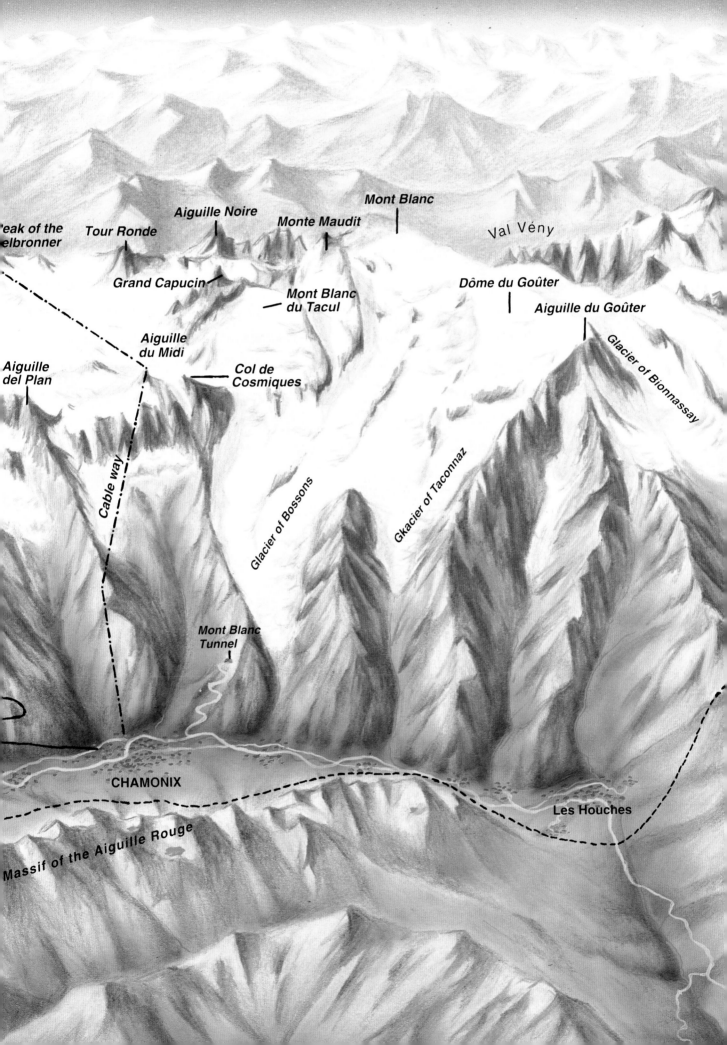

Peak of the
Elbronner

Tour Ronde

Aiguille Noire

Monte Maudit

Mont Blanc

Val Vény

Grand Capucin

Mont Blanc
du Tacul

Dôme du Goûter

Aiguille du Goûter

Aiguille
del Plan

Aiguille
du Midi

Col de
Cosmiques

Glacier of Bionnassay

Cable way

Glacier of Bossons

Gkacier of Taconnaz

Mont Blanc
Tunnel

CHAMONIX

Les Houches

Massif of the Aiguille Rouge

USEFUL INFORMATION

Duration: 11 days, which can be cut to 7 by making use of the public transportation that runs along the valley floor.

Elevations: ranging from the 985 metres of Les Houches to the 2,665 metres of the Fenêtre d'Arpette and the Col des Fours.

Season: from July to September. At the beginning of the season, one finds snow on the trail. Be aware in September of the closing dates of hotels and huts.

Signage: red and white with the indication TMB for the French section of the trail, and local trailmarkers in Italy and in Switzerland.

Degree of difficulty: minimal in the heart of the season. At the beginning of the summer, it is possible to encounter some fairly steep snow beds.

How demanding: average, with a few particularly long and fatiguing climbs.

Equipment: normal mountain gear, ice axe until mid-July.

Peaks: among the easy vantage-points that can be reached by brief detours, we should mention the Punta Léchaud (3,127 metres), which can be reached from the Elisabetta hut, and the Buet (3,099 metres), a remarkable point of view which can be reached from Vallorcine, via the Refuge de la Pierre à Bérard. From the Col de Balme, via the Albert Ier hut and the Glacier du Tour, one can climb up to the Aiguille du Tour. But the logical conclusion of the Tour is to climb up Mont Blanc (4,810 metres) along the French standard routes or the Italian one.

How to get there: from France, take a train as far as Chamonix (quick connects from Paris to Sallanches), or else by the highway Lyon-Annecy-Chamonix. From Switzerland, one can take a train from Martigny to Chamonix, a regularly scheduled bus from Martigny to Champex and La Fouly, a bus direct from Geneva to Chamonix. From Italy, one can take a train as far as Pré-St.-Didier (very slow), or a regularly scheduled bus from Aosta, Turin, and Milan to Courmayeur.

How to get around: bus run by the Chamonix Bus Co. from Chamonix to all the villages along the valley, local buses from Courmayeur to the valleys of Vény and Ferret, postal buses run through the Swiss valleys. There are ski lifts running up to the Flégère, Planpraz, Brévent, Prarion, Bellevue, and Chécrouit. The Mont Blanc Tramway runs up from St. Gervais to Bellevue and to the Nid d'Aigle.

Overnight accommodations: huts of the CAI, CAF, private owned huts, hotels and bed-and-brekfasts. Especially on the French side there are many gîtes d'étape dormitories.

If you want to camp out: there are a number of camping areas on the valley floor, and one can also camp freely at high elevations.

Alpine Guides: in Italy, the Society of Guides of Courmayeur (39) (165) 842064; in France, the Bureaux des Guides at Chamonix (33) 50530088, at Argentière (33) 50540012, at Les Houches (33) 50545076, and of the Vallée de Montjoie (33) 50585357, and the Association Indépendante des Guides du Mont-Blanc (33) 50532705; in Switzerland, the Bureau des Guides of La Fouly (41) (26) 832583, or else (26) 831643.

Information Offices: Chamber of Tourism of Courmayeur (39) (165) 842060, Tourist Bureau of La Fouly

61 The head of the high valley of Malatrà, which can be reached easily from the houses of La Vachey, offers a classic vista of the Italian slope of Mont Blanc, and the woods and meadows of the Val Ferret. Photograph by L. Raimondi/K3

FIRST DAY

From Courmayeur to La Vachey
Distance climbed: 1,670 metres
Distance descended: 1,260 metres
Time: 7 hours

This is a long stage in remote areas, offering remarkable views of the Grandes Jorasses and other nearby peaks. Many walkers make the mistake of avoiding this route along the Val Ferret. Lovely and solitary are the high valleys of Sécheron and Malatrà, dominated by the spires of the Grand Golliaz. It is possible to break up this stage by spending the night at the Bertone hut. From the village (1,228 metres), one follows the road to Lower Villair (1,282 metres) and Upper Villair (1,327 metres), and beyond that, one takes the dirt road along the Val Sapin, running through splendid woods. At a crossroads, one turns to the left, climbing up to the Bertone hut (1,991 metres). One continues along the extremely spectacular mountain crest, which is quite steep as far as the Mont de la Saxe (2,348 metres), becoming less steep after that point. After crossing the Testa della Tronche (2,495 metres), one descends to the Col Sapin (2,436 metres) and to the Alpe Sécheron (2,260 metres). A further climb takes one up to the Pas-d'Entre-Deux-Sauts (2,524 metres), and from there one climbs down to the isolated Vallone di Malatrà. After reaching the Upper Alp of Malatrà (2,213 metres) and the Alpe Gioè (2,007 metres), one descends, following the signage of the High Route number 1 of Val d'Aosta, with a splendid view of the glacier of Frébouze, all the way to La Vachey (1,642 metres). It is possible to descend directly to the Val Vény, either from the Bertone hut or from Sécheron.

(41) (26) 832717, Tourist Bureau of Champex (41) (26) 831227, Bureau of Tourism of Trient (41) (26) 224623, Tourist Bureau of Argentière (33) 50540214, Tourist Bureau of Chamonix (33) 50530024, Maison de la Montagne di Chamonix (33) 50532208, Tourist Bureau of Les Houches (33) 50555062, Tourist Bureau of Les Contamines (33) 50470158.

Useful phone numbers: Bertone hut (39) (165) 844612, Restaurant Club-Alpine Champex (41) (26) 831161, Youth Hostel Champex (41) (26) 831423, chalet du Val d'Arpette Champex (41) (26) 831221, chalet CAF Le Tour (33) 5040416, chalet UCPA Le Tour (33) 50540058, overnight information at Les Moulins Montroc (33) 50540537, overnight information at La Boerne Montroc (33) 50540414, Refuge du Lac Blanc (33) 50534914, Refuge de la Flégère (33) 50530613, Refuge de Bellachat (33) 50534323, Les Chavants hut, Les Houches (33) 50544107, hotel Bellevue (33) 50781324, chalet du Miage (33) 50780716, chalet du Truc (33) 50783739, chalet CAF Nivorin (33)

50470088, chalet du Nant Borrant (33) 50470357, chalet de la Balme (33) 50470354, Refuge de la Croix du Bonhomme (33) 79070528, Refuge des Mottets (33) 79072422, Elisabetta hut (39) (165) 843743.

Weather Forecasts: Météo Chamonix (33) 50536300, Météo Ginevra Cointrin (41) (22) 7178206.

Mountain Rescue: in Italy, dial 115 (Protezione civile) or the Soccorso Alpino Valdostano (39) (165) 238222. In France call the PGHM (High-Mountain Gendarmerie) of Chamonix (33) 50531689, PGHM St.-Gervais (33) 50717881, PGHM Bourg-St-Maurice (33) 7970507. In Switzerland, call the Gendarmerie of Orsières (41) (26) 831106, or the Garde Aérienne Suisse de Sauvetage (41) (1) 3831111.

Maps: the best map is the *Massif du Mont Blanc*, on a scale of 1:25,000, by the IGN of France, in two sheets. Also good is the Swiss CNS 1:50,000, sheets 282 *Martigny* and 292 *Courmayeur*. Adequate but less good are the maps 1:5000 by Kompass, IGC, and Didier & Richard.
The "tables" 1:25,000 by the IGM of

Italy are not well updated and are very expensive.

Book guides: *Tour of Mont Blanc* by Andrew Harper (Cicerone Press) - out of print. *Chamonix to Zermatt, The walker's Haute Route* by Kev Reynolds (Cicerone Press). In French, *Tour du Mont Blanc* by the Comite National des Sentiers de Grande Randonnée.

Readings: Among the many books devoted to Mont Blanc and its valleys we recommend *Voyage autour du Mont Blanc* by Rodolphe Toppfer (first published in 1886, reprinted by Le Livre du Mois, Losanna) about our tour. However it would be better to read a short story about the adventures on the massif walls; the real or fanciful ones by Walter Bonatti, René Desmaison, Edward Whymper, Roger Frison-Roche and many other mountaineers and authors who offer a wide array.

SECOND DAY
from La Vachey to La Fouly
distance climbed: 890 metres
distance descended: 940 metres
time: 5 hours 45 minutes

This is not a lengthy stage, which features a number of splendid views of the Jorasses, the Aiguille de Leschaux, and the Dolent; this stage introduces the walker to the tranquil atmosphere of the Swiss slopes of Mont Blanc. Wooden huts, perfectly manicured meadows, and Swiss flags fluttering in the breeze dot the landscape between Ferret and La Fouly. From La Vachey, one takes the paved road (there are bus lines) all the way to Arnouva (1,759 metres), and, from there, runs a broad dirt track. Where the track turns sharply to the right, one has a direct view of the sérac of the glacier of Pré de Bar. After reaching the new Elena hut (2,062 metres), one continues along a clearly

marked trail, which runs steeply all the way to the shepherds' huts of Tramail de Pré de Bar, and then obliquely along the slope all the way to the Col du Grand Ferret (2,537 metres), a great vantage point overlooking all of the peaks that enclose the Val Ferret.
One descends along the Swiss slopes,

following a good trail that skirts the high Vallon de Peule, drops down to the shepherds' huts with the same name, and then runs to a bridge (1,775 metres) over the Drance de Ferret. Along the paved road, one climbs down to Ferret (1,700 metres), and then on down to La Fouly (1,610 metres).

THIRD DAY

from La Fouly to Champex
distance climbed: 410 metres
distance descended: 550 metres
time: 3 hours 15 minutes

A short and interesting stage, which many walkers skip by taking a bus (which runs through Orsières), but which allows one to complete one's exploration of the Swiss slopes of the massif, where most of the inhabitants still make their livings from agriculture rather than tourism. The trail follows the left bank of the Drance, flows past the foot of the rocky Valle de l'Amone, runs across a number of mountain streams, and then runs through Praz de Fort (1,151 metres), where it crosses over to the right bank, following it as far as Issert (1,074 metres), the most traditional village in the valley. Just outside of the village, a marked trail begins on the left, running up through the mountain summer meadows of Affe (1,324 metres) and Niolet (1,319 metres), running into the paved road at the entrance to Champex (1,466 metres), a resort town overlooking the lake of Champex. The dirt road that begins alongside the base of the cable car leads to Arpette (1,627 metres), at the bottom of the high valley through which one will run the following day.

FOURTH DAY

from Champex to Trient
distance climbed: 1,200 metres
distance descended: 1,340 metres
time: 5 hours 15 minutes

A long stage in a daunting setting, which begins with a lengthy, exhausting climb. Once one has reached the Fenêtre d'Arpette, one can take a good close look at the spectacular sérac of the Glacier du Trient. The climb up is also interesting and quite spectacular; it runs along very steep and very close to the glacier. Before reaching Trient, it is worthwhile to take a look at the *bisse*, a water conduit running obliquely along the slope from here to the Col de la Forclaz. From Arpette, one begins to climb the Vallon d'Arpette, which is overlooked by the Pointe des Ecandies and the Pointe d'Orny. The route is always well marked: stick to the right

at a fork in the path (2,100 metres), and the trail climbs steeply upward amidst scree and snowfields, all the way up to the Fenêtre d'Arpette (2,665 metres), a magnificent point of view overlooking the very nearby Glacier du Trient. The trail runs further on, at an oblique angle, reaching the sheepherds' huts of Vésevey (2,096 metres), and then, with another long traverse, the huts of Ourtiers. After reaching the Chalet du Glacier (1,583 metres), one follows the trail along the stream that runs to Trient (1,297 metres).

FIFTH DAY

from Trient to Montroc
distance climbed: 860 metres
distance descended: 830 metres
time: 3 hours 30 minutes

The Col de Balme, which lies on the boundary between France and Switzerland, offers a walker what is likely to be one of the most spectacular moments of the day. From here, in fact, standing alongside a venerable old tavern that has been transformed into a hut and recently restored, one can gaze out over one of the most complete and spectacular panoramas of the Mont Blanc massif, with the jaggedly serrated Chamonix Aiguilles silhouetted against the glaciers that flow down from the summit. The climb up to the pass is difficult, but the climb down just couldn't be any easier. The climb up to the Albert Premier hut (2,702 metres, 3 hours 30 minutes, round trip) is quite

62 A group of walkers is shown heading across the meadows of the Mont de la Saxe. Edward Whymper, first man to climb the Matterhorn and the author of the first guide to Mont Blanc, in 1896 called this 2,300-metre peak "one of the finest vantage-points in the Alps." Photograph by Philippe Bonhème

interesting; this is the point of departure for the walk to the Aiguilles de Chardonnet and de Tour. It also offers an excellent view of the Glacier du Tour.
After reaching the bridge of Le Peuty, one follows the trail leading to the Col de Balme.
A steep climb obliquely along the slope leads along a traverse of the high valley of the Nant Noir, beyond which one emerges from the woods, skirting the mountain summer meadow of the Herbagères (2,033 metres), and then one reaches the Col de Balme (2,191 metres).
After a well deserved halt, one descends along a fairly easy trail, running parallel with the cable car. The trail leads all the way to Le Tour (1,453 metres). It is of course possible to use the cable car, which takes one up — though one can hardly bring heavy loads — to the Albert Premier hut.

SIXTH DAY

from Montroc to La Flégère
distance climbed: 1,000 metres
distance descended: 480 metres
time: 4 hours 15 minutes

63 top The crossing of the Fenêtre d'Arpette (2,665 metres), on the stage that runs entirely through Swiss territory and runs from Champex to Trient, offers some dazzling close-up views of the glacier of Trient.
Photograph by M. Lanfranchi/Overseas

63 centre The Col de Balme and its venerable hut, at an altitude of 2,204 metres, on the boundary between Switzerland and France, allows one to admire another celebrated vista over the Alps. For those who are climbing up from Trient, this is a view that appears unannounced after three hours of very tiring trail.
Photograph by M. Lanfranchi/Overseas

63 bottom At an altitude of 2,702 metres, the venerable hut that commemorates Albert Premier, the King of Belgium who was also known as an enthusiastic mountain climber, overlooks the glacier of Tour. In the background is the massif of the Aiguille Verte.
Photograph by Stefano Ardito

64 top Despite the cable car, the Aiguille du Midi (3,820 metres) remains a splendid mountain. Here, seen from Chamonix, is the dramatic north face, crisscrossed by demanding mountain climbing routes.
Photograph by René Robert/ Agence Freestyle

With this stage, the Tour of Mont Blanc runs through the best-known panoramic trail in all of the Alps: the trail runs from the foot of the Aiguilles Rouges, cutting obliquely along the slope of the valley of the High Arve above Chamonix and Argentière. After passing the slabs of the Aiguillette a number of trails running parallel allow one to choose the route one prefers: in any case, the views are spectacular everywhere. The more contemplative of walkers are well advised to spend the night at Lac Blanc, far from the cable car, in a hut alongside the romantic waters of the lake. More energetic walkers may select the variant of the Vallon de Bérard and the summit of Buet (3,099 metres), and the panoramic Mont Blanc des Dames. One returns to the Brévent along the base-trail. From the resort of Montroc, the trail climbs up to Trélechamp (1,417 metres), and then runs through a wood over wood which loom the jagged boulders of the Aiguillette d'Argentière. After skirting the base of these looming towers, one climbs up some cables and then comes to a fork in the trail at 2,145 metres. One takes the right-hand fork, skirting the little lakes of the Chéserys, and one thus comes to Lac Blanc (2,352 metres), alongside which stands the hut bearing the same name. High above tower the Aiguille de la Pérséverance and the Aiguille du Belvedère. A steep and rocky trail runs down to the Flégère (1,877 metres), linked by a cable car to the valley.

SEVENTH DAY

from La Flégère to the Col de Voza
distance climbed: 710 metres
distance descended: 1,580 metres
time: 5 hours 45 minutes

The panoramic trail overlooking the Arve Valley and Mont Blanc continues through this stage, which is very difficult in the brief climb (one can simply take a cable car, instead) from Planpraz to the Brévent. After this stretch, one can enjoy a great silence along with the lovely views. A long descent, running concurrently along the GR 5 — the *Grande Traversée des Alpes* from Lemano to Nice — brings one to Les Houches. For those who

love a fine view, we suggest spending the night at the hotel of Bellevue, which is truly worthy of its name. One starts out along the trail, which runs obliquely along the slope down to the hollow of Charlanon (1,812 metres), then one passes a trail that branches off to Lac Cornu, continuing on to Planpraz (2,020 metres), an intermediate station on the cable car of Brévent. A steeply climbing trail, with a beautiful view of Mont Blanc, leads to the Col du Brévent (2,368 metres), where one encounters the GR 5. One follows the GR 5 on the left as far as the summit of Brévent (2,525 metres), perhaps the best known

64 bottom Mont Blanc and the daunting sérac of the glacier of Taconnaz serve as a backdrop to the meadows of the nature park of Merlet, which marks the beginning of the descent toward Les Houches.
Photograph by M. Lanfranchi/Overseas

observation point with a view of Mont Blanc. From here, it is possible to look at details of the standard route from Chamonix to the peak, along the Grands Mulets, the Grand Plateau, and the Vallot hut. Proceeding along, and leaving the terminus of the cable car the trail begins to descend: one leaves the Lake of Brévent on one's right, one reaches the plateau of Bellachat (2,152 metres), and continues along until reaching the zoological park of Merlet, where mountain goats and chamois live in large enclosures, within view of the massif. One walks past the statue of Christ the King (1,268 metres), and then descends to Les Houches (1,003 metres), the traditional starting point for the Tour of Mont Blanc for those who arrive from the north.

To reach the Col de Voza (1,653 metres) and to reach Bellevue, one should definitely take the cable car: on foot, this distance will take 1 hour 45 minutes more. The view of the Aiguille de Bionnassay from here is simply splendid.

EIGHTH DAY

from Bellevue to Les Contamines
distance climbed: 610 metres
distance descended: 1,240 metres
time: 5 hours

A fairly short stage, dominated at the outset by the splendid ice face of the Aiguille de Bionnassay one of the most exciting aspects of the Tour. After crossing the Col de Tricot, one finds the hollow of the Chalets de Miage, which marks the beginning of a gloomier area of Mont Blanc: this stretch of darker terrain runs all the way to the Col de la Seigne. A brief descent takes one to a grassy saddle, and from here a trail leads to the woods, running close to the glacier, and crosses the issuing mountain torrent over a hanging bridge (1,720 metres). After reaching a grassy plateau, one climbs along a trail that leads in among the meadows to the Col de Tricot (2,120 metres), where one has a spectacular view of the North Face of the Dômes de Miage. It is also possible to climb up to the nearby, panoramic Mont Vorassay (2,299 metres), 45 minutes, round trip). A steep, zigzagging descent takes to the Chalets de Miage (1,559 metres),

an excellent halting place. One runs along a dirt track for a while, and then one climbs off to the left all the way up to the plateau and the Chalet of Truc (1,720 metres). One sets out again along the dirt track that leads to the meadow, veering off onto a trail through the woods, dropping down all the way to Frasse (1,263 metres) and Les Contamines (1,164 metres).

NINTH DAY

from Les Contamines to Les Mottets
distance climbed: 1,660 metres
distance descended: 850 metres
time: 7 hours 30 minutes

The longest stage in the Tour of Mont Blanc leads one to excellent views of the isolated high valleys that run down toward the Tarentaise and the Beaufortain. Among magnificent ridges and solemn high valleys, the dolomitic Aiguilles de La Pénaz jut high, along with the curious mound of the Plan des Dames, which from close-up is reminiscent of a *chorten*, while all around stretch the panoramic views, particularly striking from high atop the Col de la Croix du Bonhomme and the Col des Fours. The day begins with walk up to the little church of Notre Dame de la Gorge (1,210 metres), where one enters the Reserve Naturelle de Les Contamines-Montjoie, and begins to climb upward along an ancient Roman road carved into the living rock. After passing the Pont de la Téna (1,392 metres) one comes to the Chalet du Nant Borrant (1,460 metres), and then continues onward until reaching the wide-open hollow and to the Chalet de Balme (1,706 metres). A steep climb among boulders and scree takes one to two forks in the path, leading respectively to the lakes of Jovet and to the Plan des Dames (2,043 metres). After walking around the mound of the Plan des Dames, one climbs along winding curves to the Col du Bonhomme (2,329 metres), and from here a trail running along the slope takes one to the Col de la Croix du Bonhomme (2,479 metres), and to the hut of the same name (2,443 metres). After returning to the Col, one follows the trail that runs to the Col des Fours (2,665 metres), and here one overlooks the Aiguille de Trélatète, and the Aiguille des Glaciers. A steep descent to the foot of an escarpment of shattered boulders leads to a first plateau (2,401 metres), to a second, steep slope, and to the sheepherds' hut of Tufs (1,993 metres). A cart-road takes one to the mountain summer meadow of Ville des Glaciers (1,789 metres). A further brief climb takes on up to the Chalet des Mottets (1,978 metres).

TENTH DAY

from Les Mottets to the Elisabetta hut
distance climbed: 590 metres
distance descended: 350 metres
time: 3 hours 30 minutes

As a sort of rest from the previous day's undertaking, this is an undemanding stage, designed to linger in the area around the Col de la Seigne and the Elisabetta hut, with an excellent view of one of the finest vistas in the Alps, described by travellers from every era. The limestone backdrop of the Pyramides Calcaires, the broad plateau of meadowlands on the Lex Blanche, and the schistose slopes of Mont Fortin and Mont Percé — all serving to frame the summit of Mont Blanc, the Aiguille Noire de Péuterey, the Dent de Géant, the Grandes Jorasses, and the series of valleys of Vény and Ferret. One begins along a winding trail that climbs through pastures alongside the mountain stream of the Grand Praz. Passing the Chalets de la Seigne on the right, one climbs up to the Col de la Seigne (2,516 metres), straddling the French-Italian border. It is possible to climb up to the right, along the ridge, toward the Gollet de la Seigne (2,694 metres), where one can enjoy an even more extensive view. One descends along a broad trail, among pastures and schist ridges, passes by a small bunker lying in ruins, and then reaches the Upper Alp de la Lex Blanche (2,285 metres). After making a circuit around the plateau of the Lex Blanche, one reaches the Lower Alp de la Lex Blanche (2,156 metres) and, on the left, the Elisabetta hut (2,200 metres).

ELEVENTH DAY

from the Elisabetta hut to Courmayeur
distance climbed: 440 metres
distance descended: 1,460 metres
time: 5 hours 45 minutes

The last stage is — at least as far as the ski areas that have spoiled the Chécrouit — one of the most spectacular and loveliest of the stages. The view overlooking the glaciers of Miage and Brenva, in particular, is quite magnificent, as is the view of the dramatic Italian slope of Mont Blanc, where the "pylons" and the séracs of Freney and Brouillard can be admired. One begins by climbing down along a dirt road (short cuts) to the plateau of Combal, crossing the plateau until one reaches a bridge

65 top The verdant Vallée des Glaciers, over which looms the Aiguille des Glaciers (3,816 metres), is the least known and least popular of the valleys of Mont Blanc. The hut of the Mottets provides an overnight stay before the crossing of the Col de la Seigne, heading in the direction of the Val Vény and Courmayeur. Photograph by Laurent Collinet/ Agence Freestyle

65 centre The Aiguille de Trelatète, an elegant snow-covered peak looming to 3,920 metres, and the intricate séracs of the glacier of the Lex Blanche loom over the marshes of the Combal and the upper Val Vény. Photograph by Riccardo Carnovalini

65 bottom The lake of Miage, set at the foot of the glacier of Miage, is the most distinctive glacial lake on the massif of Mont Blanc, and one of the loveliest in the Alps. Photograph by Stefano Ardito

(1,950 metres); on the other side of this bridge are the dirt road and the trail leading to the Lake of Miage, which is certainly worth another detour. Before the bridge, one follows the trail that immediately runs past the Lower Alp of Arp Vieille (2,072 metres), in ruins, and then one continues among the meadows as far as the Upper Alp with the same name (2,303 metres).

After leaving the trail for Mont Fortin on the right, one keeps to one's left, following another trail that climbs up a grassy shoulder (2,365 metres). This trail then traverses for quite some way obliquely along the slope, the entire distance offering a magnificent panorama of the Mont Blanc massif. Along the ski slopes, one can reach the lake (2,165 metres) and the Col Chécrouit (1,956 metres). From here, it is possible to get down to Courmayeur, first by chairlift and then on by cable car. On foot one follows a cart-road to the Plan Chécrouit (1,697 metres), and from there a trail through the woods leads down to Dolonne (1,216 metres). One can reach Courmayeur from here, on foot or by bus.

THE TRAIL OF THE WALSER

The circuit of the "four-thousand-metre peaks" of Monte Rosa, on the trail of an ancient migration

66-67 The tenuous light of dawn mantles with delicate hues the Punta Parrot (4,436 metres), the Punta Gnifetti (4,554 metres), the Punta Zumstein (4,563 metres), the Punta Dufour (4,633 metres), and the Punta Nordend (4,609 metres), the highest and most dramatic ones on Monte Rosa. Here we see them from close-up in a spectacular aerial photograph. Photograph by Marcello Bertinetti/ White Star

This is the heart of tourism in the Alps. Between Zermatt and Cervinia, Gressoney and Saas Fee lies the greatest concentration of peaks towering over the elevation of four thousand metres to be found in the Alps, surrounded by a profusion of hotels, roads, local high-elevation railroads, and cable car, practically unrivalled throughout the Alps. Here modern climbing came into the world, with the first adventuresome climbs of the young men of Gressoney toward the high elevations of Monte Rosa. World renown came to this area with the tragic victory of Edward Whymper over the Matterhorn in 1865. Then came tourism, walking, and skiing. Around the glaciers of Monte Rosa, the Matterhorn, the Lyskamm, the Dent Blanche, the Weissmies, and the other great peaks of the Pennine Alps sprang up huts, hotels, and buildings of every sort. The high hollows of the Breuil — now occupied by Cervinia — of Saas Fee, and of Zermatt are monuments to the modern Alps and to mass tourism. Nonetheless, these valleys and these peaks tell the story, moving and ancient, of one of the most interesting peoples in Europe. These are the Walser (the name comes from Walliser, people from Valais), mountain folk who descend from an ancient nomadic people, who settled long before the year 1000 in the Goms valley, at the foot of the Oberland Bernese, between Brig and the Furka Pass. From there, the Walser begin to move southwest. In the thirteenth century, we find them already settling throughout much of the Vallese. In the following century, encouraged by the mild climate and by the retreat of the glaciers, their settlements spread out over the southern slopes of the Alps, from the Val Formazza to the Valle d'Ayas. Gressoney, Alagna, Macugnaga, Carcoforo, Ornavasso, and Rimella — among other villages — date from this period. Later, a second wave of migration pushed into the Val Formazza, affecting the high valleys of the Rhaetia, the Vorarlberg, and the border with the Tyrol.

USEFUL INFORMATION

Duration: 8 days.

Elevations: ranging from the 1,100 metres of Riva Valdobbia to the 3,317 metres of the Teodulo hut.

Season: from July to September.

Signage: there is nothing specific for the Alta Via. Signs and trailmarkers are local in Switzerland, while there are red-and-white GTA trailmarkers in Piedmont, and yellow trailmarkers for the High Route No 1 in the Valle d'Aosta.

Degree of difficulty: the base-route runs entirely over easy trails, with the exception of the crossing of the Colle del Teodulo, over an elementary ice route. There are many variant trails across the glacier.

How demanding: average, but look out for the elevation.

Equipment: normal mountain gear as far as Champoluc, then heavy boots and ice axe for the crossing of the Colle del Teodulo.

Peaks: the Breithorn (4,165 metres), at a distance of less than two hours from the Plateau Rosa, is accessible to anyone who has any experience with an ice axe and crampons. More difficult, but still accessible to any walker accompanied by a guide, are Weissmies (4,023 metres) from Saas Grund, the Punta Gnifetti (4,554 metres) of Monte Rosa from Alagna or Gressoney, the Castor (4,226 metres) from Gressoney. Tougher still, but extremely satisfying, is the climb up to the Matterhorn (4,474 metres) along the Italian or Swiss standard routes.

How to get there: Brig, on the Simplon railroad line, can be reached easily by train from Switzerland (Martigny, Lausanne, Geneva) or from Domodossola and Milan.
From Zermatt, another railroad line runs down to Tasch (parking area) continuing along the Mattertal and the Vispertal as far as Visp, on the main line and eight kilometres from Brig.

How to get around: postal buses from the Simplon Pass to Brig and from Saas Almagell to Visp, cable car from Gspon to Stalden, regularly scheduled buses from Macugnaga to Gravellona Toce, from Alagna and Carcoforo to Varallo Sesia and Vercelli, from Gressoney, Champoluc, and Cervinia to St. Vincent, Aosta, and Turin; cable car from the Plateau Rosa to Cervinia.

Overnight accommodations: hotels, bed-and-breakfast in the low valley, huts of the CAI and CAS (Swiss Alpin Club), Simplon Hut.

If you want to camp out: you can, except for the Colle del Teodulo.

Alpine Guides: the Alpine guide office at Macugnaga (39) (324) 65170, the Alpine guide office at Saas Grund (41) (28) 571444, the Alpine guide office at Saas Fee (41) (28) 572348, the Alpine guide office at Alagna (39) (163) 922988 or else 91310, Society of guides at Gressoney (39) (125) 366143, Society of guides at Ayas (39) (125) 307194, Society of guides at Cervinia (39) (166) 948169, the Alpine guide office at Zermatt (41) (28) 673456.

Mountain Rescue: in Switzerland, dial 117, in Piedmont, call (39) (163) 922977 or (39) (324) 65013, in the Valle d'Aosta call (39) (165) 362543.

Information Offices: Tourist Bureau of Valtournanche (39) (166) 92029, Tourist Bureau of Saas Grund (41)(28) 572403, Tourist Bureau of Saas Almagell (41) (28) 572653, Tourist Bureau of Macugnaga (39) (324) 65119, Tourist Bureau of Alagna (39) (163) 922988, Tourist Bureau of Gressoney-St.-Jean (39) (125) 355185, Tourist Bureau of Champoluc (39) (125) 307113, Tourist Bureau of Cervinia (39) (166) 949136, Tourist Bureau of Zermatt (41) (28) 661181, the Zermatt-Trockener Steg cable car (41)(28) 672520.

Useful phone numbers: Monte Moro cable car, Macugnaga (39) (324) 65050, Matterhorn cable cars, Cervinia (39) (166) 948424, Oberto hut (39) (324) 65544, Città di Casale St.-Jacques hut (39) (125) 307668, Teodulo hut (39) (166) 949400, hut of the Guides of the Matterhorn, Plateau Rosa (39) (166) 948369.

Guide books: published by Bugra Suisse with the Swiss National Tourist Bureau, *The Great Walser Trail*, in four different languages, offers the best information about the route. Among the others we recommend *The Grand Tour of Monte Rosa* (Vol. I and II).

Maps: the best maps are the Swiss CNS 1:50,000 n. 274 *Visp*, n. 284 Mischabel, and n. 294 *Gressoney*, or else the CNS 1:25,000 n. 1309 *Simplon*, n. 1329 *Saas*, n. 1349 *Monte Moro*, and n. 1348 *Zermatt*. Not bad are the Kompass 1:50,000 n. 89 and n. 88 *Monte Rosa* and the IGC 1:50,000 n. 11 *Domodossola-Val Formazza*, n. 10 *Alagna-Macugnaga*, n. 5 *Cervino-Monte Rosa*. Not very up-to-date and very expensive are the IGM 1:25,000 of *Iselle*, *Pizzo d'Andolla*, *Pizzo Bottarello*, *Macugnaga*, *Rima S. Giuseppe*, *Alagna*, *St. Jacques*, *Valtournanche*, and the *M. Cervino*.

To the west, other groups of Walser continued their long slow walk, finally reaching and settling in the Haute Savoie. "The German colonization of the Goms can fairly be termed the first true attempt on the part of the medieval peasant to create a permanent settlement in the high mountains... With their experience as colonists of the high mountains, the Walser were particularly sought after by feudal lords who owned high-elevation lands that were still yielding nothing... One thing that helped encourage the Walser to migrate was the strong pressure to keep their landholdings together, and not split up by inheritance," wrote Enrico Rizzi in his introduction to his book, about these people.

The end of the migration coincided with the end of the Middle Ages, when the Alps — at this point completely reclaimed — offered no new opportunities for migration. Extending over thirty-four stages — to which a number of variants can be added — ranging from Zermatt all the way to the Austrian border, the Grande Sentiero Walser is one of the most interesting and varied trails in all the Alps. Here, we describe its southwesternmost section, between the Simplon Pass and Zermatt, at the foot of the high peaks of Monte Rosa, the Mischabel, and the Matterhorn. It is in this area that the Pennine Alps display their most grandiose landscapes: glaciers of Himalayan dimensions, walls of rock and ice, huge forests, majestic waterfalls. And it is precisely along the circuit route around Monte Rosa that the power and the solidity of the culture of the Walser become most clearly evident.

The big wooden houses (which are joined by a stable-farm and a granary in the Walser villages of the Vallese) are quite similar, whether at Saas, Alagna, Macugnaga, Champoluc, or Zermatt, and quite different from the houses, generally made out of stone, of the lower-dwelling mountaineers of the lower Vallese, of the Valle d'Aosta and the Piedmont regions. Here, too, dialect, costumes, and traditions bind the various valleys together.

This walk, however, is not only a voyage among wooden houses and ancient paved mule-tracks. Step by step, and pass after pass, one admires many of the most celebrated vistas in all the Alps, and a great many of the tallest peaks of the entire chain. Those who choose to complete the walk by climbing up to the magic elevation of four thousand metres have only the problem of choosing the peak. Breithorn, despite the harshness of its north face, offers one of the shortest and easiest normal route in the Alps. Walkers with a modicum of familiarity with ice axe and crampons, if they are in the company of a more experienced friend or a guide, can reach the elegant Castor, the lofty Weissmies, or the Punta Gnifetti of Monte Rosa, where the Capanna Margherita stands, the highest-elevation hut in all of Europe.

The most unmistakable challenge, however, is the Matterhorn.

Its standard routes normally over the ridges of the Hörnli and the Leone, which are reached respectively from Zermatt and from Cervinia, are long, not easy, and over treacherous terrain. Once on the peak, the satisfaction and the sense of accomplishment are remarkable.

70-71 In the final descent from the Colle del Teodulo to Zermatt, the little glacial lakes at the edge of the Oberer Theodulgletscher offer a pleasant halting place and a remarkable view of the entire chain of Monte Rosa. Photograph by Gianluca Boetti

71 top This picture features the classic view of the Valle d'Aosta slope of Matterhorn (4,474 metres) from the hollow of the Breuil. The Italian normal route runs across the lofty Italian ridge of the Leone, on the left in the photograph.
Photograph by
Marcello Bertinetti/
White Star

70 bottom The Colle del Teodulo, despite its 3,316-metre elevation, is one of the richest in history in all of the Alps. From the pass, by the light of dawn, walkers admire the nearby and impressive massif of the Breithorn.
Photograph by
Gianluca Boetti

71 bottom The heat of the sunlight sculpted this curious block of ice teetering over the glacier of Grenz, at the foot of Monte Rosa and the Breithorn. In the background is the pyramid of the Matterhorn.
Photograph by
Gianluca Boetti

FIRST DAY
from the Simplon Pass to Gspon
distance climbed: 820 metres
distance descended: 920 metres
time: 5 hours

This is a short stage, which can take one up to Simplon Pass in a morning's walk. It is also possible to spend the night in the old Hut, founded in 1245, which can accommodate as many as sixty. From here, there is an incredible view of the north face of the Fletschhorn. From Gspon, there is a magnificent panorama of the Mischabel and the entire Saas Valley. One begins from the Hut (1,997 metres) along the trail that crosses the plateau to the west of the building, and then one climbs up the meadows and moraines of Bistine as far as the Bistinepass (2,417 metres). A series of switchbacks leads one down into the Nanztal, passing by Grosse Lager (2,115 metres) and Bistitafel (1,899 metres). After crossing the mountain stream of Gamsa at the Mattwe bridge (1,800 metres), one climbs back up along the slope to the Gebidumpass (2,201 metres), a broad grassy saddle served by the ski lifts of Visperterminen. Without climbing down to the village, one continues along the slope southward to Gspon (1,893 metres), a lovely village linked by a cable car with Stalden.

SECOND DAY
from Gspon to Saas Almagell
distance climbed: 750 metres
distance descended: 970 metres
time: 3 hours

This pleasant stage features a great deal of climbing and descending, and runs level on the orographic right of the Saas Valley, offering spectacular views of the opposite slope, and featuring the Nadelhorn, the Dom, the Taschhorn. There are of course many variant trails that allow one to shorten the total distance walks by descending to the valley floor.
The trail begins by running slightly uphill, mostly through the woods, emerging from the trees just before the wooden houses of the Finilu (2,039 metres). A steeper climb leads around the ridges that drop down to the west of

this peak. One descends to where one can cross (2,300 metres) the stream of the high valley of Mattwald. Another climb leads up to the higher sheepherds' huts of Rachti (one can make a detour toward Saas Balen here) and to the mountain stream that runs down from the Gruebegletscher, beyond which one finds the chalets of Gruebe (2,300 metres). One continues along to the edge of the woods, where one has a close-up view of the Mischabel, as far as reaching Chrisbode (2,397 metres), an intermediate station of the cable car Saas Grund-Hohsaas. One can ride down to the village, and from there one can quickly reach Saas Almagell. Otherwise, one can continue along the trail around the crests that run down from the Trifthorn, and descends to the Almagellertal and on down to the Saas Almagell (1,673 metres).

THIRD DAY
from Saas Almagell to Macugnaga
distance climbed: 650 metres
time: 3 hours

The stage that brings the walker from Switzerland into Italy via of Monte Moro Pass crosses one of the most important passes in the Pennine Alps, and it is the only pass around Monte Rosa that is not occupied by a glacier. This is a short stage if — as we definitely recommend — one takes a bus all the way up to the dam, and a cable car from the Col to Macugnaga. Otherwise, one should add five hundred metres of uphill climbing, as well as 1,550 metres of downhill walking, adding up to at least four

hours' time. Magnificent and rocky, the Swiss high valley of Talli is partly occupied by the manmade lake of Mattmark. From Saas Almagell, then, one takes a bus up to the dam (2,203 metres hotel). As an alternative, one can get up there by following the trails that run off to the right (east) of the road, in a two-hour walk. On foot, one follows the little lane that skirts the basin, which then gives way to the trail that climbs up to the shepherds' huts of Talliboden and to the pass of Monte Moro (2,868 metres). Immediately beyond that pass, on the Italian side, is the Oberto hut (2,796 metres) and the station of the cable car that climbs down to Staffa di Macugnaga (1,317 metres). If one wishes to make the descent on foot, the trail — which runs across the ski slopes at several points — takes two-and-a-half hours.

FOURTH DAY
from Macugnaga to Alagna
distance climbed: 1,500 metres
distance descended: 1,550 metres
time: 8 hours

Long and harsh, the walk that is required to pass from one of the Piedmontese valleys of the Monte Rosa to another offers interesting views in all directions, limited however in the direction of the massif by the nearby looming bulks of the Corno di Fàller and the Punta Grober. The abandoned gold mines of the Val Quarazza are also quite interesting. On the Valsesia side, a very steep descent takes one down to the idyllic woods around the Pastore hut. From Staffa, one must follow the road all the way to Isella (1,226 metres), continuing from there along an uphill trail to Motta (1,285 metres). After reaching the lake of the Fate (1,315 metres), one follows a little road running

monotonous climb up a trail, partly eliminated by landslides, leads to the Colle del Turlo (2,738 metres). One descends sharply beyond in the high valley of the Acqua Bianca, passing by the lakes of Turlo (2,492 metres), and then one continues on until one reaches the Alpe Fàller (1,969 metres), where the trail splits. The finest trail runs down to the mountain summer meadows of Mittentheil (1,928 and 1,943 metres respectively), while off to the right run the forks leading to the Barba-Ferrero hut and the very nearby Pastore hut, finally reaching the paved road within sight of the Acqua Bianca waterfall. Four kilometres of paved road takes one to Alagna (1,161 metres).

FIFTH DAY
from Alagna to Gressoney-St.-Jean
distance climbed: 1,370 metres
distance descended: 1,180 metres
time: 7 hours

Another long and alluring stage, which allows one to explore the gentle and verdant Val Vogna, one of the loveliest valleys in the Pennine Alps, with its splendid wooden Walser houses. On the Colle di Valdobbia stands one of the oldest huts built in the Alps: this hut was built in 1823 by the canon Nicolao Sottile, and it bears a commemorative dedication in his name. One begins by descending rapidly to Riva Valdobbia (1,112 metres), the ancient "Pietre gemelle" described by the abbot Gnifetti, the first man to climb Monte Rosa, as "the loveliest and most attractive vantage-point in the valley." Along the paved road, or else along marked shortcuts, one

around the lake and leading up to the abandoned gold mine (1,360 metres). A trail running through the woods leads to the Alpe La Piana (1,613 metres), and then climbs sharply to the Alpe Schena (2,037 metres), traversing to the right toward the camp ground Lanti (2,150 metres). A steep and

climbs up to the mouth of the Val Vogna. From the end of the road to S. Antonio (1,381 metres) one continues at length along the slope, running by a number of villages with wooden houses. After passing Peccia (1,529 metres) and an arched bridge, one leaves the main mule-track, which runs up to the Maccagno Pass, taking the track that runs off to the right, running by the Alpi Larecchio (1,900 metres) and Pastore (2,125 metres), and climbing up through an austere high valley to Colle di Valdobbia (2,480 metres) and Ospizio Sottile. After making a stop, one must set off on the long descent toward the meadows of Cialfrezzo and the Lys Valley, which one reaches just south of Gressoney-St.-Jean (1,385 metres).

SIXTH DAY

from Gressoney-St.-Jean to Champoluc
distance climbed: 1,390 metres
distance descended: 780 metres
time: 5 hours

In order to pass from the valley of the Lys to the valley of the Evançon, walkers nowadays can choose among a number of high passes. For the Walser colonists, the most frequented pass was Colle della Bettaforca, to the north of which loomed the moraines and the glaciers of the Monte Rosa. Nowadays, the Colle della Bettaforca is served by ski lifts from both sides, and it is worthwhile to take the trip only if one is heading from the Sella hut and the Castore, or if one is interested in crossing over into the Val d'Ayas without having to climb. To those who want to reenact the exploration of the valleys experienced by the Walser, we would instead suggest climbing the Colle di Pinter, to which one climbs up along an unspoilt high valley, and beyond which one can visit the pleasant lakes that lie within view of the distant Mont Blanc. From Gressoney-St.-Jean one begins down toward the trail along the valley, which runs parallel to the road, all the way to the houses of Chemonal and to the trail of the High Route No 1 of the Valle d'Aosta, which runs up toward the high valley of Pinter. One follows this trail, climbing up to the houses of

Alpenzù Grande (1,779 metres), the Alpe Mehr (1,856 metres), Lower Montil (2,001 metres), Lower Loasche (2,355 metres), and Upper Loasche (2,466 metres), and from there a rocky high valley leads to the Colle di Pinter (2,777 metres). Beyond that, a short descent takes one down to the lakes of Pinter (2,692 metres), and from there one continues into the broad high valley of Cunéaz, in the shadows of the rocks of Testa Grigia and Sarezza, all the way to the houses and the cable car of the Crest (1,979 metres), which

takes one down to Champoluc (1,568 metres). If one wishes to walk for another hour, one can take the trail that leads to Mascognaz (1,822 metres), one of the most distinctive towns in the valley, and from there one descends quickly to Champoluc.

SEVENTH DAY

from Champoluc to the Colle del Teodulo
distance climbed: 1,750 metres
distance descended: 100 metres
time: 7 hours

This is a long and interesting stage. The first part, which runs up along the solitary high valley of Cortod, presents the Valle d'Aosta of yesteryear, and one can admire

among other things the Ru Cortod, a canal built in the fourteenth century, which still functions perfectly, and which cuts across much of the valley. Beyond the Cime Bianche, which have been described in what can only be called a bit of a stretch as the "Dolomites of the Valle d'Aosta," one enters the realm of the Matterhorn. From Champoluc to St.-Jacques (1,689 metres) the best idea without a doubt is to take one of the regularly scheduled buses. One climbs on foot up to the houses of Fiéry (1,878 metres), and from there one continues along the trail that runs into the high valley of Cortod obliquely along the slope; far below one can see the first stretch of the

74 centre Gressoney-la-Trinité, at the base of the southern slope of Monte Rosa, is one of the most popular resorts in the Valle d'Aosta, as well as being the point of departure for walkers and climbers heading up toward the peaks and glaciers of Monte Rosa.
Photograph by Marco Milani/K3

manmade canal that takes water toward Emarèse and St. Vincent. After passing by the mountain summer meadows of Ventina (2,179 metres), Varda (2,336 metres), and Mase (2,400 metres), a steeper climb leads up to the enchanting Gran Lago (2,808 metres), which is often frozen over. After climbing the Upper Colle of the Cime Bianche (2,982 metres), one has a fine view of the Matterhorn, but also of the *domaine skiable* of Cervinia. By following tracks running from ski slope to ski slope, and not always clearly, one passes above the lake of the Cime Bianche, and then only climbs obliquely as far as the Colle (3,301 metres) and the hut (3,317 metres) of Teodulo. It is also possible to climb down to the Cime Bianche station of the cable car, and then take this up to the Plateau Rosa, descending to the Teodulo along the ski slopes. One can thus avoid a climb of some four hundred metres,.

EIGHTH DAY
from Colle del Teodulo to Zermatt
distance climbed: 50 metres
distance descended: 1,780 metres
time: 4 hours

The last of the stages of the Sentiero dei Walser (Trail of the Walser) can be shortened in a number of ways, either by heading down toward Zermatt by taking one or another of the cable cars that run down toward the Trockener Steg, the Furgg, and the Schwarzsee. The remarkable spectacle of the peaks of Monte Rosa, the Matterhorn, the Mischabel, and the vast chain that runs from the Dent Blanche to the Weisshorn, however, provides another good reason to savour with calm this descent through one of the most thrilling areas in the Alps, which has remained unspoilt despite the blight of track and cable lifts. From the hut, just a brief descent takes one to the Colle del Teodulo, and from there one heads north along the Oberer Theodulgletscher, at the edge of the summer ski slopes, with a remarkable view of the pyramid of the Matterhorn. Further along, the track turns to the right and leads to the rocks surrounding the Gandegghutte (3,029 metres). A trail leads from there down to the station of the cable cars of the Trockener Steg (2,939 metres), and then continues on to the Furgg station (2,432 metres). Here, one climbs up to the left for a short distance, and then

one traverses until one reaches the trail that leads down from the Schwarzsee to Zermatt. With a little extra effort, it is without a doubt worth climbing to the lake, a splendid vantage-point on the Matterhorn, and a point of departure for the Hornlihutte and the standard route to the peak.
The last part of the climb down, along an easy little lane, runs past a number of wooden huts typical of the Walser culture. A very short climb leads up to the centre of Zermatt (1,616 metres).

AT THE FOOT OF THE BERNESE OBERLAND

Along the Hintere Gasse, in the shadow of the Wetterhorn, the Eiger, the Mönch, and the Jungfrau

The Maiden, the Monk, and the Orge (respectively, the Jungfrau, the Mönch, and the Eiger) loom over the most spectacular valleys in the Bernese Alps. The first of these peaks, the Jungfrau, rises sheer with a daunting ice face: unrivalled mistress of the winding valley of the Weisse Lutschine — where Murren, Lauterbrunnen, and Wengen stand — the Jungfrau can be seen clearly from as far away as Interlaken and the banks of the lakes of Brienz and Thun. Mönch, in turn, overlooks Grindelwald and the Kleine Scheidegg with a massive face, near which rises the rounded ridge of the Eisnollen, the so-called "ice nose," over which there is a demanding ascent route. On clear days, one can see the entire face from as far away as Berne. It is the third peak in the group, however, the Eiger, which has been the most famous mountain in the massif for the past fifty years. Its grim north face, shaken and swept by incessant rockslides, rises up nearly two thousand metres to dominate the Kleine Scheidegg and Grindelwald. A major legend of the European mountain climbing of the Thirties, finally scaled in 1938 by the Austrian and German party of mountaineers including Heckmair, Kasparek, Harrer, Vorg, it has acquired — with its dozens and dozens of victims — the slightly morbid status of superstar in world climbing. Today, this face boasts about twenty different routes, and the classic route that was conquered in 1938 is climbed quickly and without problems by many parties every year. Many tourists, however, watch the climbers on the face in the expectation of accidents and rescues. The three great peaks are not isolated. Behind them rises the massif of the Oberland, the "little Himalayas" of the Swiss Alps. Among the summits of the Oberland is the incredible Finsteraarhorn (4,274 metres) and the icy Aletschhorn (4,195 metres), which rise to greater elevations than the Jungfrau and are surrounded by huge glaciers like those of the Aletsch —

the longest glacier in Europe — the Fiescher, the Oberaar, and the Unteraar. Less fashionable among modern climbers, to the north loom other rocky peaks such as Schreckhorn (4,078 metres) and Wetterhorn (3,701 metres), renowned challenges to the climbers of the turn of the century. At the easternmost tip of the massif, the granite slabs that descend to the edge of the lake of Grimsel and the limestone faces of the Engelhorner offer extreme challenges even for the most skilful of climbers. The ski lift facilities and the ski runs at the foot of the northernmost face of the Oberland have played a major role in the history of skiing. All of the slopes of the massif, and especially the uncanny basin of Aletsch, feature remarkable routes, perfect for alpine skiers and mountain climbers who are not daunted by long distances and extremely steep climbs both up and down. In many routes, the glacial saddle

76 bottom A group of shepherds' huts can be seen on the gentle meadows running between Alpiglen and the Kleine Scheidegg. Over this pastoral setting stand some of the most dramatic rock faces in the Alps, starting with the north face of the Eiger. Photograph by Gianluca Boetti

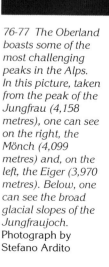

76-77 The Oberland boasts some of the most challenging peaks in the Alps. In this picture, taken from the peak of the Jungfrau (4,158 metres), one can see on the right, the Mönch (4,099 metres) and, on the left, the Eiger (3,970 metres). Below, one can see the broad glacial slopes of the Jungfraujoch. Photograph by Stefano Ardito

of the Jungfraujoch, at an elevation of 3,475 metres serves as an excellent base camp, served by a rack railway that runs up from Grindelwald and Wengen. The railway, which zigzags up through the nooks and crannies of the Eiger, allows its passengers to look into the great void of the north face through a natural window. From the saddle, both Jungfrau and Mönch can be climbed with no major difficulties. The Oberland, however, is not the exclusive domain of those who love to move on snow with crampons or on skis. Around the massif, hundreds of panoramic trails lead to vantage-points of remarkable beauty. To the north, in the verdant valleys that drop down as far as Interlaken and its many lakes, the contrast amongst the forests, the meadows, and the grim rock and ice faces is particularly interesting to observe. For these reasons, the Hintere Gasse — the walking route that connects Meiringen with Grindelwald, Murren, Kandersteg, and Gsteig — is one of the most popular in Switzerland. In its complete version, the route extends for one hundred twenty-two kilometres taking over fifty hours of walking, and offers a daily vertical distance, climbed and descended, of nearly twelve hundred metres. There are ways of shaving those distances and measurements considerably.Over the first section of the walk, especially, rack railways and postal buses allow one to reduce the burden quite a bit. The overnight accommodations — many of which are hotels down in the valley, while others are comfortable private huts — are quite numerous, and they make it possible to spend two or three more days to walking. On the other hand, the proximity of the Jungfraujoch and of the enormous expanse of the

Aletsch encourage one to climb a bit further on. To those who are able to climb safely on alpine routes grades PD (peu difficile) level, or for those who can afford it, and who choose to hire a guide, we would certainly recommend climbing both Jungfrau and Mönch, extending the overall walk by two days. Equally alluring — and different in character and charm — is the descent from the Jungfraujoch to the Konkordia hut along the broad but crevasse-ridden slopes of the Aletsch, continuing on from here toward the Rhône valley. Everybody, however, ought to venture out onto the glacier at least once. One need only wander away from the hill for a few minutes, leaving behind the station crowded with tourists and walkers from all over the world, and one is soon in the midst of one of the most enchanting high-mountain landscapes in all of Europe.

USEFUL INFORMATION

78 On the southern slope of the Oberland, which runs down toward the Vallese and the river Rhône, winds the glacier of Aletsch.

This glacier with a Himalayan appearance is the lengthiest in all Europe. Photograph by Gianluca Boetti

Duration: from 5 to 7 days.
Elevations: ranging from the 595 metres of Meiringen to the 2,835 metres of the Blumlisalp hut (as a variant, one can climb up to the 4,099 metres of the Mönch, or to the 4,158 metres of the Jungfrau).
Season: from July to September.
Signage: yellow signs and white-and-red trailmarkers.
Degree of difficulty: minimal, except for the snow fields at the beginning of

the season on the Hintere Gasse; the standard routes of the Jungfrau and the Mönch are PD (peu difficile) not difficult.
How demanding: quite, due to the length of various stages.
Equipment: normal mountain gear, ice axe useful throughout much of July.
Peaks: there are none along the base-route. With brief detours, however, one can climb up to vantage-points such as the Gemschberg (2,658 metres) from the Grosse Scheidegg, the Lauberhorn

(2,472 metres) from the Kleine Scheidegg, or the Ammertenspitz (2,612 metres) from the Ammertenpass. The best way of concluding the crossing is the climb up along the standard routes of the Mönch (4,099 metres) and/or the Jungfrau (4,158 metres), accessible to experienced walkers, accompanied by a guide.
How to get there: Meiringen and Kandersteg are linked by railroad with Interlaken.

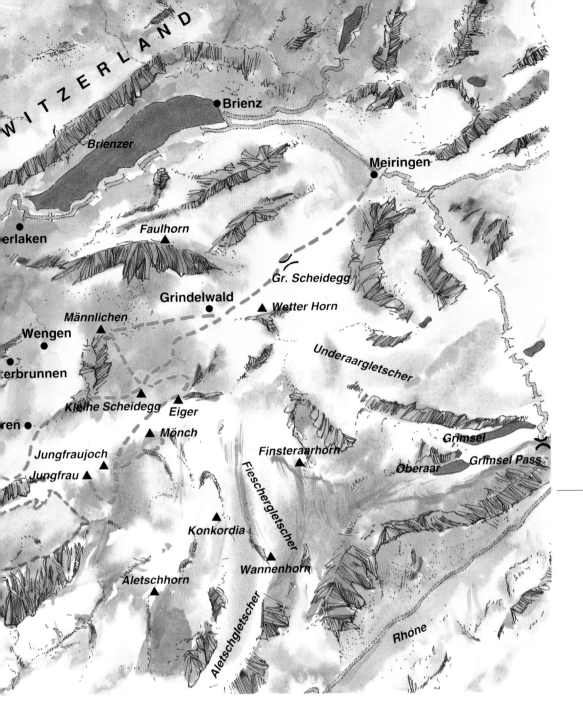

How to get around: trains and postal buses run to Grosse Scheidegg, Grindelwald, Kleine Scheidegg, and Stechelberg.

Overnight accommodations: privately owned huts and hotels, the Blumilisalp hut belonging to CAS and the Mönchsjoch hut belonging to the Guides of Grindelwald.

If you want to camp out: there are a great many restrictions, and the great length of a number of stages complicates things still further.

Alpine Guides: at Grindelwald (41) 36535200, at Wengen (41) 36551775, at Murren and Kandersteg (41) 33752210, or else 33751358 or (41) 36552395.

Weather Forecasts: they can be obtained by calling 162 throughout Switzerland.

Mountain Rescue: call the Police (dial 117) or else the Garde Aerienne Suisse de Sauvetage (41) (1) 3831111.

Information Offices: Tourist Bureau of Grindelwald (41) (36) 531212, Tourist Bureau of Murren (41) (36) 551616, Tourist Bureau of Wengen (41) (36) 551414, Tourist Bureau of Kandersteg (41) (33) 751272.

Useful phone numbers: Berghaus Schwarzwaldalp (41)(36)713515, Touristenlager Grosse Scheidegg (41) (36) 531209, Hotel Bellevue Kleine Scheidegg (41) (36) 551212, Mönchsjoch hut (41) (36) 713472, Rotstock hut (41) (36) 552464, Bundalp (41) (33) 761216, Blumlisalp hut (41) (33) 761437.

Maps: the excellent Swiss CNS is available in a scale of 1:50,000 (n. 255 Sustenpass, 254 *Interlaken*, and 264 *Jungfrau*) or else a scale of 1:25,000 (n. 1210 *Innerkirchen*, 1229 *Grindelwald*, and 1248 *Murren*).

Guide Books: *The Bernese Alps, Switzerland* by Kev Reynolds (Cicerone Press) - covers walks round Grindelwald, Lauterbrünnen and Kandersteg; *Footlose in the Swiss Alps* by N. Reif Snyder (Sierra Club) or *Bernese Oberland* by M. and M. Teal (Corwood Press, 1990). For those who are interested in alpinistic variant trails, *Guide des Alpes Bernoises* by Maurice Brandt (CAS, 1982)

Readings: any book about the history of the North wall of Eiger is interesting. Suggested are the publications by Rébuffat, Harrer, Hiebeler and others.

80 top *From the trail running between the Kleine Scheidegg and the Mannlichen, stands the glacial triangle of the* Silberhorn (3,695 metres), *a secondary peak at the base of the Jungfrau. Photograph by Gianluca Boetti*

FIRST DAY
From Meiringen to Grosse Scheidegg
Distance climbed: 510 metres
time: 2 hours

A short opening stage, running along the dirt road up the valley, which runs to the idyllic Schwarzwaldalp and then on to the panoramic view of the Grosse Scheidegg, at the base of the wild northern slopes of the Wetterhorn and the Mittelhorn. The road begins in the village of Meiringen, climbs up to Zwirgi, and then continues on to Gschwantenmad (1,304 metres) and to the Schwarzwaldalp (1,454 metres). We suggest taking a bus this far. One then continues along the solid mule-track that climbs up to the pass and on to Grosse Scheidegg hotel (1,961 metres).

SECOND DAY
from Grosse Scheidegg
to Kleine Scheidegg
distance climbed: 1,020 metres
distance descended: 740-930 metres
time: 5-6 hours

Another stage in which it is possible to reduce the effort involved considerably, because it is possible to take buses and rack railways. The route begins with a handsome descent along a trail that runs on the right side of the road, passing through numerous pastures, with splendid views of the Eiger, the Wetterhorn, and the hollow of Grindelwald. From Im Brendli (1,228 metres) we recommend making a detour toward the cave existing at the base of the Unterer Grindelwald Gletscher, and one can get to the village of Grindelwald (1,034 metres) by bus. There is a very nice climb up to Brandegg (1,332 metres), Alpiglen (1,616 metres), and the spectacular saddle of the Kleine Scheidegg (2,061 metres).
Among the easier solutions, we recommend riding up in the cable car that runs up to the Mannlichen, and then taking the splendid trail that runs from here to the Scheidegg, facing the Mönch, the Jungfrau, and the Eiger.

80 centre
The light of sunset colours the wild north face of the Eiger (3,970 metres). First scaled in 1938 by four German and Austrian climbers, today this face is crisscrossed by nearly thirty routes, *and remains legendary as a symbol of danger at high elevations. Photograph by Marco Milani/K3*

80 bottom *From Kleine Scheidegg, one enjoys a splendid view of the very steep north face of the Mönch* (4,099 metres). *The northwest face was climbed by Hans Lauper in 1921; the ice ridge* of the Nollen (right) had already been scaled by 1866. *Photograph by Mario Verin*

VARIANT TRAIL OF THE SUMMITS
from the Jungfraujoch to the Mönch and the Jungfrau
distance climbed: 500-1,600 metres
time: 3 hours 30 minutes -
10 hours 30 minutes

From the high pass of the Jungfraujoch (3,575 metres), which one reaches by train from the Kleine Scheidegg, begin the handsome standard routes up the Mönch (4,099 metres) and the Jungfrau (4,158 metres). One can climb the first peak in a single stay, reaching the broad saddle of the Mönchsjoch and the base of the south ridge, which leads up to the peak with a climb over snow and small rocks: the final crest is quite exposed. This climb will take three-and-a-half hours, round trip. If one wishes to climb the Jungfrau, it is advisable to spend the night at the Mönchsjoch hut, setting out very early the next morning: one descends along the glacier, reaching the base of a rocky spur (3,411 metres). One climbs the spur, and then continues along the glacier, climbing a steep slope that leads up to the Rottalsattel (3,885 metres). Another steep and dangerous slope, then large boulders and snow-fields take one on up to the peak. This climb will take six hours, round trip.

THIRD DAY
from Kleine Scheidegg to Rotstock hut
distance climbed: 710-1,220 metres
distance descended: 1,240 metres
time: 5-7 hours

After leaving the very popular Kleine Scheidegg, one passes quite close to Wengen and Murren — both of which are among Switzerland's most exclusive ski resorts — and then one begins the more desolate and solitary section of the Hintere Gasse.
One begins by descending to the Wengenalp (1,874 metres), and from there a steep trail leads downhill among meadows and forests to the valley of the Lauterbrunnental, joining that valley at Trummelbach (819 metres). One can ride up on the cable car of the Schilthorn, from Langwald (868 metres) to Gimmelwand (1,393 metres), and there one returns to the trail that climbs up along the Sefinen Tal, in the shadow of the faces of the dramatic Gspaltenhorn, all the way up to the Boganggen Alp and the Rotstock hut (2,039 metres).

FOURTH DAY
from Rotstock hut to Obere Bundalp
distance climbed: 920 metres
distance descended: 1,120 metres
time: 4 hours 30 minutes

This is one of the shortest stages in the entire walk, where one travels from the massif of the Gspaltenhorn to that of the Blumlisalphorn, where handsome rocky towers are interspersed with impressive snow arêtes, at the westernmost tip of the Oberland. One climbs up to the Sefinen Furke (2,612 metres), and then one descends through the pleasant Kiental, across moraines and then alongside a mountain stream. After passing by the shepherds' huts of Ober der Berg (1,930 metres) and Hubeln, one reaches the valley of the Gamchibach at Bundsteg (1,488 metres). A further, gradual uphill climb takes one to the Obere Bundalp (1,840 metres), a pleasant privately owned hut among meadows teeming with marmots.

FIFTH DAY
from Obere Bundalp to Kandersteg
distance climbed: 990 metres
distance descended: 1,040-1,660 metres
time: 5 hours 30 minutes -
6 hours 30 minutes

This stay begins with a climb up to the Hohturli Pass and on to the Blumisalp hut, continuing with a descent to the Oeschinen See and on to Kandersteg. Riding on the chairlift for the last stretch here will make this stage easier on the legs, and it gives the walker more time to explore the area around the hut. One begins with a gradual climb up to the Hohturli Pass (2,778 metres) and to the nearby Blumlisalp hut (2,834 metres), an excellent base camp for climbs up to the Blumlisalphorn. One climbs down to the huts of Ober Bergli (1,981 metres) and Unterer Bergli (1,767 metres), and then on to the shores of the Oeschinensee (1,578 metres). From the hotel, the trail descends to Kandersteg (1,175 metres). Otherwise, a track running up the slope leads to the upper station of the chairlift.

81 top The Swiss flag flutters before the distinctive Blumlisalp Hutte (2,837 metres), on the crest that separates the Kandertal from the Kiental. Here, far from the crowds and the railroads of Grindelwald, one finds anew the tranquillity that was typical of the Oberland in years gone by.
Photograph by Franz Hauleitner

81 bottom
The northwest face of the Blumlisalphorn (3,664 metres), one of the peaks of the western section of the Oberland, is shown here from a vantage point on the Oschinen See. None of the routes on this mountain is easy. The way up the north face, made in 1924, is exceedingly elegant.
Photograph by Ernst Höhne

FROM THE TICINO CANTON TO THE GRISONS

From Airolo to Davos along the migratory route of the Walsers to the east, running along the Via Mala and the source of the Rhine

82 The bridge built between 1738 and 1739 still crosses the impressive gorge of the Via Mala. The road that links Ticino and Lombardy with Coira and northern Switzerland across this gorge is one of the most spectacular bridges in the Alps. Photograph by Stefano Ardito

"The high valley was familiar to him in every aspect, with its spires, its ridges, the rocky faces, with the jutting formation on the left pierced by the Brembuhl, whose crest ran down obliquely toward Davos and whose slopes were covered by dense woods, and there were mountain formations on the right. The names of these formations were well known to him, as well known as the face of the Altein which, seen from there, seemed to close off the valley to the south." In these words, Thomas Mann described the hollow of Davos, the pearl of the Grisons, well within sight of the Austrian border and the oddly shaped peaks of the Silvretta. In the route that we describe here, Davos is only the final destination of the voyage. It can be reached after ten days of walking along the eastern branch of the *Grande Sentiero dei Walser* (Great Trail of the Walser), which we have already encountered in the high valleys around the Monte Rosa, the Mischabel, and the Matterhorn. First of all, along the trail that begins from Airolo, from the mouth of the Saint Gotthard tunnel, and from the Val Leventina, there is a magnificent procession that begins with the uplands of Campo Blenio, continuing with the verdant valley through which runs the Hinterrhein, a stream that has gouged out with the Via Mala, one of the most astounding gorges in the Alps, then the romantic towns of Thusis and Zillis, the tranquillity of Vals, and the glittering social whirl of Arosa. In Switzerland, what catches the attention is usually the rich landscape. The area that we describe here is certainly no exception to that rule, and in particular we would mention the peaks of the Adula (3,402 metres) and the peaks around the Splügen Pass, the Albula, and the peaks between Davos and Arosa. If one pays close attention to the geography here, the valleys through which this walk runs are principally a trip from the Mediterranean basin to that of the North Sea. After leaving the banks of the river Ticino not far from where it rises, one passes into the valley of the Rhine. As early as 1574, Josias Simler, author of *De Alpibus Commentarius*, the first treatise on the Alps, had distinguished between the principal branches of the river Rhine, nowadays known respectively as the Hinterrhein *(Rein posteriur*, in Romansch), the

83 A group of walkers is shown working along the ancient and easy trail that runs across the pastures between Vals and the Valserberg. A number of different pastures punctuate the route from the 1,252 metres of Vals Platz, and the 2,504 metres of the Valserberg. Photograph by R. Carnovalini

Vorderrhein *(Rein anteriur)*, and the Valserrhein *(Rein de Vals)*, in addition to such tributaries as the Sumvigtrhein *(Rein de Sumvigt)* and the Averserrhein *(Rein d'Avers)*. Only from Coira on does the river become a single stream. Here there is more than just nature, however. Far from the highest and the most spectacular peaks, this part of Switzerland reminds us just how ancient and solid is the history of humanity among these mountains. The transition from the Ticino Canton, with its Italian language and traditions to the valleys of the Grisons, where the German language and culture has been long at work, eroding the space left to Romansch, clearly reveals how this area is a meeting place of civilizations. The history of the Walser, who came here beginning in the thirteenth century from the Vallese (they reached Davos in 1284), makes this story yet more interesting. In the central portion of the trip, aside from the splendid medieval church of Zillis, the featured

stars, so to speak, are the valley of the Rhine and the Via Mala, a canyon that is five kilometres in length, with vertical faces rising hundreds of metres sheer. We have no idea when the first road was built here. We do know that a Roman army passed through here in A.D. 398, while a tract on geography written in 1219 mentions this road. The two splendid arched bridges which run parallel with the bridges of the modern superhighway date from 1738 and 1739, and they were both masterpieces built by Christian Wildener, the renowned master builder of Davos. In 1822, lastly, the engineers of the Ticino drove the road that crossed the pass of San Bernardino and the Ticino through the Verloren Loch, the "forsaken hole" which had impeded for centuries direct contact between Rongellen and Thusis. Everywhere along this trail, the presence of centuries of history is shown by remarkable and very beautiful

churches, historical bridges like those of the Hinterrhein and the Via Mala, castles such as the very impressive ones around Thusis. The wooden houses of the Walser, which are found in the central and final portion of the walk, are certainly very handsome and interesting, though they may be a bit of a disappointment to the walker who is familiar with those found in the Vallese and in the valleys of Alagna and Ayas. The exception to this observations consists in the truly spectacular houses of Tschiertschen, a village through which one passes on the stay between Churwalden and Arosa. Pleasant, slightly zigzagging, not difficult despite the occasional rough high pass, this trail is an ideal place for partial routes lasting one day or just a weekend, a solution that is made far easier by the excellent local system of transportation in Switzerland.

USEFUL INFORMATION

Duration: 11 days.

Elevations: ranging from the 130 metres of Greina to the 1,400 metres of Campo Blenio.

Season: from July to October.

Signage: yellow signs and white-and-red trailmarkers.

Degree of difficulty: minimal.

How demanding: average.

How to get there: Airolo is at the southern mouth of the railroad tunnel of the St. Gotthard Pass (the line Lucerne-Bellinzona-Milan); from Davos one continues by train via St. Moritz and Tirano, Andermatt, and the St. Gotthard Pass or else via Bad Ragaz and Zurich.

How to get around: trains to Thusis and Arosa, regularly scheduled buses to Campo Blenio, Vals, Hinterrhein, Splügen,

Safien Platz, Zillis, and Lenzerheide.

Overnight accommodations: hotels and bed-and-breakfast in the valley. The Motterascio and Terri huts belong to CAS.

If you want to camp out: there are camping areas in some of the places one passes by. There are major problems with camping out in the wild.

Alpine Guides: at Davos and Arosa: contact the bureaus of tourism.

Weather Forecasts: in Switzerland they can be obtained by calling 164.

Mountain Rescue: call the Police (dial 117) or else the Garde Aerienne Suisse de Sauvetage (41) (1) 3831111.

Information Offices: Tourist Bureau of Vals (41) (81) 9351242, Tourist Bureau of Splugen (41) (81) 621332, Tourist

FIRST DAY

From Airolo to Acquacalda
Distance climbed: 720 metres
Distance descended: 520 metres
time: 5 hours

One begins at Airolo (1,175 metres), following obliquely along the slope the well-known *Strada alta*, or high road of the Val Leventina, one of the most popular mid-mountain trails in the entire Ticino. After reaching Altanca (1,390 metres), one rides up by cable car — the steepest one in the world, by the way, at a gradait of 88% — to Piora (1,793 metres). One continues by skirting to the north of Lake Ritòm (1,850 metres), and working through the solitary Val Piora, which has been thoroughly sculpted by ancient glaciers, all the way to the Pass of the Sole (2,376 metres). From this pass, a short descent brings one to Acquacalda (1,753 metres), set in the broad valley that climbs up to the Lucomagno Pass, where there is an Ecological Centre open during the warmer season.

SECOND DAY

from Acquacalda to Campo Blenio
distance climbed: 320 metres
distance descended: 860 metres
time: 3 hours 30 minutes

This stay is quite short, and runs through magnificent meadows, at all times offering a pleasant and relaxing walk. One begins by crossing a first pass (1,917 metres), and then continues down through the charming meadows of Dotra (1,748 metres) and Anveuda (1,678 metres). One climbs back up to and across the pass of Cantonil (1,937 metres). Then one descends through the extensive meadows of the Val di Campo, along a narrow lane, which turns into a mule-track, finally reaching Campo Blenio (1,204 metres).

85 At an elevation of 1,215 metres Campo Blenio, which lies within sight of the dam of Luzzone, is one of the highest villages in the valley of the same name. Over the entire region, one can see the peaks of the massif of Adula.
Photograph by Riccardo Carnovalini

Bureau of Thusis (41) (81) 811134, Tourist Bureau of Arosa (41) (81) 311621, Tourist Bureau of Davos (41) (81) 452121.
Maps: the excellent Swiss CNS, available on a scale of 1:50,000 (n. 266 *Val Leventina*, 267 *San Bernardino*, 257 *Safiental*, and 258 *Bergun*) or else 1:25,000 (n. 1254 *Hinterrhein*, 1215 *Thusis*, 1216 *Filisur*, 1196 *Arosa*, and 1197 *Davos*).
Guide books: *Central Switzerland - A Walking Guide* by Kev Reynolds (Cicerone Press) - Luzern to the St. Gottard Pass including Engelberg and Klausen.

FOURTH DAY

from Greina to Vals
distance climbed: 350-400 metres
distance descended: 1,050 metres
time: 4 hours

With this stage, after leaving the breathtaking plateau of the Greina, one crosses into the basin of the Vorderrhein, and all its tributary streams. At the end of this tour, the lonely village of Vals, defended from anything downhill by an astounding

the Vorderrhein, and then one climbs up to Vals (1,252 metres). As an alternative, one can continue on foot, passing through Surin and Surcasti, then taking the bus only for the stretch from Uors to Vals.

FIFTH DAY

from Vals to Splugen
distance climbed: 1,250 metres
distance descended: 1,250 metres
time: 6 hours 30 minutes

This stay has two faces, so to speak, the first one dedicated to crossing the Valserberg, and involving a relaxed and interesting tour of the valley floor between Hinterrhein and Splugen. Waterfalls, large stones and desolate high gravel valleys are found throughout the first section of the trip.
At Hinterrhein is one of the most distinctive bridges in the Grisons, as well as one of the most photographed. One sets out obliquely along the slope on the orographic right side of the valley, then climbs up to the Alpe Walletsch (1,875 metres) and continues along until one reaches the

THIRD DAY

from Campo Blenio to Greina
distance climbed: 1,400 metres
distance descended: 130 metres
time: 6 hours

This is a long stage that runs through particularly isolated country, taking one over the border between the Ticino and the Grisons through some of the most unspoilt valleys of the Lepontine Alps. Of special interest at the beginning of the trail is the broad lake of Luzzone, followed by the dramatic hollow in which are nestled both the mountain summer meadow and the CAS hut of Motterascio. The meadows and the marshes of the Greina are as pristine as they still are, thanks in part to the rallying of environmentalists against the construction of new dams. One climbs along the paved roads until one reaches the dam of Luzzone (1,597 metres), then walks around the south shore of the lake, and climbs along a broad high valley until one reaches the Alp of Motterascio (CAS Michela hut), 2,172 metres). There is a gentler climb up to the pass of Crap la Crusch (2,259 metres), then one enters the Grisons and continues on through the lovely Plaun de la Greina, all the way on to Chamanna di Terri (2,470 metres).

rocky gorge, is the bulwark and bastion of the Walser civilization in the Grisons — as the town's name suggests.
The distinctive "double houses" of the central square are especially lovely, while the little museum of local history is very interesting.
One begins by leaving the Greina across the pass of Diesrut (2,428 metres), and from here one descends to the mountain summer meadows of Diesrut (1,899 metres), to the houses of Puzzatsch (1,667 metres), and then down to Vrin (1,448 metres).
By bus, one can ride down to Ilanz (699 metres), on the valley floor of

86 top The dark and entrancing evergreen forests at the bases of the Piz Terri and the Piz Medel frame the man-made lake of Luzzone, at the beginning of the long climb up toward Motterascio and the Chamanna from Terri.
Photograph by Riccardo Carnovalini

86 bottom A group of picturesque wooden and stone houses stands in one of the pastures near Vals. In this valley, very difficult to reach until recent times, the Walser people first arrived at the beginning of the fourteenth century.
Photograph by Riccardo Carnovalini

Valserberg (2,504 metres); from here, the landscape opens out suddenly over the valley of the Hinterrhein, the passes of the Splügen and San Bernardino, and over the distant shapes of the Rhaetian Alps. From here, one descends steeply and quickly to the valley floor, at Hinterrhein (1,620 metres), and then one continues along on the river's right bank, which is largely wooded and very pleasant, despite the proximity of the road. After passing by Nufenen and Medels, one reaches Splügen (1,457 metres).

SIXTH DAY
from Splugen to Safien Platz
distance climbed: 1,130 metres
distance descended: 1,270 metres
time: 5 hours 30 minutes

Another long stage, which takes one from the crowded valley of the Hinterrhein, running up to the solitary Safienthal, one of the least frequented valleys in the Grisons. The first part of the stay consists of the long steep climb up to the pass of Safienberg (2,486 metres). The climb down on the other side is only steep at first. After reaching the valley floor at

around 1,800 metres, one leaves on the left the trail that leads from Vals heading for the Tomulpas (a possible variant trail that will shorten this walk by one day), and then one reaches Thalkirch (1,686 metres), where there is a handsome little church dating from 1503.

From here, one can reach Safien Platz through the little road along the valley.

It is more pleasant, however, to walk the trail that runs obliquely along the slope, and then drops down gently, with a splendid panorama of the rocky slopes of the Bruschghorn and the Piz Beverin, leading eventually to the town Safien Platz (1,315 metres).

SEVENTH DAY
from Safien Platz to Thusis
distance climbed: 540 metres
distance descended: 1,050 metres
time: 4 hours 30 minutes

Far more gentle than the preceding ones, this stay runs to the alluring town of Thusis, gate to the Via Mala looking northward, which deserves a visit to see the nearby castles of Hohenratien (twelfth-century, on a site that has been fortified since prehistoric times) and Burg

Ehrenfels. One begins by climbing through the woods, then over open ground, to the Glaspass (1,846 metres), and then down to the houses at Tschappina (1,577 metres), Urmein, and Thusis (723 metres). It is possible to spend a few hours touring Thusis, or else one can set out directly on the following stay, leading to Zillis. A circuit on foot that runs out to both castles and the pass of Crap Carschenna will take three hours more.

EIGHTH DAY
from Thusis to Zillis
distance climbed: 560 metres distance descended: 350 metres
time: 4 hours

Short but interesting, this stage on the Via Mala is inexplicably missing from the "official" descriptions of the *Grande sentiero Walser*, but it is certainly worth walking. The steep trail, which climbs among the rocks of crapteig, is a worthy introduction to the savage atmosphere that pervades this stage. After one reaches a saddle (1,065 metres), things become a little gentler until one reaches the houses of Ober Rongellen (1,005 metres); from here, a little road leads on to the true and full-fledged Via Mala. One tours the most impressive section of the canyon along a tourist trail, with an access fee, and then one continues for some way along the old road, with an immediate crossing of a bridge that spans the dizzying gorge. After passing through the village of Reischen (high above looms the castle of Haselstein) one descends to the quiet little town of Zillis (945 metres), where one can visit the splendid church of St. Martin, with its ceiling frescoes dating from the twelfth century.

88 top
The reformed church of St. Martin at Zillis was built in 1130 on the foundations of a Roman temple. The building is, even now, one of the most important monuments in the Grisons. The ceiling is adorned with 153 panels of pine and larch, painted around 1160.
Photographs by Stefano Ardito

NINTH DAY
from Zillis to Churwalden
distance climbed: 920 metres
distance descended: 960 metres
time: 5 hours

This is a stage that spans two different worlds; it begins with a lovely walk through the woods, then continues along with a varied and interesting climb down, ending with a bus ride. Of particular interest are the churches that line the route. After returning to Reischen, one climbs at considerable length through a lovely forest until one reaches the shepherds' huts of Samest — there is a wonderful view of the Via Mala from on high — and then the pass and the houses of Obermutten (1,860 metres), where there is another splendid eighteenth-century church. From here, without a doubt, it is worth taking a little side-trip to the summit of the Mutten Hohi (2,000 metres, forty-five minutes, round trip).

88-89 In these pictures, it is possible to admire three panels from the church of St. Martin. The artist who created these masterpieces has remained nameless, but the influence of the Bavarian style is quite evident. The paintings represent the cycle of the life of Jesus Christ, and the most significant moments of the life of St. Martin. It is interesting to note that, on the edges of the panels, mysterious monsters and marine creatures with a terrifying appearance are depicted.
Photographs by Stefano Ardito

Beyond that point, one descends as far as Mutten, and from there one continues toward Stierva (1,375 metres, a handsome Gothic church), Mon (1,231 metres), and Tiefencastel (908 metres); it may be worthwhile to take a detour to the church of St. Ambrogio at Mistail (forty-five minutes, round trip).

One then takes the bus to Churwalden (1,299 metres), where one can tour yet another lovely church.

TENTH DAY
from Churwalden to Arosa
distance climbed: 1,090 metres
distance descended: 580 metres
time: 6 hours

This is a relaxing and very pleasurable stage, that follows a varied route, that runs uphill and downhill quite a bit, running through the lovely village of Tschiertschen, with its stout wooden houses in the finest Walser tradition. At the end of the day's walk is the quiet and exclusive ski resort of Arosa, one of the highest resorts in the Grisons, towering to 1,815 metres. One begins with a long and pleasant walk along an oblique trail across the slope, skirting the spurs of the Gurgaletsch. A further descent leads to Praden (1,161 metres), and from there one climbs up to Tschierschen (1,343 metres), which is worth a pretty thorough tour. One sets off again uphill through the Urden Tal, leaving that valley at the shepherds' huts of Loser (1,683 metres), continuing along a lengthy and panoramic oblique traverse along the slope. After passing close to the Ochsenalp (1,936 metres) and walking across the meadows of Uf Pratsch (1,985 metres), one climbs down to Maran and Arosa (1,739 metres).

ELEVENTH DAY
from Arosa to Davos
distance climbed: 750 metres
distance descended: 950 metres
time: 5 hours

The last stage along this trail has as its destination one of the greatest ski resorts in Europe: with its three hundred twenty kilometres of

downhill slopes, Davos lies at the heart of one of the most extensive *domaines skiables* in Switzerland and all of the Alps. This route, however, allows one to skip almost entirely the areas equipped for skiing, and it still features a lovely alpine landscape. One begins by descending to the valley floor of the Plessur, and then by climbing beyond through a dramatic high valley all the way to the Maienfelder Furgga (2,440 metres).

The trail runs down obliquely along the slope on the orographic left of the Chummertalli, then runs into the woods and on down to the valley floor of the Landwasser, which one encounters at Frauenkirch.

WALKING OVER GRANITE

Ten days through the wilderness
and over the massifs of Màsino,
Disgrazia, and Bernina

"The most handsome alpine landscape that I know of. Verdant meadows, quaint mountain farmhouses, dense stands of evergreens, over which loom the severe silhouettes of mountains clad in ice... What mountain climber has not dreamed at least once of daring the pale-hued faces of the Badile, Cengalo, Gemelli, Sciora, Trubinasca, and many of the other summits here?" With these words, in his autobiography *Le mie montagne* — or "My Mountains" — the great italian climber Walter Bonatti describes the allure of the granite massifs of the Masino. Straddling the border between the Italian Valtellina and the Swiss Engadine, these peaks have been considered for over a century to be the finest training ground for the alpinists of Lombardy, while at the same time they are a magnificent terrain for walkers seeking spectacular and dramatic places to explore, and who do not fear to encounter rough landscape or steep climbs. This is still full wilderness, but one need not be a virtuoso climber to find it. Even among climbers, the trails that lead up to the huts in this area — the Omio, the Gianetti, base for the Piz Badile; the old Allievi, alongside which the new and comfortable Bonacossa has been built — are notoriously tough and tiring endurance trails. This is just one more good reason to remain at altitude for a number of days at a time: it is no accident that this is the region that gave birth to the "Sentiero Roma" in the Thirties, one of the first marked walking routes in all the Italian Alps. Later on, the High Route of the Val Malenco was added, acclaimed by its creators as an open-air museum, leading in eight stages to the foot of the Disgrazia and the Bernina. The two routes, both of which are much-frequented classics, have now been incorporated into the Lombard stretch

of *Sentiero Italia*, the great walking trail that links Calabria, in the extreme south of Italy, with Trieste, in the far northeast, across the Apennines and the Alps. One begins on the banks of the lake of Mezzola, situated between the mouth of the Valtellina and Chiavenna, and one immediately finds oneself in the harsh and singular Val Codera, one of the last of the high Alps that are inhabited year round but are not linked by roads. The granite large slabs that

prevent access are clear signs that the reason for no road system is technical, more than ecological; in fact, over the last few years the mountain people have had harsh disagreements with environmentalists over the uses to which the valley should be put. In the future, a cable car from the valley floor to Codera ought to allow everyone to come to an agreement. After crossing the Passo dell'Oro, one enters the broad and pristine Val Masino, with a fine view of the Badile and Cengalo. One after another, the great peaks of the border crest stand like so many reminders for passing walkers of the great achievements of Aldo Bonacossa, Alfonso Vinci, Riccardo Cassin, Walter Bonatti, and the "young lions" of modern climbing. After making one's way around the mighty pyramid

90 top
The astonishing granite walls of t he Ligoncio (3,038 metres) and the Sfinge serve as a backdrop to the traverse of the Passo dell'Oro (2,526 metres), a lofty pass linking the Val Codera and the Val Masino.
Photograph by Gianluca Boetti.

of Mount Disgrazia (the name, in Italian, may seem to invite terrible bad luck — it means "disgrace," or "disaster" — but it is actually just a corruption of the word *desglacià*, which means "free of ice") one enters the gentler Val Malenco, with its quarries where talc and porphyry are extracted, its pastures, its forests and peaks. Such idyllic spots as the Piano del Ventina, the areas surrounding Lake Palù, and the Val Poschiavina are interspersed among

90 bottom
The Bonacossa hut,
which rises at an
altitude of 2,385
metres at the head of
the dramatic Val di
Zocca, is one of the
most isolated huts in
the Val Masino. This
marks the beginning
of the routes
climbing up to the
Cima di Castello
(3,376 metres), the
Punta Allievi (3,012
metres) and the
narrow Punta Rasica
(3,350 metres).
Photograph by
F. Raiser/K3.

91 The snowy
ridges of the
Disgrazia (3,678
metres) can look at
times like something
out of the
Himalayas. The
name of this
mountain may seem
somewhat grim and
foreboding, but in
reality it comes from
the word desglacià,
which means "free of
ice." This is an
accurate description,
if one compares the
peak with the
nearby and taller Piz
Bernina.
Photograph by
F. Raiser/K3.

other, harsh and rocky landscapes, as one moves toward the foot of the Piz Bernina, the elegantly shaped mountain that rises just to the north of St. Moritz, attracting climbers from all over with its elegant ridges of snow, including the splendid Biancograt. From the comfortable Marinelli-Bombardieri hut, one of the huts most loved by Lombard walkers and mountain climbers, it is possible to spend a day — perhaps accompanied by a guide — climbing up to the lofty Marco and Rosa hut, certainly one of the finest vantage-points in the Alps, and on up from there to the summit of the Bernina, which, at 4049 metres, is the easternmost four-thousand metre peak in all of the Alps. The final climb down to Poschiavo and the railroad of the Bernina Pass is a long one, fairly hard on the legs, and it is made more complicated by a bureaucratic problem: if one crosses the border over a non-official pass, one may find oneself in hot water with the Swiss authorities. It is therefore a good idea to enquire with the Swiss border police (the phone number is printed below), and descend towards Chiesa Valmalenco. The Sentiero Italia, which runs at a safe distance from the border, through the high Val Fontana, the Cederna-Maffina hut and Prato Valentino, offers another solution. While waiting for the Swiss, people with a tradition of freedom, to discover that even walkers can be harmless.

USEFUL INFORMATION

Duration: 10 days.

Elevations: ranging from the 212 metres of Novate Mezzola to the 2,983 metres of the Bocchetta di Caspoggio.

Season: from July to September.

Signage: red and white trailmarkers along the Lombard stretch of the Sentiero Italia, yellow trailmarkers of the High Route of the Valmalenco, red crosses along the Sentiero Roma, and various local trailmarkers.

Degree of difficulty: climbing passages that range up to the second degree of difficulty on the Sentiero Roma, snow fields — and steep ones — for much of the summer.

How demanding: quite, considering the length of the stages and the considerable steep climbs and descents, the difficult terrain (stone fields and snow fields), especially along the Sentiero Roma. The small steep glacier of Caspoggio, which one crosses during the tenth stage, is an easy glacier, which requires adequate equipment and gear and some experience.

Equipment: normal mountain gear. Ice axe and in some cases crampons may be useful for the small steep glacier of Caspoggio and, especially at the beginning of the season, for certain high passes along the Sentiero Roma.

Peaks: many of the most enchanting and elegant peaks in the chain that separates the Engadine from the Valtellina can be reached from the huts along this route: none of them however is truly easy. A walker accompanied by a guide Mount Disgrazia (3,678 metres) Piz Bernina (4,049 metres),

Piz Badile (3,308 metres) from the Gianetti hut, is a long grade II/III rock climb.

How to get there: Novate Mezzola is on the railroad line Milan-Lecco-Colico-Chiavenna, while Poschiavo is on the "railroad of the Bernina" running from St. Moritz to Tirano and Sondrio.

How to get around: regularly scheduled buses from the Val Masino and the Val Malenco to the Valtellina and Sondrio.

Overnight accommodations: in privately owned and CAI huts.

If you want to camp out: camping is not forbidden in the areas this walk runs through. There may be some problems in terms of weight because the trail is quite demanding and the

terrain is quite rocky.

Alpine Guides: Alpine guides of Bormio/Valtellina (39) (342) 910991, Guides of the Val Malenco, c/o the APT (Local Bureau of Tourism) of Chiesa (39) (342) 451150.

Weather Forecasts: contact the tourist bureaus.

Mountain Rescue: the headquarters of the CNSA c/o Elilario Piateda can be contacted by dialing 113 or 118.

Information Offices: APT of the Val Malenco (39) (342) 451150, Tourist Bureau of Poschiavo (41) (82) 50571.

Useful phone numbers: Gianetti hut (39) (342) 645222, Bonacossa and Allievi huts (39) (342) 614200, Ponti hut (39) (342) 611455, Bosio hut (39) (342) 451655, Porro-Gerli hut (39) (342) 451404, Longoni hut (39) (342)

Piz Bernina
Piz Scerscen
Piz Roseg
Piz Palù

A. dell'Oro

Alpe Gera • Poschiavo

Pirola
Palù
Campomoro

Piz Scalino

Val Malenco

Mt. Disgrazia
acier of
eda Rossa

A. Pradaccio • Caspoggio

Chiesa

Airale Valley

Valtellina

ITALY

93 From the Bernina Pass (2,323 metre) over which runs the old road that once linked the Valtellina with the Grisons, one's gaze wanders over the peaks of the Pizzi Cambrena. Photograph by Gianluca Boetti and Daniele Castellino

451120, Carate hut (39) (342) 453297, Marinelli-Bombardieri hut (39) (342) 511577, Bignami hut (39) (342) 451178.
Guide Books: *Walks in the Engadine, Switzerland* by Kev Reynolds (Cicerone Press) - Bernina and Bregaglia.
Maps: it is enough to have the Kompass 1:50,000 n. 92 *Chiavenna - Val Bregaglia*, n. 93 *Sondrio - Bernina*, and n. 676 *Sentiero Italia - Lombardia nord*. The best maps are the Swiss CNS 1:50,000 n. 268 *Julierpass* and n. 278 *M. Disgrazia*, to which one may add the CNS 1:25,000 n. 1296 *Sciora* and n. 1277 *Piz Bernina*. As always, not updated are the IGM 1: 25,000 of *Verceia, Villa di Chiavenna, Piz Badile, M. Disgrazia, Piz Bernina,* and *Chiesa.*.

FIRST DAY

From Novate Mezzola to Brasca hut
Distance climbed: 1,100 metres
Time: 4 hours

This is a fascinating stage, warm in the summer during the first part because of the southern exposure and the altitude. The Val Codera is one of the last valleys in the Alps that is inhabited year round, and yet is not served by a road. The reason appears quite clearly if one walks some distance along the trail, which is literally carved into the huge granite slabs. The upper section of the valley is more restful, as one walks among dense woods dominated by the rocks of Pizzo Ligoncio and the Sfinge. From Novate Mezzola (212 metres), one climbs very quickly up to the village of Mezzolpiano and to the end of the road (316 metres).
One continues along a trail that is quite steep - and with steps carved into long stretches of it - which climbs up to a granite quarry and a little chapel, and then enters a wood. A further climb takes one to the houses of Avedée (790 metres), and then one continues diagonally all the way to Codera (825 metres), a small village with a tavern that remains open during the summer as well.
The trail continues through the open, rocky valley, reaches the houses of Saline (1,085 metres), and then gives way to a fairly unlovely cart-road that was built in 1989; this track runs on through woods and beautiful meadows, passing through Stoppadura and Bresciadega, finally winding up at the Brasca hut (1,304 metres).

SECOND DAY

from Brasca hut to Gianetti hut
distance climbed: 1,250 metres
distance descended: 200 metres
time: 5 hours 45 minutes

A not excessively lengthy day, in a savage surrounding, with splendid views of the Piz Badile and Cengalo, which allows one to travel from the wooded Val Codera to the rocky and savage Val Porcellizzo, the first taste of the spectacular environment of the high Val Masino and the Sentiero

94 top The little hamlet of Codera, a picturesque little village at an altitude of eight hundred twenty-five metres, is one of the few in the Alps that is not served by a road. Even nowadays the only way up is along the ancient mule-track that has been dug into the living rock. Photograph by F. Raiser/K3.

94 bottom The Gianetti hut, base for the standard route up the Piz Badile, stands at an altitude of 2,534 metres in a stark and rocky setting, marking the beginning of the Sentiero Roma, one of the most classic walking routes in the Central Alps. Photograph by G. Miotti/K3.

Roma. The climb up to the Passo dell'Oro is the only fatiguing part, and it is possible to shorten the length of the stage by heading directly to the Omio hut. There are no particular technical difficulties, which are present in some substantial number, however, in traversing the Pass of the Barbacan, the shortest passage between Val Porcellizzo and Val Codera. From the hut, one reaches the Alpe Coeder, and one leaves the trail, heading for the Vaninetti camp ground, and climbing up among the fir trees of the Valle dell'Averta. After passing by the Alpe Pisci (1,636 metres) and the Alpe Averta

(1,957 metres), one quickly reaches a plateau and a fork in the paths (2,120 metres).
After leaving the trail to the Pass of the Barbacan on the left, one climbs yet higher up the high valley, one goes off to the right, and one proceeds up a rocky gully as far as the Passo dell'Oro (2,526 metres). One climbs down, proceeding beyond the meadows, until one crosses the Sentiero Risari, following it on the left along a steep gully as far as the the South Pass of the Barbacan (2,650 metres), beyond which an equipagged ledge and a little trail lead on to the Gianetti hut (2,534 metres).

THIRD DAY

*from the Gianetti hut
to Bonacossa and Allievi huts
distance climbed: 670 metres
distance descended: 500 metres
time: 6 hours*

This is a classic stage, through the rocky setting of the upper Val Masino, within sight of the elegant spires of the Monte di Zocca, of the Cima di Castello, of the Punta Rasica and the Punta Allievi, all criss-crossed by classic rock-climbing routes over the granite.
The descent from the pass of Camerozzo, which is steep and fairly exposed, requires great care. From the hut, one reaches the base of the Spigolo Vinci of the Cengalo (one of the most classic climbs of the Màsino) one climbs up through stone fields and small rocks to the pass of Camerozzo (2,765 metres), and then one climbs down into the high Valle del Ferro along ledges and a small equipped gully with fixed ropes.
A pleasant route running obliquely along the slope through the stone fields and large granite slabs of the high Valle del Ferro (about halfway up one passes, low and to the right, the campground Molteni-Valsecchi), leads one to the gentle slope that climbs up to the pass of Qualido (2,707 metres). One descends on the far side (fixed ropes and pitons), one crosses a large gully, and climbs back up on the other side with fixed ropes to the pass of the Averta (2,540 metres). A system of equipped ledges allows one to climb down into the Val di Zocca, where one skirts the Spigolo Parravicini of the Torrione di Zocca, and one reaches the huts of Bonacossa and Allievi (2,395 metres).

FOURTH DAY

*from the Bonacossa hut to the Ponti hut
distance climbed: 810 metres
distance descended: 500 metres
time: 6 hours 30 minutes*

The last stage in the Sentiero Roma, also in a wild setting with rather steeper climbs and descents than previously, offers a number of fairly challenging stretches of rock climbing, due to the disappearance of the snowfields and the little glacier that used to make it easier to climb up to the pass of Cameraccio and the Bocchetta Roma. One begins by traversing almost on the level all the way to the pass of Torrone (2,518 metres), beyond which one begins to climb down along the Val Torrone along a rocky gully. One traverses it

until reaching the large rock alongside of which is the rest point Manzi (2,538 metres), and from there begins the steep ascent (first and second degree, equipped trails) to the Cameraccio Pass (2,950 metres). Within sight of the elegant Mount Disgrazia, one descends obliquely along the slope, and continues among stone and snow fields on the head of the Val di Mello. At the end, a gully (snow or ice, crampons), then a number of equipped passages lead to the Bocchetta Roma (2,850 metres). By this point, the pyramid of the Disgrazia is near: one climbs down across rocky ground at the foot of the mountain, until one reaches the Ponti hut (2,559 metres).

climbers can cross after taking the morning to climb up the standard route of Mount Disgrazia (6 hours round trip), and which for others will be a welcome piece of cake after the exhausting walk of the preceding day. The environment is solitary and wild. Those who have some experience with glaciers may choose to take the variant running up to the Porro hut across the small steep glacier of the Ventina. From the hut, one follows the trail that runs across the moraine of the glacier of Preda Rossa, and then one climbs up a gully dotted with reddish rocks (there is snow here at the beginning of the season) all the way to the pass of the Corna Rossa (2,836 metres); just beyond

95 top The rocky pillars of the Cima di Zocca (3,175 metres) are shown here as photographed from the Passo dell'Averta (2,540 metres), one of the most difficult high passes on the Sentiero Roma, in the heart of the wild mountains of the Val Masino. Photograph by G. Miotti/K3.

FIFTH DAY

*from the Ponti hut to the Bosio hut
distance climbed: 280 metres
distance descended: 750 metres
time: 3 hours*

A short linking stretch between the Sentiero Roma and the Alta Via of the Val Malenco, which solid mountain

95 bottom On the third stage, just before reaching the Bonacossa hut, one can admire the imposing granite

walls of the Val di Mello, one of the temples of rock-climbing in the Alps. Photograph by Gianluca Boetti.

that pass is the Desio hut. A high valley leads down to the Val Torreggio. Alongside a waterfall, at a fork in the paths, one leaves the trail to the Porro hut behind on one's left, and one crosses the small steep of the Ventina. The easiest trail runs along the foot of a strip of rocks, and leads on to the Bosio hut (2,086 metres), along a terrace at the edge of the woods.

SIXTH DAY

from the Bosio hut
to the Gerli-Porro hut
distance climbed: 900 metres
distance descended: 1,200 metres
time: 7 hours 30 minutes

Harsh and tiring, the first long day of the High Route of the Val Malenco extends over a considerable bit of mileage, while the vertical distance covered is confined to the sheer vertical leap of the Val Sassersa. The area, which receives very few walkers or visitors, is an alternation of dense forest and stone terrains and meadows. There are numerous signs of human activity, ranging from talc, asbestos, and porphyry quarries, and a number of meadows in use as pasture. From the hut, one crosses a hollow dotted with huge boulders, one climbs up to the Alpe Airale, and continues toward the Alpe Mastabbia (2,077 metres). Further along, the trail runs through a series of abandoned talc quarries, then drops down among the larches, leading on to the meadows of the Lago di Chiesa and Giumellino (1,756 metres). A lengthy traverse at the foot of the Pizzo Cassandra leads to the Alpe Pirlo (1,600 metres), and then on to the Alps of Prato and Pradaccio (1,725 metres). One climbs up the steep and difficult Gully of Sassersa, first of all covering a rocky terrain, and then running past three little lakes, and finally over snow, all the way to the Pass of Ventina (2,575 metres). A steep descent — blanketed by snow over much of the summer — leads past a panoramic view of Mount Disgrazia to the moraine of the steep glacier of the Ventina and to the Alpe Ventina, where the hut of the same name and the Gerli-Porro hut are located (1,960 metres).

96 top The summit of Mount Disgrazia (3,672 metres) looms at the head of the hollow of Preda Rossa. The standard route to the summit runs along the left-hand ridge, while the walking route runs around the massif to the right, crossing the wild pass of Corna Rossa. Photograph by F. Raiser/K3.

96 bottom The Alpe Prato, at an altitude of 1,725 metres, along the stage that runs between Bosio and Gerli-Porro hut, is one of the most isolated and distinctive in the Val Malenco. In this area, there are a great many quarries, most of them abandoned, where talc, porphyry, and asbestos were mined. Photograph by Riccardo Carnovalini.

SEVENTH DAY

from the Gerli-Porro hut
to the Longoni hut
distance climbed: 750 metres
distance descended: 160 metres
time: 4 hours

A brief linking stretch of trail, with a splendid view of the north face of Mount Disgrazia, which can be extended (by nearly five hours) with the variant trail of the Val Sissone, or else by heading directly to the lake of Palù. The idyllic clearings around the Mallero are inviting, and one may choose to make an extended halt. The Pass of the Muretto was once part of a major route linking Valtellina with the Engadine. One begins by climbing down along the mule-track that leads to the hut, and then leaves the track almost immediately to head down to the huts at Forbicina (1,700 metres) and the fork in the path for the Val Sissone. A dirt lane leads to a bridge over the river Mallero, beyond which one can quickly reach Chiareggio, off to the right. A climb up through the meadows leads to the ancient mule-track of the pass of the Muretto, which one takes all the way to the Alpe dell'Oro (2,010 metres), another balcony overlooking the Disgrazia. An extended stretch of trail running obliquely along the slope leads to the Alpe Fora (2,059 metres), and from there one can climb to the Longoni hut (2,450 metres).

EIGHTH DAY

from the Longoni hut
to the Lago Palù hut
distance descended: 400 metres
time: 4 hours

This is a brief stage, without any climbing, in one of the most picturesque and least popular corners of the Val Malenco, among magnificent forests. Handsome and pleasant are also the areas surrounding lake Lago Palù, the classic destination of the picknickers and summer visitors of Chiesa. It is possible to cut one day's walk off the walk by climbing up to the Marinelli-Bombardieri hut along the lower glacier of Scerscen.

A brief descent takes one to the dirt road that links S. Giuseppe with the hut and the summer ski slopes of Entova-Scerscen. One climbs uphill for two kilometres until reaching a switchback (2,380 metres), from which one begins a long tour across meadows and scree that leads to the Alpe Sasso Nero (2,304 metres). A short way beyond, a steep descent through stands of mugo pines leads to the Lago Palù hut (1,947 metres).

NINTH DAY

from the Lago Palù hut
to Marinelli-Bombardieri hut
distance climbed: 1,400 metres
distance descended: 150 metres
time: 7 hours

This is a long stage and is relatively monotonous at the beginning, when it runs through meadows and across ski slopes, but it becomes more interesting as one passes the Bocchetta delle Forbici, and from that point one is walking through high mountain terrain.
At the foot of the Piz Bernina, the Marinelli-Bombardieri hut is one of the most popular huts in the Lombard Alps; it is not very easy to find solitude and silence here. One begins with a steep climb up to the Bocchel del Torno (2,203 metres), a little saddle from which one descends and crosses the ski slopes. A trail leads to the open space of Campascio (1,828 metres), which was damaged by the great flood of 1989. After climbing up to the Alpe Musella, (2,021 metres) one continues along the exhausting ramps of the "seven sighs," which are great morainic steps that live up to their name and which lead to the Carate hut (2,636 metres) and to the nearby Bocchetta delle Forbici, where the environment changes with great suddenness. Facing one are the Piz Bernina, the Piz Roseg, and the other peaks of the massif; one descends at length obliquely along the slope, passes by the small steep glacier of Caspoggio, and then climbs steeply back up to the Marinelli-Bombardieri hut (2,813 metres).

TENTH DAY

from the Marinelli-Bombardieri hut
to the Poschiavo hut
distance climbed: 630 metres
distance descended: 2,310 metres
time: 7 hours 30 minutes

A very lengthy and interesting stage — which can be split up into two sections, with an overnight stay at the Bignami hut — which runs southward around the highest peaks of the Bernina,

skirts the dramatic man-made lake of Campo Gera, and then climbs up to the pastureland as high as the ridge running along the border, where a long descent leads one to Poschiavo. It is worth pointing out that only Swiss walkers can cross the Passo Confinale without any bureaucratic difficulties. Italian walkers — and those from other nations — must call ahead at least 24 hours in advance, applying to the border police of Samedan (tel. 41.82.65775). Otherwise, it is possible to return to the Val Malenco via Campo Moro and Franscia. From the hut, one descends to the small steep glacier of Caspoggio, climbing it up to the Bocchetta of Caspoggio (2,983 metres). One descends along inconvenient small earthy rocks, and then along the broad high valley that leads to the Alpe Fellaria and the Bignami hut (2,401 metres). Here one descends toward the left, running around the lake of Campo Gera, finally reaching the Alpe Gembrè (2,224 metres). Passing the trail to the lovely Val Poschiavina, leading off to the right, one climbs along barely visible paths among the pastures all the way to the Border Pass. A clearly marked trail runs off to the left as far as the huts of Sommodosso (2,160 metres). Along the road, one descends to Poschiavo (1,019 metres).

97 top A broad and popular trail runs up to the 2,813-metres elevation of the Marinelli hut, an overnight accommodation on the walking route and the point of departure for mountain climbers heading for the summit of the Piz Bernina, the easternmost "four-thousand" in the Alps. Photograph by Stefano Ardito.

97 bottom The light of dawn enhances even more the spectacular view of the rocky walls of the Piz Roseg (3,936 metres), one of the highest and most magnificent peaks in the massif of the Bernina. Photograph by Gianluca Boetti.

THE RING OF THE ÖTZTAL ALPS

A spectacular, high-altitude tour of the "roof of the Tyrol" and a hunt for the ancient "Similaun man"

It was the chance discovery of "Otzi," the mysterious prehistoric man of the Similaun, found in the ice in 1991, that made world-famous the ridges and passes that separate Austria's Ötztal from Italy's Val Senales and the Venosta in Alto-Adige. The mummified remains of the ancient wanderer received rough treatment at the hands of tourists and amateur archeologists, and were badly damaged. The prehistoric clothing, the basic but effective equipment, and even his presence at such high altitude, gives us remarkable information about prehistoric life in the Alps, and more information will probably be obtained as studies of "Otzi" proceed. For mountain climbers, walkers, and skiers, however, the mountain chain along the border, between the Palla Bianca (Weisskugel) and the Similaun, has been well known for many years. The same is true of the huge massif of the Wildspitze, which is the highest mountain in the Tyrol, at 3,772 metres and in all of Austria only the Grossglockner is taller. These mountains had all been thoroughly explored by the middle of the nineteenth century — the exploits of Franz Senn, parish priest of Vent and the first man to climb many of the peaks in this area, are justly famous — and were equipped with an excellent network of mountain huts before the First World War, a network which is still used extensively in all seasons of the year. The skier will find splendid winter slopes here, as well as the summer *domaines skiables* of Similaun, Solden, and Mittelberg, splendid routes for traverses on skis along peaks and glaciers. In comparison with the expanse of the massifs and the altitude, the difficult mountain climbing routes are not very numerous. The low- and mid-

elevation walking routes that begin from Solden, Obergurgl, Vent, and the villages of the Val Senales, in Italy, on the other hand, are very pleasant. There can be no doubt, however, that the best way to see these mountains is through high-elevation walking, via huts and glaciers, with the occasional climb up to the more spectacular, higher peaks such as the Similaun and, of course, the Wildspitze. This is exactly the sort of route that we are suggesting here. This is a route that runs a broad circuit around the Ötztal, offering extraordinary views in all directions — particularly noteworthy is, to the south of the Val Venosta, the impressive massif of the Ortles, while in the distance one can see the Dolomites — as well as offering, in the area around the Brandenburger Haus and along the extensive and nearly level Gepatschferner, authentic and surprising whiffs of Greenland. Here we will discover thrills, peaks, and vistas similar to those of the Hohe Tauern, between the Gross Venediger and the Grossglockner. Those who are familiar with these mountains knows full well that high-elevation alpine walking is a very popular activity in Austria, as it is along the Western Alps. To any reader feeling daunted by the altitude and the abundance of glaciers along the walk, we would point out that this route is accessible to any walker in decent shape, as long as that walker is properly equipped and accompanied by an experienced guide. Lastly, the route offers a number of different approaches: those who have had enough of high elevations can take the "low circuit" via the Mittelberg, while those who wish to add the Wildspitze to their collections of peaks can also make that climb, and then descend to Solden, or else to Vent.

98-99 *From the modest elevation of the Polleskogel, one's gaze wanders over the Wildspitze (3,774 metres) and its glaciers. The highest peak in the Ötztal Alps (and the second highest in all of Austria) can be reached from the valleys of Vent and Taschach.*
Photograph by Ernst Höhne

99 bottom left *In the valleys at the base of the Wildspitze, despite the importance that tourism has attained during recent years, agriculture and livestock still play a major role in the local economy.*
Photograph by G. Veggi/White Star

99 bottom right *This picture shows a distinctive shepherds' hut in the Patznautal, at the base of the mountains of the Ötztal. Those who decide to walk through this section of the Tyrol can admire handsome traditional buildings everywhere.*
Photograph by G. Veggi/White Star

USEFUL INFORMATION

Duration: 7 days.

Elevations: ranging from the 1,734 metres of the Mittelberg to the 3,606 metres of the Similaun or to the 3,772 metres of the Wildspitze.

Season: from late June to mid September. Beware of crevasses, which can open up greatly in late summer.

Signage: red and white along the trail O2 and the local trails along the parts that do not run over glaciers.

Degree of difficulty: long stretches across glaciers at relatively high elevations. This is an easy route merely alpinistic.

How demanding: average, but look out for the altitude!

Equipment: gear for walking on a glacier, with ice axe, crampons, and climbing rope.

Peaks: in this route is included a climb up the Similaun (3,606 metres) along the easy standard route over the glacier. The perfect conclusion for this route would be to climb up the Wildspitze (3,772 metres), the tallest mountain in the western Tyrol. Among the detours, let us mention the steep climb up to the Punta di Finale (Fineil

Spitze, 3,516 metres), and the rocky ridge of the Wassertalkogel (3,247 metres), an easier alternative to the standard route of the Wildspitze.

How to get there: Solden can be reached by bus from Innsbruck, along the railroad line Verona-Brenner-Munich, or from the station of the Ötztal, on the railroad line Innsbruck-Bregenz. It is possible to reach here from Italy via Merano, the Val Passiria, and the pass of the Rombo, or also via the cable car of the Similaun, riding up from Maso Corto to the Bellavista hut, and beginning the circle from there. There are frequent scheduled buses between Solden, Obergurgl, and the ski lifts of the Rettenbachferner.

How to get around: buses from Vent to Solden, from the Gepatschhaus to Prutz and Landeck and from the Mittelberg to Wenns and Imst. From the Bellavista hut, one can climb down to Italy (Val Senales) by cable car, and continue by bus to Merano.

Overnight accommodations: privately owned and OEAV and DAV huts.

Alpine Guides: at Solden (43) (5254) 2364, at Vent (43) (5254) 8106.

Weather Forecasts: (43) 5121567.

Mountain Rescue: at Solden (43) (5254) 2534, at Vent (43) (5254) 8119.

Information Offices: Tourist Bureau of Solden (43) (5254) 2212, Tourist Bureau of Vent (43) (5254) 8193.

Useful phone numbers: Ramolhaus (43) 5256223, Martin Bush Haus (43) (5254) 8130, Similaun hut (43) (4738) 9711, Bellavista hut (43) 88048, Hochjoch Hospitz (43) (5254) 8151, Brandenburger Haus (43) (5254) 8108, Gepatsch Haus (43) (5475) 215, Taschachhaus (43)(5413) 8239, Riffelsee hut (43) (5413) 8235, Braunschweiger hut (43) (5413) 8236.

Maps: the best maps are the 1:25,000 of the Alpenverein, n. 30/2 *Otztaler Alpen-Weisskugel* and n. 30/6 *Otztaler Alpen-Wildspitze*. Otherwise, there are the Kompass 1:50,000 n. 43 *Otztaler Alpen* or the Freytag-Berndt 1:50,000 n. 251 *Otztal-Pitztal-Kaunertal-Wildspitze*.

100 Another view of the Wildspitze: this great mountain in the Ötztal was climbed for the first time in 1848 by L. Klotzo, a peasant from Rofenhoffe, along with a fellow-climber whose name has been lost to posterity.

The year before, the brothers Schlagintweit — who had crossed the Himalayas and Karakorum in 1845 on behalf of the king of Prussia —had attempted to scale the peak.
Photograph by G. Veggi/White Star

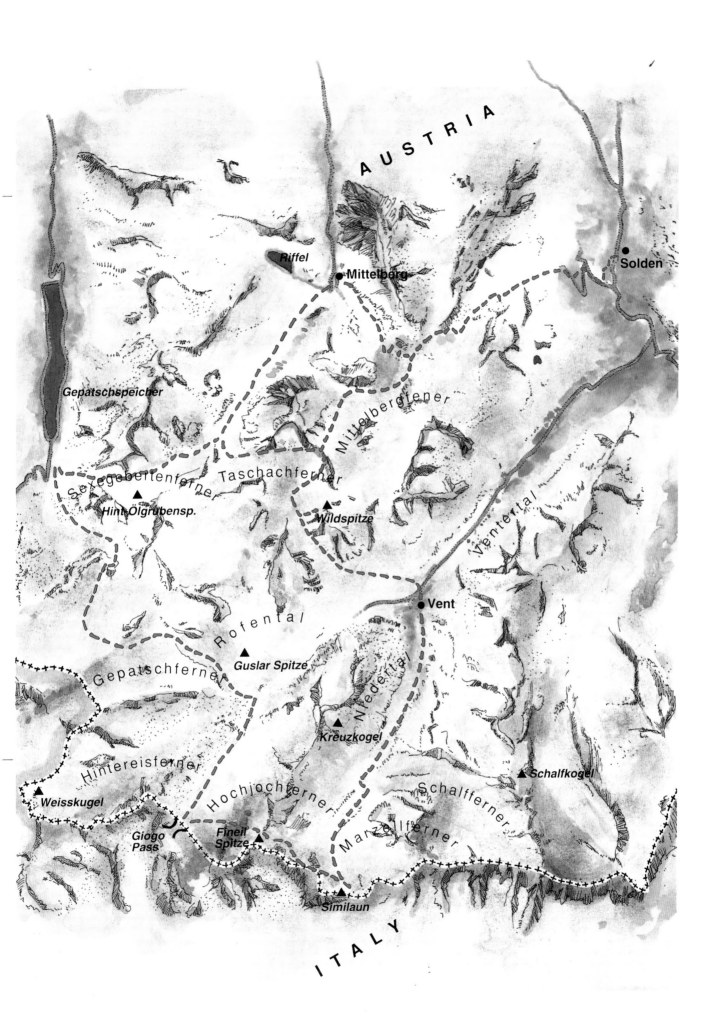

AUSTRIA

Solden

Riffel

Mittelberg

Gepatschspeicher

Mittelbergferner

Sexegettenferner

Taschachferner

Ventertal

Hint. Ölgrubensp.

Wildspitze

Rofental

Guslar Spitze

Niedertal

Vent

Gepatschferner

Kreuzkogel

Hintereisferner

Schalfkogel

Weisskugel

Hochjochferner

Schalfferner

Giogo Pass

Fineil Spitze

Marzellferner

Similaun

ITALY

101

FIRST DAY

From Vent to Martin-Busch hut
Distance climbed: 510 metres
time: 2 hours 45 minutes

This brief stage serves as an introduction to some very wild mountains, with a climb up from Vent to the comfortable Martin-Busch hut (also known as the Samoar hut) along the lovely and relaxing Niedertal. The location of the hut is splendid, at the confluence of the very impressive glacial flows of the Schalfferner, the Marzellferner, and the Niederjochferner. From Vent (1,896 metres), one follows the clearly marked mule-track (the Hermann Kuchling Weg) which runs up the Niedertal, at first through woods and later through open ground. After running past the Schafer hut (2,230 metres), one climbs up to the Martin-Busch hut (2,510 metres).

SECOND DAY

from the Martin-Busch hut
to the Similaun hut
distance climbed: 1,100 metres
distance descended: 580 metres
time: 6 hours

This is a long and interesting stage, devoted to climbing the easy summit of the Similaun, which offers a splendid vista; this is one of the most popular peaks in the eastern Alps, straddling the border ridge between Austria and Italy. This is an easy route, over a fairly crevasse-free glacier, with a slightly steeper final section that still presents no major problem. The ridge that leads up to the summit is lovely and easy. Starting from the hut, one follows the trail that leads to the Similaun hut, leaving it immediately for another trail that climbs off to the left all the way up (2,800 metres) to the grassy Marzellkamm ridge. One can walk along it, enjoying the excellent view of Schalfkogl, the Cime Nere (Hintere Schwarze), the Punta di Finale (Fineil Spitze), and the Kreuzspitze. Where the ridge ends (3,149 metres) one descends briefly to the glacier, climbing it up to the right of the broad north ridge of the Similaun, reaching the track that runs from the Similaun hut. A steep slope leads to the summit ridge and the peak itself (3,606 metres), where one can look out over the Val Senales. The descent to the Similaun hut (3,016 metres), surrounded by ugly buildings, is very short.

THIRD DAY

from Similaun hut to Hochjoch Hospiz
distance climbed: 50 metres
distance descended: 650 metres
time: 6 hours

Another splendid stage at high
elevations, along a route that was
once classic, but which nowadays has
been largely forsaken. This route
features spectacular vistas of the
massifs of the Wildspitze and the Palla
Bianca (Weisskugel). Expert climbers,
or those who are accompanied by
guides, can climb up to the Cima di
Finale (Fineilspitze, 3,516 metres),
the toughest of the great summits that
seal off the hollow of the Ötztal.
One begins along the marked trail that
climbs up to the ridge of the Jochkofel
(3,143 metres), and then continues
along a bit to the right (north) of the
crest. After crossing a snow-field, one
climbs up to the Hauslab Joch (Giogo
di Tisa, 3,279), where the standard
route to the Cima di Finale begins
(3,516 metres, 2 hours 30 minutes,
round trip). The track continues through
a level area of the Hochjochferner,
rising over a rocky ridge, and leading
to a trail (3,144 metres) across
moraines. At the end of the descent
(2,900 metres), one climbs back up to
the base of the Similaun ski lifts, and
then one crosses the glacier all the
way to the Bellavista hut (Schone
Aussicht Schutzhaus, 2,842 metres),
in the territory of Alto-Adige. After
returning to Austria, one can do
nothing more than to follow the
excellent trail that descends along the
left side of the valley all the way to the
Hochjochs Hospiz (2,412 metres).

FOURTH DAY

from Hochjoch Hospiz
to Brandenburger Haus
distance climbed: 900 metres
time: 3 hours

After leaving the valley behind one, a
long but gentle uphill climb takes one
to the solid and friendly-looking
Brandenburger Haus, at an elevation
of 3,272 metres atop the ridge that
separates the enormous
Gepatschferner from the smaller —
though still impressive —
Kesselwandferner. There is a
magnificent view over the Palla Bianca
(Weisskugel), the tallest peak along
the border-straddling mountain chain.
One can compete the stage by
walking along the Gepatschferner,

*103 top This is a
section of the climb
up to the Wildspitze
from the
Taschachhaus: the
climb, which runs
through one of the
most unspoilt and
spectacular settings
in the Austrian
Alps, presents no
major difficulties,
aside from the
nearly fourteen
hundred metres of
vertical distance.
Photograph by
A. Gogna/K3*

*103 bottom Seen
from the moraines of
the Taschachferner,
the northern slope of
the Wildspitze
appears particularly
impressive.
The peak is two-
headed: the higher
of the two summits
is the right-hand, or
southern one.
Photograph by
A. Gogna/K3*

climbing one of the low peaks in the surrounding area, or simply by sunbathing on the terrace of the hut, surrounded by a sea of ice that is almost unrivalled in the Alps.
One follows the trail — the Deloretten Weg — that climbs zigzagging up the slopes of the stone terrain Guslar Spitzen, doglegging to the northwest toward the Kesselwandferner.
One can admire the peak from a lofty trail, and then one crosses a stone terrain, climbing up over the ice almost all the way to the Brandenburger Joch. One stops short of that peak, and then one follows the trail that leads off to the left, all the way to the Brandenburger Haus (3,272 metres).

FIFTH DAY
from the Brandenburger Haus
to the Gepatsch Haus
distance climbed: 50 metres
distance descended: 1,350 metres
time: 5 hours 30 minutes

This is a stage that is as lovely and as panoramic as the preceding ones, especially the vista of the great séracs of the Gepatschferner. From the beginning of August onward, this stage is almost entirely over bare ice: of course, this reduces the problems posed by crevasses, but it may create some problems of orientation, especially in the case of low clouds, or fog.
One begins by venturing out in a slight descent along the Gepatschferner, along a track that runs gradually to the right, and then reaches the boulders of the Rauher Kopf, where a trail across the moraines leads to the very panoramic views that can be had from the Rauhekopf hut (2,732 metres). A steep trail leads to the edge of the lower strip of the glacier, is crossed heading for an impressive waterfall.
An awkward earth slope and then a beautiful trail take one out over the man-made Gepatsch lake.
Continuing along through meadows, and along paved road for a short stretch, one comes to the Gepatsch Haus (1,928 metres).

SIXTH DAY
from the Gepatsch Haus
to Taschachhaus
distance climbed: 1170 metres
distance descended: 650 metres
time: 5 hours 30 minutes

After leaving behind the border chain of the Venoste, we enter the Wildspitze massif, with the steep climb that leads up to the Olgruben Joch, whence one can climb down to the Taschach Haus, a comfortable hut, and yet another lovely vantage-point along this walk, directly opposite the northern face of the Wildspitze. The trail climbs steeply toward the peaks of the Kaunergrat, among scree and snow fields where it is easy to spot chamois and marmots. After reaching the Olgruben Joch (3,095 metres), with its wooden cross, one descends off to the left of the little Sexegertenferner, venturing into the dramatic Taschach Tal. After crossing a colossal huge boulder field terrain, the trail climbs gently up to the Taschach Haus (2,434 metres), a splendid balcony overlooking the northern face of the Wildspitze.

SEVENTH DAY
traversing the Wildspitze
from the Taschachhaus to Vent
distance climbed: 1,330 metres
distance descended: 1,440 metres
time: 8 hours

At the foot of the Wildspitze, as we were saying, there are at least three possible routes. The first one, which is also the most attractive, consists of a climb up the Wildspitze across the Mittelbergjoch, the Taschachferner, the Mitterkar Joch, and the eastern slope, followed by a descent to the Breslauer hut, and on to Vent. This is the most satisfying solution, clearly alpinistic in nature, and should be attempted by expert climbers or those who are travelling in the company of a guide. The two alternative routes are described as follows.
One begins by climbing up and traversing (2,600 metres) the Taschachferner, which one then follows on the orographic right (trail) all the way to Mittelberg Joch (3,166 metres). Here one turns to the right (southwest) along the upper plateau of the glacier, and then one veers to the left in the direction of the Mitterkar Joch, and then to the left again along the fairly undemanding ridge that leads up to the summit (3,772 metres). After making a halt to admire the incredible vista, one descends quickly to the Mitterkar Joch, to the Breslauer hut (2,840 metres), and on to the chairlift (2,356 metres) that takes one back to Vent.

SEVENTH DAY
traversing the Mittelberg Joch
distance climbed: 730 metres
distance descended: 410 metres
time: 5 hours 30 minutes

The "middle solution," which includes a stretch along the glacier, and which offers a splendid close-up view of the northern slope of the Wildspitze, begins with a climb up the route to the Mittelberg Joch (3,166 metres), as described above. One descends beyond alongside the ski slopes of the Mittelbergferner, then one traverses to the right above the sérac of the glacier, continuing along on a good track that leads to the Braunschweiger hut (2,750 metres). It is possible — but not advisable — to link this stage up to the following stage by crossing the Pitztaler Joch and descending directly toward Solden.

lower route across the Mittelberg
distance climbed: 950 metres
distance descended: 690 metres
time: 5 hours 30 minutes

The easiest solution follows the handsome valley of the Taschach Tal all the way to the very popular ski area of the Mittelberg, climbing up from here along a lengthy route running through a somewhat wilder landscape to the Braunschweiger hut. The trail drops steeply beneath the hut, joining (2,043 metres) a dirt road that runs all the way to Mittelberg (1,734 metres). From here, one sets out along another dirt road, climbing all the way to the Gletscherstube (1,891 metres), and then one undertakes the steep and winding climb to the Braunschweiger hut (2,759 metres). There are also two interesting variant trails. The first one follows the Fuldaer Hohenweg — instead of following the valley — obliquely along the slope, with a splendid wide-ranging view, and then descends to the Mittelberg along the Riffelsee (one-and-a-half hours longer). As an alternative, one can walk directly to the Mittelberg, ride up by cable car to the Mittelbergferner (2,841 metres), and then climb to the hut along the last section of the route described above (saving an hour's walk).

EIGHTH DAY

*from Braunschweiger hut
to Solden
distance climbed: 250 metres
distance descended: 490 metres
time: 1 hour 30 minutes*

The short crossing of the Pitztaler Joch can certainly be completed during the previous day's walk. It is more interesting, however, to join this walk with the partial or full walk of the Mainzer Hohenweg, the alpine trail over rock - an easy route featuring a few brief equipped stretches that runs north toward the Wildes Mannle (3,063 metres) and the Wassertalkogel (3,247 metres). The complete walk takes five hours, round trip.

104 Among the possible bases for the climb up to the 3,772-metre summit of the Wildspitze, the Breslauer hut is the one that allows one most greatly to reduce the vertical distance climbed. In the background, one can see the peak of the Brochkogel.
Photograph by Ernst Höhne

105 top From Mittagskogel, an easy summit towering to an elevation of 3,142 metres, and which can be reached from the Mittelberg ski slopes, an exceptional panorama opens out of the Wildspitze and the great icy expanse of the Brunnenkogel.
Photograph by Ernst Höhne

*105 bottom In this picture, it is possible to recognize the dramatic eastern slope of the Watzespitze (3,533 metres).
This daunting peak can be reached from the 2,811-metre elevation of the Kaunergrat hut, along a difficult route over the crevasse-ridden, demanding glacier of the Planggerossferner.*
Photograph by Ernst Höhne

THE KING LUDWIG TRAIL

Through Bavaria and on to the Alps,
in the footsteps of a surprising
sovereign

Baroque palaces and towers with fantastic battlements, Italian-style gardens dotted with statues and little man-made lakes. Monuments and environments that are quite different from the dramatic limestone peaks of the Eastern Alps await all those who choose to leave the Bavarian plains and climb mountainward, along a remarkable trail called the King Ludwig Trail , a trip through the landscape but also through time, which takes five days to walk. Ludwig succeeded to the Bavarian throne in 1864 at the age of eighteen — and was the second-to-last king — and was found dead in the waters of the lake of Starnberg on 13 June 1886, just before his fortieth birthday. King Ludwig II was one of the strangest and most contradictory characters in all of nineteenth-century Europe. Even today, Ludwig is considered by many Bavarians to be a symbol of national identity, and without a doubt he fell victim to the ambitious plan for the unification of Germany, devised and implemented by Otto von Bismarck. Educated in literature and the fine arts (but absolutely ignorant of politics and the art of governing) Ludwig succeeded his father Maximilian II on the Bavarian throne at a time of difficulties for himself and for Bavaria. Ludwig's father had already devoted himself to developing the architecture of Munich and other major cities in Bavaria — rather than to its military strength or political well-being.

As soon as Ludwig took the Bavarian throne, he summoned Richard Wagner to his court, and over the following months he financed the composer himself and the costly productions of his works. The popular protests at the lavish expenditures forced Ludwig to send Wagner away at the end of 1865: in those few months, however, there had been a production of *Tristan und Isolde*, and Wagner had completed a first draft of *Parsifal*. Even then, Ludwig's interest in politics was scanty, in comparison with his interest in the Middle Ages and the great High German epic of the Nibelungenlied. And the course of history did little to aid him in the difficult tasks of kingship. In 1866, Bismarck's Prussia defeated Bavaria, and during the Franco-Prussian war (1870-1871), Bavaria almost completely lost its independence. In 1871, Bavaria completely and definitively lost its independence. Ludwig devoted himself to art and architecture. With the example of Versailles before him, he ordered the construction of the palaces of Linderhof and Herrechiemsee. The castle of Neuschwanstein — with its bizarre mix of Romanesque, Byzantine, and late Gothic — was meant to be a tribute to such German heroes as Parsifal and Lohengrin. The hundreds of performances of French operas and his imitations of Louis XIV (the "Roi Soleil," or Sun King, of France) brought Ludwig ineluctably to the final chapter of his

reign. In June 1886, King Ludwig was officially declared insane, and a commission was sent to Starnberg to arrest him. Three days later, the king was found dead in the waters of the lake. The trail that is dedicated to the memory of King Ludwig is one hundred twenty kilometres in length. It was inaugurated in 1977, and links the two places that best symbolized the earthly voyage of the mad king: the lake where he was found dead, and the castle that constitutes his most visible monument. There is more. Ludwig was, in all likelihood, the king who was fondest of walking in the entire history of Europe, and he loved to spend days and weeks walking through forests and mountains.

The trail, therefore, is perhaps the most fitting monument to this strange sovereign, allowing walkers to visit in an unusual and fitting manner the castles that are now one of the biggest tourist attractions in all of Bavaria. Aside from the various historical considerations, this trail offers a pleasant and relaxing route through quiet villages, cultivated fields, and forests. The Alps can be seen in the distance throughout the walk, but the setting is anything but "Alpine." There are no lofty stretches of trail, no Dolomitic saddles, no steep uphill climbs. Once one reaches Fussen and Neuschwanstein, however, it is hard not to yield to the temptation to push on toward the Alps of Garmisch, the mountains of the Lechtal, and the Karwendel.

107 The castle of Neuschwanstein, the great creation of King Ludwig of Bavaria, marks the end of this pleasant route along the base of the Alps, along the border between Germany and Austria. Photograph from the Archives of the Kurverwaltung Füssen

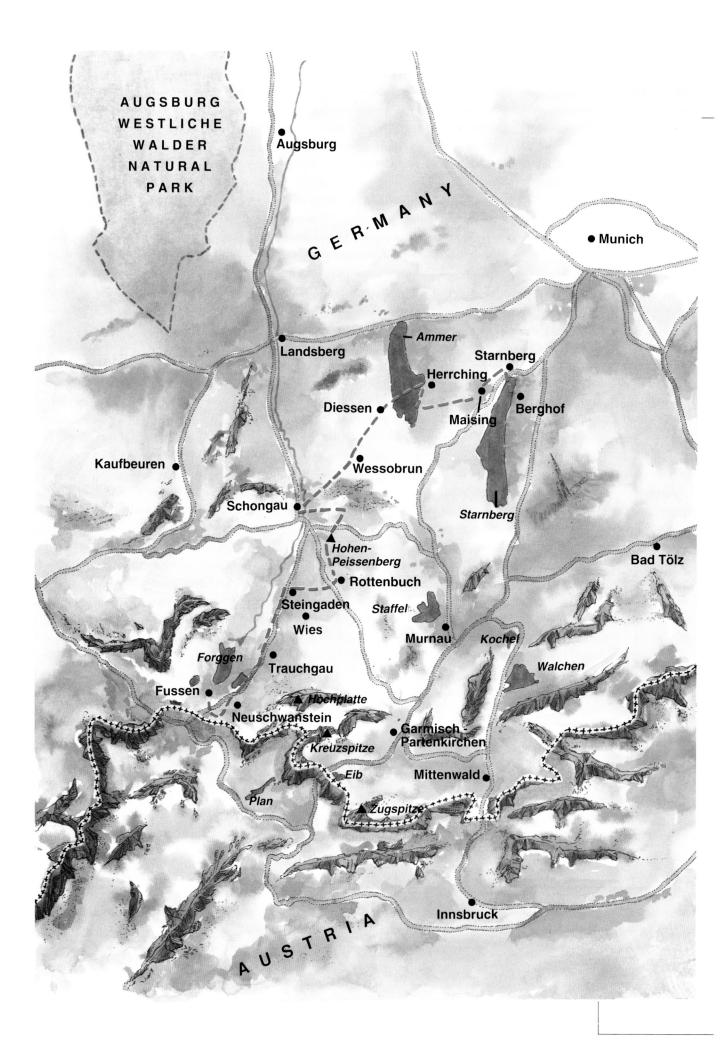

AUGSBURG
WESTLICHE
WALDER
NATURAL
PARK

● Augsburg

G E R M A N Y

● Munich

● Landsberg

— *Ammer*

● Herrching

● Starnberg

● Diessen

● Maising

● Berghof

● Kaufbeuren

● Wessobrun

Starnberg

● Schongau

▲ *Hohen-Peissenberg*

● Bad Tölz

● Rottenbuch

Staffel

● Steingaden

Kochel

● Wies

● Murnau

Forggen

● Trauchgau

Walchen

● Fussen

▲ *Hochplatte*

● Neuschwanstein

● Garmisch-Partenkirchen

▲ *Kreuzspitze*

Eib

● Mittenwald

Plan

▲ *Zugspitze*

● Innsbruck

A U S T R I A

108

Duration: 5 or 6 days.

Elevations: one reaches an elevation of 988 metres.

Season: year round, though spring and fall are the best times.

Signage: signs with a dark-blue "K" and local trailmarkers.

Degree of difficulty: minimal.

How demanding: from moderate to average.

Equipment: low- and medium-elevation walking gear.

Peaks: there are none along the route.

How to get there: Starnberg can be reached from Munich with the line number 6 (via Tutzing) of the S-Bahn. The return by train from Füssen to Munich is comfortable and quick.

How to get around: buses allow one to leave the route at virtually any point. Diessen is on the railroad line Augsburg-Gettendorf-Weilheim-Garmisch.

Overnight Accommodations: hotels and bed-and-breakfasts in all of the towns along the trail.

If you want to camp out: we recommend that you do not, since much of the land is privately owned.

Alpine Guides: there are many in Munich. Contact bureaus of tourism.

Mountain Rescue: in case of accidents, contact the Police (dial 110).

Information Offices: Füssen Kurverwaltung (49) 83627077, Trauchgau-Verkehrsamt (49) 8368890, Wald Gemeinde (49) 8302473, Nesselwang Gaste Information (49) 8361750, Prem Am Lech Verkchrsant (49) 88627256, Weissensee Kurverwaltung (49) 83626500.

Guide Books: in English, *King Ludwig Way* by Fleur and Colin Speakman, Cicerone Press 1987.

Maps: the best maps are topographic ones made by the Bayerisches Landesvermessungsamt 1:50,000, n. L1 *Ammersee, Starnberger See und Umgebung*, n. L3 *Pfaffenwinkel, Staffelsee und Umgeburg*, n. L10 *Füssen und Umgebung*, or else 1:25,000 n. 8033, n. 8034, n. 8032, n. 8132, n. 8232, n. 8231, n. 8331, n. 8330, n. 8430.

109 top In this picture, one can see the walls and the towers of the castle of Hohenschwangau, considered a jewel of the famous "Romantic way". In this castle, King Ludwig lived as a child.
Photograph from the Archives Kurverwaltung Füssen

109 bottom During the last few kilometres of the route, one can enjoy the view of the castle of Hohenschwangau and the Alpsee. This mansion, which dates from the Renaissance, was rebuilt between 1832 and 1837 at the orders of Maximilian II, the father of Ludwig.
Photograph by Ernst Höhne

110 A number of sailboats ply the tranquil waters of the Ammer See, one of the most enchanting lakes in Bavaria. One can take a boat across from Herrsching to Diessen, at the conclusion of the first full day of walking along the King Ludwig Trail. Photograph from the Archives of Landkreis Landsberg/Lech

Hohenpeissenberg all the way to St. Leonhard im Forst. After passing through the forest of fir trees of Schongau, a steep uphill climb takes one to the summit of the Hohenpeissenberg (988 metres), and from here one walks rapidly downhill to the town of the same name, at the heart of an ancient mining region.

FIRST DAY
The tour of the Schloss Berg
no distance climbed or descended
time: 1 hour 30 minutes

The King Ludwig Way begins on the banks of the Starnbergsee, with a pilgrimage to the cross that stands where Ludwig was found dead in 1886; one can make this outing in the morning of the first day of walking, or else in the afternoon of the day before. The best way of proceeding is to reach the Schloss Berg by boat from Starnberg, to tour the Schloss Berg at one's leisure, and then to return on foot to Starnberg, a distance of five kilometres over asphalt, yet quite a pleasant walk.

SECOND DAY
from Starnberg to Herrsching
distance climbed: 533 metres
time: 5 hours

The trail proper begins from the Vodermuhlgasse, right in the heart of Starnberg, and then runs out to the edge of town, continuing from there into the wooded gorge of the Maisinger Schlucht, running by the village of Maising and a hotel, and then on to the lake of Maising, which forms part of a protected nature reserve, inhabited by a great many species of birds. One continues through evergreen forests and mountain meadows until one reaches Aschering, passes on one's right a trail that leads to the zoological

institute that was founded by Konrad Lorenz, and then one continues along a stretch of paved road until one reaches Andechs, which features one of the loveliest medieval abbeys in Bavaria. A last stretch of trail running through the woods leads to Herrching, on the banks of the Ammersee. It is possible to complete the stage by crossing the lake by boat, and by touring the church of Diessen.

THIRD DAY
from Diessen to Hohenpeissenberg
distance climbed: 430 metres
distance descended: 270 metres
time: 6 hours 30 minutes

This is a long and fairly exhausting stage because of the steep final section. One begins by crossing the lake and touring the monastery of Diessen, founded in A.D. 815 but rebuilt during the seventeenth century. One continues through a urbanized area, and then on into the woods of the Waldehrpfad. After coming to the hot springs of Mechtild, one enters the protected forest of Bayerdiessen. A stretch of trail running through the meadows leads to Wessobrun. The baroque monastery here is magnificent. The site is well known, among other reasons, because the earliest known inscription in German was found here: a prayer dating from A.D. 814. One continues through a second wooded ravine, the Schnittbachgraben, and continues along within sight of the

FOURTH DAY
from Hohenpeissenberg to Wildsteig
time: 6 hours

Another stage of considerable interest, perhaps the finest in the whole walk, considering the magnificent gorge of the Ammer and the extensive evergreen forests. One begins among meadows, and one soon enters the woods, where fir trees, holm oaks, and beechwood alternate, leading on to a shepherds' hut, and on to the waters of the Ammer. After passing over a dam, one enters the gorge, passing over a wooden bridge, and then continuing along a little trail that is quite exposed, and at certain points quite slippery — one should use great caution here. Then one descends back down to the river, and then veers away on the trail that climbs up to the hill of the Schweinberg, a first-rate vantage-point over the Alps, quite near by this point. After reaching the village of Moos and the monastery of Rottenbuch, one continues on through forests and meadows, within sight of the mountains, all the way to Wildsteig.

FIFTH DAY
from Wildsteig to Berghof
or to Bayer-Niederhofen
time: 5 hours

This stage is shorter than the previous stages, but it can be lengthened by a good ten kilometres,

two-and-a-half hours), including the circuit of Steingaden. One begins by passing by a handsome little baroque church, then by crossing a brook, and entering the forest of Schwarzenbach, beyond which one comes to the eighteenth-century church of Wies. This is where one runs into the variant trail of Steingaden. The shortest route runs on through the nature reserve of Klaperfilz, reaching a series of meadows which offer splendid views of the mountains.

One comes to Trauchgau almost at a level, passes over the river Ach,

and emerges onto a paved road. It is best to avoid this road (though the "official" route follows it); we recommend shifting over onto the trail FP 118, which leads on to the twin towns of Berghof and Bayer-Niederhofen.

SIXTH DAY
from Berghof to Fussen
time: 5 hours

The final stage takes one to the border between Germany and Austria, and especially to the castle of Neuschwanstein, the best known and the most spectacular among all the castles built by King Ludwig II. One begins along a little road from which one can see the castle in the distance, then skirts the lake of Hegratsried, passes by the village of Brunnen, and one comes to a paved road.

Along the river, one comes to the stunning gorge of the Pollat. Emerging from this gorge, one finds oneself at the foot of the castle of Neuschwanstein. Before touring the castle — and the crowds are a stark divergence from the peace of the previous days — it is worthwhile venturing out onto the Mariabrucke, a bridge swaying over the gorge, which offers the best view of the castle.

After touring the castle itself, one descends quickly to Hohenschwangau. On the last stretch toward Füssen, we recommend abandoning the road and taking the little trail of the Alpenrosenweg.

111 top The area surrounding Trauchgau, where there is a splendid forest protected by a nature reserve, provides one of the most pleasant parts of the stage that runs from Wildsteig to Berghof.
The mountains are clearly visible from here.
Photograph from the Archives of the Landkreis Landsberg/Lech

111 bottom left The King Ludwig Trail allows one to walk through the relaxed and tranquil landscape of southern Bavaria.
In this photograph, a number of walkers work their way along the Autchen Weg.
Photograph from the Archives of the Landkreis Landsberg/Lech

111 bottom right Nature and history merge at every step along the lovely King Ludwig Trail.
In this picture, we see the route followed by the last stage, not far from the castle of Neuschwanstein.
Photograph by Ernst Höhne

FROM SALZBURG TO
THE WILDER KAISER

Through the spectacular limestone
massifs on the border between
Austria and Germany

Elegant limestone peaks and dense forests of fir trees, lakes of a dark, romantic beauty, huts that abound in history. At the border between Bavaria and Austria, the massifs across which this trail runs are among the most spectacular in all the Alps, featuring popular trails, with panoramic views, offering enormous excitement. Between the Untersberg — which separates Salzburg from Berchtesgaden — and the wild spires of the Wilder Kaiser, the settings for a thousand of the greatest adventures in climbing history, runs the daunting face of the Watzmann — the tallest and the most spectacular peak in the Bavarian Alps — the desolate limestone uplands of the Steinernes Meer, and the solitary and little known massif of the Loferer Steinberge. Between these separate and dramatic high-mountain landscapes, the route includes long stretches running through meadowland and forestland, and valley rich in history. At the beginning, the churches and the museums of Salzburg, the "city of Mozart," gives one a chance to immerse oneself in sightseeing and culture. For walkers whose native tongue is German, many of the places through which this route runs are well known. The legends and the vistas of the Königssee, the feats of Preuss, Dulfer, and Rebitsch on the faces of the Totenkirchl, the Predigstuhl, and the Ellmauer Halt, the forests surrounding Hinterbarenbad and the Karstic uplands straddling the border between Germany and Austria, all are clear and substantial attractions. For those who arrive from southern Europe — and especially for Italian walkers — the landscapes, the rocks, and the villages of the northern limestone Alps offer new surprises with every day that passes. The route that we describe here is a brand-new linkage of a number of the better known "official" walking routes of this area. By making use, as one progresses, of the E4, its alpine variant, the O1, and a great many

local trails, one passes and reviews a number of the most popular trails in this part of the Alps. It is certainly not an easy matter to find much solitude during the climb up from the Griesner Alm to the Stripsenjoch, as unspoilt as the Steinerne Rinne, and on around the Ingolstader hut or along the shores of the Königssee. Nonetheless, this route offers a great many quiet nooks and crannies, many moments of perfect solitude, and much powerful feeling to be pondered in silence. It is completely intentional that this is the case, and indeed this walk reviews a long procession of the most interesting protected areas of the limestone Alps. The best known of these areas is the Natural Park of the Alps of Berchtesgaden, an old hunting reserve that belonged to the sovereigns of Bavaria, under state administration and protection ever since 1930, covering 20,800 hectares. Here, among bare boulders, lakes, and splendid red fir, larch, and Swiss pine forests, live chamoises, stags, marmots, and golden eagles, and plans call for the introduction of the lynx and the bearded vulture. Beyond the border, the Austrian Natural Park of the Mitterkaser protects the southern slope of the Steinernes Meer and the forests around the man-made lake of Diesbach, extending further east to include the upland of the Hagen Geb and the spurs that run down to the banks of the Salzach. At the end of the crossing, the spires, the forests, and the uplands of the Wilder Kaiser form part of another Nature Reserve of enormous beauty and interest. Those who wish to walk further along the E4 can pass by both Kufstein and the highway that runs from Munich to the Brenner Pass, and thus go on to the Karwendel, the wildest of all the great limestone massifs of the Tyrol, before climbing on down to Innsbruck. Along the entire route, there are a great many possibilities for mountain climbing variants or equipped trails, so that one can make one's way up to the

tallest and most spectacular peaks of the various massifs. We have chosen to suggest as a base-route a path that is easy and accessible to one and all, and which only occasionally requires to tackle a few simple equipped passages (crossing of the Loferer Steinberge, the Steinerne Rinne and the Ellmauer Tor). It is not until the end, on the Wilder Kaiser, that the route that runs directly to the heart of the massif, crossing the Ellmauer, was described alongside the other, alternative route — far easier — that runs from the Grütten hut down to Kufstein along the Hintersteiner See.

112-113
The Grütten hut
(1,620 metres) is
one of the most
comfortable and
welcoming
mountain huts on
the Wilder Kaiser.
Unlike the
Stripsenjoch hut, at
the beginning of
the Steinerne
Rinne,
it is particularly
popular with
walkers.
Photograph by
A. Gogna/K3

113 bottom
The Königssee, the
most romantic lake
in the Bavarian
Alps, is shown here
as it appears from
the Halskopfl. Set at
the foot of the great
wall of the
Watzmann, it is a
major attraction to
the many tourists
who come to
Berchtesgaden.
Photograph by
Ernst Höhne

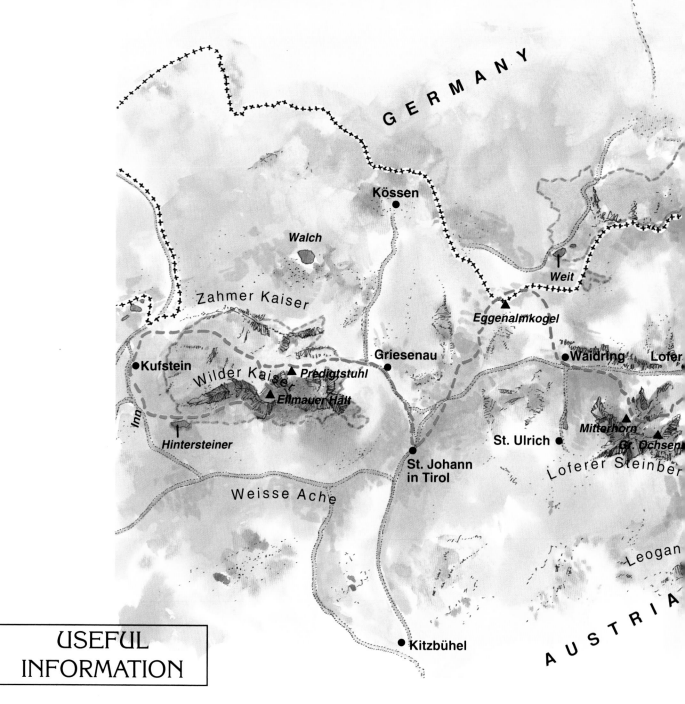

GERMANY

Kössen

Walch

Weit

Zahmer Kaiser

Eggenalmkogel

Griesenau

Waidring

Lofer

Kufstein

Wilder Kaiser

Predigtstuhl

Ellmauer Halt

Mitterhorn

St. Ulrich

Gr. Ochsen

Inn

Hintersteiner

Loferer Steinber

St. Johann
in Tirol

Weisse Ache

Leogan

AUSTRIA

Kitzbühel

USEFUL INFORMATION

Duration: 9 days.
Season: from July to October.
Elevations: ranging from the 424 metres of Salzburg to the 2,344 metres of the Ellmauer Halt.
Signage: white and red for the trails E4, O4, and O1 and for the local trails.
Degree of difficulty: equipped and easy-climbing trails (first and second degree) concentrated in the crossing of the Loferer Steinberge and the Wilder Kaiser.
How demanding: average, but in full summer the low-altitude stretches can be somewhat tiring.
Equipment: normal mountain gear, with body shape harness, little rope, screw gate karabiner, and abseil device.
Peaks: along the base-route are the

Ellmauer Halt (2,344 metres), the highest peak in the Wilder Kaiser, and the twin peaks of the Salzburger Hochtron (1,853 metres) and the Berchtesgadener Hochtron (1,972 metres), the highest peaks of the Untersberg. As detours, it is possible to head up, from the Karlinger Haus, to a number of easy peaks of the Steinernes Meer — the Funtenseetauern (2,579 metres); the Grosse Hundstod (2,594 metres), the two highest peaks of the Loferer Steinberge, the Grosses Ochsenhorn (2,511 metres) and the Mitterhorn (2,506 metres); and other, more difficult peaks of the Wilder Kaiser.
How to get there: Salzburg can be reached easily by train or car from Munich, Innsbruck, and Vienna; there is an international airport. Kufstein is on

the railroad line Verona-Brenner-Innsbruck-Munich.
How to get around: regularly scheduled buses to Lofer, Waidring, and St. Johann Im Tirol (via Salzburg, Kitzbuehel, and Innsbruck), railroad from Berchtesgaden to Salzburg and Munich and from St. Johann Im Tirol to Innsbruck, Villach, and Vienna.
Overnight accommodations: huts of the OEAV, DAV, and private owners, bed-and-breakfasts and hotels in the low valleys.
Alpine Guides: (49) (662) 329294 Salzburg, (43) (6564) 247 Krimml.
Weather Forecasts: (43) (662) 6263010.
Mountain Rescue: (43) (662) 830888, Landbüro 620506, Stadtbüro 88987203.

FIRST DAY
From Salzburg to Berchtesgaden
Distance climbed: 500 metres
Distance descended: 1,560 metres
time: 4 hours 30 minutes

From the center of Salzburg (423 metres), one can take a bus to the little village of St. Leonhard (459 metres), and from here take the Untersberg cable car to the Geiereck (1,806 metres), a traditional and splendid vantage-point overlooking the city of Salzburg.

A little way downhill and to the north is the Zeppezauer hut (1,668 metres). One continues on foot along the broad trail (markers of the trails E4 and O4) that runs up to the peak of the Salzburger Hochtron (1,853 metres). The trail continues along the ridge that marks the border between Austria and Germany, and then runs over the Grosses Heuberg (1,852 metres), dropping down to the broad Mittagscharte. At this point the trail

115 The wild limestone peaks of the Wilder Kaiser - shown here is the Ackerlspitze, which rises to an elevation of 2,331 metres - among the most alluring in the Alps. Their crags and walls have been the site of many of the most important events in the history of European alpinism.
Photograph by Ernest Höhne

is running through German territory; it cuts south, leaving behind on the right the impressive limestone uplands of the Untersberg. The trail then climbs to the Berchtesgadener Hochtron (1,972 metres), and drops down to the Stohr Haus (1,894 metres). Another practically level stretch of trail takes one to a fork, where one leaves the E4 (this trail continues toward Bad Reichenall), and one heads south to the Kalter Brunnen and the houses of Ober Gern. From the Theresien Klause hotel (750 metres) one can walk or take a bus down to Berchtesgaden (572 metres).

Information Offices: Tourist Bureau of Salzburg (43) (662) 80987331-6205060, Tourist Bureau of Berchtesgaden (49) (8652) 9670, Tourist Bureau of Lofer (43)(6588) 321, Tourist Bureau of Waidring (43) (5353) 5242, Tourist Bureau of St. Johann Im Tirol (43) (5352) 2218, Tourist Bureau of Kufstein (43)(5372) 62737-62207.
Useful phone numbers: Zeppezauer hut (43) (6246) 3346, Toni Lenz hut (49) (8650) 208, Stohr Haus (49) (8652) 7233, Karlinger Haus (49) (8652) 2995, Ingolstadter huy (43)(6582) 8353, Grütten huy (43) (5358) 2242.
Maps: the Kompass 1:50,000 n. 14 *Berchtesgadener Land-Chiemgauer Alpen*, and n. 9 *Kaisergebirge*.

SECOND DAY
*from Berchtesgaden
to the Karlinger Haus
distance climbed: 1,130 metres
time: 3 hours 30 minutes*

This is a fairly brief stage, entirely within the boundaries of the National Park of the Alps of Berchtesgaden; it is devoted to a pleasant boat trip across the Königssee, and then on to the almost-as-relaxing climb up to the Karlinger Haus, at 1,630 metres. The landscape is dominated by the dramatic east face of Watzmann, the most renowned peak in the Alps of Berchtesgaden. Rising 1,800 metres, in height (the central peak of the Watzmann rises to an elevation of 2,713 metres), crisscrossed by gullies and ledges, the face looms over the woods of St. Bartholomä. It was climbed for the first time in 1881 by a guide named J. Kederbacher, accompanied by O. Schuck, along a lengthy and complex route; today a number of other routes have been blazed. One begins by taking a bus to the Königssee, and by boarding one of the boats that cross this mountain lake, taking one directly to St. Bartholomä (605 metres). One follows the trail that runs along the lakeshore, and then cuts uphill into the valley of the Schrain Bach, passing by a privately owned hut (866 metres) and a number of pastures. After passing by the trail that leads off to the right to the Wimbachgrieshutte and emerging from the woods (about 1,000 metres), one continues along the dramatic Saugasse, at the foot of the boulders of the Simetsberg, and then climbing steeply up to the Ofenjoch. A short descent brings one to the Karlinger Haus (1,630 metres), on the shore of the Funten See. One can finish the day with a climb to the Feldkogel (1,882 metres, 1 hour 30 minutes round trip, the trail begins directly in front of the hut), with its panoramic views, or else continue toward the Ingolstader hut.

THIRD DAY
*from the Karlinger Haus
to the Hirschbichl
distance climbed: 750 metres
distance descended: 1,230 metres
time: 6 hours*

This is a long stage, with a great deal of climbing and descending, which features two very different types of environment. From the Karst expanses of the Steinernes Meer, one moves on through the woods that surround the manmade lake of Diesbach and then stretch away toward Hirschbichl. The trail climbs gently toward the northwest, runs by the foot of the Hirsch, and runs by the Schonbichl Alm. One climbs up through an exceedingly solemn and desolate landscape to the Hundstodscharte (2,010 metres), one turns leftward, entering Austria, and one finally fetches up at the Ingolstader hut (2,119 metres). On the steep path that leads to the hut, one descends westward along the trail-markers of the E4 (Alpin), and then reaches a dirt road, following it all the way to the manmade lake of Diesbach (1,415 metres). One then skirts the lake, walking off to the left, crossing the dam, and then heading off to the right, taking a fork in the path and descending into the woods of the Weissbach Tal. This takes one to the road along the valley (980 metres), which one follows uphill all the way to the pass and the privately owned hut of Hirschbichl (1,148 metres).

FOURTH DAY
*from Hirschbichl to Lofer
distance climbed: 150 metres
distance descended: 580 metres
time: 3 hours 30 minutes*

This is a short stage, largely on dirt roads and forest tracks, which takes one in the direction of Austria, the Saalach valley, and the handsome and venerable centre of the village of Lofer. From the pass, one follows the little road that runs gently uphill to Hutnagei and to the Eiblkapelle (1,261 metres). One descends sharply westward along another little road, one continues alongside the ravine of the Wildenbach, emerging to reach — at a practically level angle of attack — the Pass

Luftenstein (856 metres). Here, the path descends on the right, skipping St. Martin bei Lofer, and hugging the right bank of the river Saalach, finally reaching the road that leads to the left bank all the way to Lofer (630 metres).

FIFTH DAY
from Lofer to the Schmidt-Zabierow hut
distance climbed: 1,180-1,350 metres
time: 3-4 hours

A short but fairly dramatic stage, at least in terms of steepness; it leads from the village of Lofer all the way up to the Schmidt-Zabierow hut, in the heart of the grim limestone massif of the Loferer Steinberge. One begins by making one's way, on foot or by bus, to the Loferer Hochtal. From the parking area to the end of the road, one continues up the clearly marked, steep, and interesting trail that climbs between the Schwarzwand and the spurs of the Eiblhorn and the Breithorn, finally reaching the hut (1,966 metres). It is possible to spend the remaining hours of the day climbing up to the Grosses Ochsenhorn (2,511 metres, 3 hours 30 minutes round-trip), the highest peak in the massif, along a steep but not particularly difficult trail.

SIXTH DAY
from the Schmidt-Zabierow hut
to the Waidring
distance climbed: 400-600 metres
distance descended: 1,550-1,750 metres
time: 4 hours 30 minutes - 6 hours

Unlike the preceding stage, this one runs almost entirely downhill, and leads to the pleasant little town of Waidring. One begins by climbing up to the saddle of the Waidringer Nieder (2,302 metres); from here, one can proceed to the nearby peak of the Mitterhorn (2,506 metres, 1 hour 30 minutes, round-trip), the second-highest peak on the Loferer Steinberge. From the pass, one sets out again along the steep trail that drops along the dramatic northern slope of the massif, entering the woods and continuing along to the Jageralm (1,065 metres). At a gentler in the angle of attack, the trail continues in the forest until reaching Unterwasser, followed by Waidring, along the road (778 metres). In town, there is an interesting piece of baroque architecture, the church of St. Veit.

SEVENTH DAY
from Waidring to St. Johann Im Tirol
distance climbed: 450 metres
distance descended: 1,160 metres
time: 4 hours 30 minutes

Among the many limestone massifs, this is a relaxing stage, among the evergreen forests that separate Waidring from Bavaria. Walkers in a hurry can take a bus to St. Johann and Griesenau, catapulting themselves into the heart of the most spectacular part of the Wilder Kaiser. It is a good idea to start the day with a ride in a bus or a taxi, riding up to the parking lot near the Alpengasthof Steinplatte. By foot, one can climb up the little lane that on the left skirts the Brenn hut, runs up to the Durchkaser Alm, and then turns off to the left all the way to the boundary between Austria and Germany and then on to the summit of the Eggenalm Kogel (1,686 metres). Then the trail runs down to the Eggen Alm, running at considerable length through the woods, finally skirting the Gernkogel, then dropping steeply down to the high valley of the Gansbache at the valley (Hausstatt, 633 metres). Here, we recommend taking a bus to St. Johann Im Tirol (665 metres), a village with remarkable houses and baroque churches.

116 bottom
This picture offers a panoramic view of Salzburg, the renowned "city of Mozart," starting point for the route. Few other routes through the Alps start from towns so rich in history and art. Photograph by Giulio Veggi/ White Star

117 top The little church of St. Bartholomä stands at the foot of the eastern wall of the Watzmann (2,712 metres). This rocky wall, the most impressive in the Bavarian Alps, was climbed for the first time in 1881. The vertical distance of 1,800 metres from base to peak still makes it a remarkable climb. Photograph by Ernst Höhne

117 bottom The last snows of the early summer whiten the undulating karst rocks of the Steinernes Meer (the "Sea of Stone"), shown here as it appears from the limestone summit of the Schneibstein. The area is one of the most distinctive of the Eastern Alps. Photograph by Ernst Höhne

EIGHTH DAY
from St. Johann Im Tirol
to the Grütten hut
distance climbed: 1,270 metres
distance descended: 370 metres
time: 5 hours 30 minutes

This is a splendid stage, which takes one into the wild setting of the Wilder Kaiser. The trail runs through easy equipped roads, passing from the Stripsenjoch to the Steinerne Rinne, and then along the road of the Jubilaums Steig, which leads along the slope to the Grütten hut. If one wishes to avoid all the harder parts, one can descend directly from the Stripsenjoch down to Hinterbarenbad and Kufstein, which will also eliminate one full day of walking. One leaves St. Johann, and takes a bus to Griesenau (722 metres), continuing on from there through the magnificent woods of the Kaiserbach Tal: the trail-markers run along a cart road on the orographic right of the mountain stream, allowing one to walk far from the traffic running along the paved road. From the parking area at the Griesner Alm (1,006 metres) one continues up along the sunny mule-track that climbs through the woods at the foot of the dizzying spire of the Predigstuhl, then passes along the base of the Steinerne Rinne, climbing from there toward the Stripsenjoch and the hut with the same name (1,580 metres). One climbs back down to the base of the last few ramps, and one turns off toward the right (stopping short of the hut, one saves fifteen minutes) along the equipped trail of the Eggersteig, which skirts the rocks of the Fleischbank, climbing up from there along the spectacular gorge of the Steinerne Rinne, over which loom faces that are very popular with climbers. After climbing up to the pass of the Ellmauer Tor (1,995 metres), an excellent vantage-point over the central part of the massif, one climbs down over scree on the slope of Ellmau. On the right, the trail of the Jubilaums Steig leads quite easily to the comfortable Grütten hut (1,620 metres), an excellent vantage-point over the southern slopes of the Wilder Kaiser.

118 top Lofer, a picturesque little town at an altitude of 649 metres, stands before a backdrop of huge mountains. The massif of the Loferer Steinberge *(the highest peak is the Grosses Ochsenhorn, (2,511 metres), is without a doubt the least known in this part of Austria. Photograph by Ernst Höhne* *118 bottom The Predigstuhl (2,115 metres), shown here as it appears from the flowering fields of the Kaisertal, is one of the most elegant* *peaks of the Wilder Kaiser. Great climbers such as Hans Dulfer and Hans Fiechtl pioneered its routes. Photograph by Ernst Höhne*

NINTH DAY
traverse of the Ellmauer Halt
from the Grütten hut to Kufstein
distance climbed: 720 metres
distance descended: 1,840 metres
time: 7 hours 30 minutes

The most spectacular way of completing this walk is by traversing the Ellmauer Halt (2,344 metres), the highest peak on the Wilder Kaiser, along a number of spectacular and not-always-easy equipped trails. There are splendid close-up views of the faces of the Ellmauer Halt itself, as well as all the other major peaks on the massif. Those who are interested in finding a more relaxing alternative (as well as being safer if the weather turns foul) can follow the other route described below. From the hut, one follows the broad trail that runs up to the handsome morainic hollow (snow until quite late in the season) at the foot of the Ellmauer Halt, and then one climbs up obliquely the rocks from right to left, at the foot of the slabs of the south face. From a fork in the trail (2,099 metres), a series

of fixed ropes and a ladder in a broad chimney lead to a small hut that is always open (the Babenstuber hut), and from there one climbs quickly up to the splendid vantage-point and to the large cross that marks the summit (2,344 metres). After climbing back down to the fork, at 2,099 metres, one finds another equipped trail which runs over the crest of the massif, running back down into the hollow of the Oberer Scharlinger Boden. Without encountering any further difficulties, one continues on to the foot of the faces of the Kleine Halt and the Gamskarkopfl, all the way to the edge of the woods. After passing by a small stream (the Mirakelbrunn) one continues climbing steeply down to the Hans-Berger Haus (936 metres) and on to Hinterbarenbad (829 metres), where the Anton-Karg Haus stands. There is nothing more to be done at that point than to follow the comfortable but lengthy cart road that runs down on the right of the Kaiserbach. From the fork following the Klaus hut (approximately 750 metres), it is best to follow the trail that leads off to the right, which may be a little longer, but which is far more scenic, and which runs by the Antonius Kapelle (867 metres) and then joins with the other trail at Pfandlhof (780 metres), where the trail starts to descend toward Kufstein.

NINTH DAY (alternative)
(via the Hintersteiner See)
distance climbed: 150 metres
distance descended: 1,270 metres
time: 5 hours 30 minutes

The easiest choice for completing the walk makes use of the easy trail running obliquely along the slope (the Grütten Weg) around to the south of the crags of the Wilder Kaiser, and then passing by the quiet Hintersteiner See. This is quite an easy route, though it is fairly long, and offers pleasant walking all the way to Kufstein. One begins with a downhill climb obliquely along the slope that takes around the massif of the Tuxeck, leaving on the left the trail to the Riedl hut. After reaching the Kaiser Hochalm (1,417 metres), at the foot of the faces of the Wiesberg and the Scheffauer, one begins to descend gently and then at a steeper grade. From the St. Leonhard Kapelle (918 metres), a little road leads down to the Hintersteiner See (844 metres) One can either walk around it to the right (north) along the road or to the left (south) along a handsome trail, and one then crosses the meadows of Hinterstein, where there are a fair number of hotels and private huts, whereupon one climbs a steep trail across the rocky gorge of the

Steinerne Stiege. Along trails and little lanes to the right, one can cross the meadows and the scattered villages of Eiberg and Egerbach, climbing over the spectacular wooded saddle where the Locherer Kapelle (590 metres) stands, and then climbing on down to Kufstein (509 metres).

119 bottom
The southern slope of the Wilder Kaiser overlooks the valley floor of Ellmau and Going. At the foot of the Ellmauer Halt, one can make out the Grütten hut.
Photograph by Stefano Ardito

119 top left The Predigstuhl (2,115 metres), one of the peaks of the Wilder Kaiser that is popular with climbers, rises over the savage gorge that rises up to the Stripsenjoch and the hut of the same name. This area, protected by a nature hut, allows one easily to observe small groups of chamois as they graze.
Photograph by Marco Milani / K3

119 top right
A walker works his way up one of the last fixed ropes on the steep equipped trail that leads up to the Grütten hut, at the 2,344 metres of the Ellmauer Halt, the tallest peak of the Wilder Kaiser.
Photograph by Stefano Ardito

119 centre The East Face of the Fleischbank (2,187 metres), climbed for the first time in 1912 by the great Hans Dulfer, is another popular "playground" for rock climbers, offering a splendid spectacle to the walkers who climb the gorge of the Steinerne Rinne.
Photograph by A. Gogna/K3

ACROSS THE HOHE TAUERN

A week of walking across the peaks, mountain huts, and glaciers of the Gross Venediger and the Gross Glockner

120 The impressive eastern slope of the Gross Glockner (3,798 metres) appears at dawn in all its massive might. The steep Pallavicini Gully, a very difficult ice route pionereed in 1876, cuts into the wall. Photograph by Ernst Höhne

121 A number of walkers climb along the easy slopes of the Obersulzbachkees, the glacier that leads up toward the Gross Venediger (3,667 metres). In 1841, the party of twenty-six persons that made the first climb up the mountain passed by here. Photograph by Gianluca Boetti

Huge spectacular mountains and tortuous glaciers, boundless forests, dramatic high valleys where the bearded vulture still hovers on updrafts — the bearded vulture was once common throughout the Alps, and has only recently been reintroduced into this part of Austria. At the border between the Tyrol, Carinthia, and the province of Salzburg, the chain of the Hohe Tauern is one of the most spectacular in Europe, and boasts — set between the Italian border and Badgastein — the splendid peaks of the Gross Venediger (3,674 metres), the Grosses Wiesbachhorn (3,564 metres), and the Gross Glockner (3,798 metres), the highest and best known mountain in Austria. The lesser massifs, such as that of the Granatsspitze (3,088 metres), are wild and spectacular. Here, humans have been intrigued by the high mountains ever since ancient times. As early as 1561, a map made by the cartographer Lazius showed the "Glocknerer" as the most important peak in the Hohe Tauern range. In a map made by the cartographer Holzwurm, in 1612, the modern name is already shown, and around the summit an uninterrupted *glacies* is designed, which one can easily recognize as the spectacular flow of the Pasterze. In part because of the retrocession of the alpine glaciers between the fourteenth and sixteenth centuries, the gold mines of the Hohe Tauern — mentioned by the Greek historian Polybius in the second century B.C. — underwent considerable development during that period. Remains of galleries and other diggings can be seen still in the area around the modern Hofmanns hut, at an elevation of twenty-four hundred metres. With the expansion of the glaciers between the eighteenth and nineteenth century,

mountain climbing was born.
In September of 1841, a party of twenty-six persons made the first climb of the Gross Venediger (the "Great Venetian"), and a few days later, a prince, Friederich von Schwarzenberg, archbishop of Salzburg, in the company of four mountain guides, reached the peak of the Grosses Wiesbachhorn. As early as 1800, at the express command of the Austro-Hungarian emperor, a party of "valiant hunters of vultures" had scaled the peak of the Gross Glockner. In the late nineteenth century and in the early twentieth century, the ice gullies and the steep rocks of the Gross Glockner witnessed remarkable feats of alpinism, such as the climb up to the Pallavicini Gully, and still today considered a great and popular challenge. Willo Welzembach, one of the great ice climbers of the Thirties, has left his mark here as well, with one of the most difficult and demanding routes on the massif. Nowadays, however, extreme climbing is certainly not the most common activity practiced in the Hohe Tauern. The rock found in this chain is often quite crumbly, and the hordes of climbers that flock to the Dolomites or the Wilder Kaiser are not found here. Springtime alpine skiing is quite popular here (excellent skiers make their way, skis on their feet, all the way up to the little saddle just a hundred metres from the peak of the Klein Glockner), and these mountains are an authentic summer paradise for walkers and climbers. The thrilling climb across the small ridge leads to the cross atop the summit of the Gross Venediger, the lofty small rocks of the standard route of the Gross Glockner, the standard routes of the other major peaks in the chain — each summer thousands and thousands of tourists and climbers venture up here, some accompanied by guides. By combining these routes, one can traverse from mountain hut to mountain hut, and follow long walking routes that are among the most alluring and charming in the Alps, like the one we describe in the pages that follow. In a long ramble among the peaks of the Hohe Tauern, one has an opportunity to observe the developing relationship of humans with these mountains. Alongside the romantic old mountain huts, the pastures, and the mule-tracks that preserve all the quite tranquillity of years gone by, one can see car-parks at the end of the "road

122 This picture shows a clearing in the wild forests of the Hohe Tauern, crisscrossed by bubbling streams. This is the Obersulzbachfalle, one of the waterfalls on the northern slopes of the massif, not far from Neukirchen.
Photograph by Gianluca Boetti

of the Gross Glockner", built during the Thirties. In the Hohe Tauern, however, alterations of the landscape are far less extensive than in the case of the Ötztal Alps or in the border-straddling chain between the Weisskugel and the Similaun.As a result, the National Park of the Hohe Tauern, which is the largest national park in Austria, is one of the "great sites" in terms of the preservation of the environment in the Alps. And anyone who sees the long flat glide of the bearded vulture understands immediately how true this is.

USEFUL INFORMATION

Duration: 8 days.

Elevations: ranging from the 1,325 metres of Kals to the 3,667 metres of the Gross Venediger.

Season: from July to September.

Signage: white and red for local trails and the trail O2, and there are long stretches over ice, with no markings at all, of course.

Degree of difficulty: long stretches over glacier, with a few passages riddled with crevices.

How demanding: average, but at considerable elevations.

Equipment: for high elevation walking, with walking boots slings, climbing rope, ice axe, and crampons.

Peaks: this route, which runs largely over glaciers, includes an easy climb up to the Gross Venediger (3,667 metres) and includes, as a brief and well marked detour, from the Erzehog-Johann hut, a climb up to the Gross Glockner (3,798 metres), along a steep and icy slope and rocks (PD+, guides are recommended). There are many other peaks, among them the Sonnblick (3,038 metres), the Granatsspitze (3,086 metres), and the Hohe Riffl (3,346 metres), which can be reached with short detours.

How to get there: Krimml, on the state road number 165, can be reached by car or by bus from Innsbruck (via Zell am Ziller), Matrei im Osttirol, and from the railroad station of Bruck on the line Villach-Badgastein-Worgl. From Kals, one can quickly reach Lienz, on the main line Bolzano-Klagenfurt-Vienna.

Overnight accommodations: huts of OEAV and of private owners, hotels in the valley.

If you want to camp out: the high elevation and many restrictions make it almost impossible to do so.

Alpine Guides: (43) (4825) 52121.

Weather Forecasts: contact the tourist bureaus.

Mountain Rescue: (43) (4824) 2233. Information Offices: Tourist Bureau of Neukirchen (for Krimml) (43) (6565) 6256, Tourist Bureau of Matrei im Osttirol (43) (4875) 6227, Tourist Bureau of Kals (43) (4876) 211, Tourist Bureau of Heiligenblut (43) (4824) 2001.

Useful phone numbers: Warnsdorfer hut (43) (6564) 8241, Kursinger hut (43) (6565) 6450, Alte Prager hut (43)(487) 56110, Venediger Haus Innegschloss (43)(4875) 6230, St. Poltener hut (43) (6562) 265, Karl Furst hut (43)(2742) 611243, Rudolfs hut (43)(6563) 8221, Oberwalder hut (43)(4824) 2546, Franz-Josef Haus (43) (4824) 2512, Erzehog-Johann hut (43) (4876) 500, Studl hut (43) (4876) 221.

Maps: the finest (by far) are the 1:25,000 maps from the Österreischer Alpenverein, n. 36 *Venedigergruppe,* n. 39 *Granatspitzgruppe*, and n. 40 *Grossglocknergruppe,* as an alternative to the Kompass 1:50,000 n. 46 *Matrei-Ostirol*, and n. 48 *Kals am Grossglockne*r, or the Freytag-Berndt 1:50,000, n. 122 *Grossglockner-Kaprun-Zell am See.*

Readings: *Mountain walking in Austria* by Cecil Davies (Cicerone Press).

123 The easy panoramic trail overlooking the glacier of the Pasterze, which begins at the end of the access road leading to the massif, *offers splendid views of the Gross Glockner, and is the most popular mountain in the Hohe Tauern.* Photograph by Stefano Ardito

Großglockner

Granatspitze

Kals

Franz-Josef-Ha

Oberwalder hut

Sonnblick

Großes
Wiesbachhorn

Rudolfs hüt

Weiß

St. Pöltener hut

Enzinger Boden

Ödtal Amertal

Kapruner Tal

Stubachtal

Felbert

Mitters

Kaprun

Niedernsill

Uttendorf

Stuhlfelden

Lengdorf

Piesendorf

FIRST DAY

From Krimml to the Kursinger hut
Distance climbed: 790 metres
Distance descended: 540 metres
time: 5 hours

The first stage of this walk offers an interesting route with a great deal of climbing and descending through the magnificent valleys of the northern slopes of the Hohe Tauern. Definitely do not miss the spectacular waterfall of Krimml, one of the most renowned in the Alps. One can also reach this point from Italy (Valle Aurina) via the Tridentina Hut (Birnlucken hut), and the Birnlucke. One begins at Krimml, taking a taxi up as far as the Inner Kees Alm (1,804 metres, 13 kilometres from the valley floor); from here a

good trail climbs up as far as the Warnsdorfer hut (2,336 metres). One starts upward again from there, on steeper ground now, through the meadows and across the moraines that lead to the broad saddle of the Krimmler Torl (2,789 metres). Before reaching the saddle in question, however, there is a detour marked off to the right, where one can climb up to the low peak of the Gamsspitzl (2,888 metres), where one has an excellent and panoramic view. One descends along the glacier and then down rocks and ledges (brief equipped passages), and then one climbs steeply uphill to the comfortable Kursinger hut (2,547 metres).

SECOND DAY

from the Kursinger hut
to the Alte Prager hut
distance climbed: 1,140 metres
distance descended: 1,180 metres
time: 5 hours 30 minutes

This is an interesting and spectacular stage, which takes one to the second highest mountain in the Hohe Tauern, with a view that beats the one from the Gross Glockner. All of the glaciers are remarkably easy, save for the occasional tough spot, and climbing up to the summit of Gross Venediger is simple, save for the last few dizzying metres up to the final ridge. For the overnight stay, one can choose between the old, Alte, and the new, Neue, Prager hut, facing the séracs of the Schlaten Kees. One begins along the

trail that climbs up the moraine that lies above the hut, leading to the edge of the Obersulzbach Kees (2,800 metres). One gets past a brief stretch riddled with crevasses, and then one continues in the direction of the glacial high valley between the Gross Venediger and the Klein Venediger. A steep slope with large crevasses takes one up to the Venediger Scharte (3,413 metres). On the right, a comfortable slope and a final ridge cut by a crevasse lead up to the summit of the Gross Venediger (3,667 metres). After descending back to the Venediger Scharte, one continues downhill along the Schlaten Kees. A short steep slope, riddled with crevices, leads one to the moraines. A trail leads on to the Neue Prager hut (2,796 metres) and to the Alte Prager hut (2,489 metres).

126 top From atop the 3,667-metre summit of the Gross Venediger one can enjoy a remarkable panorama. In this picture, we can see the slopes of the Klein Venediger, the vast expanse of the Obersulzbachkees, and the peak of the Hohe Furleg (3,244 metres). Photograph by Gianluca Boetti

126 bottom left The comfortable and welcoming Kursinger hut (2,547 metres), overlooking the séracs of the Obersulzbachkees, is the base for the north route up the Gross Venediger. Equally easy and interesting are the routes that climb up from the Prager hut and the Defregger Haus. Photograph by Stefano Ardito

128 top A steep trail running along the slope leads from the Karl-Furst hut to the crest of the Rabenstein, after which one can climb to the easy summit of Sonnblick. This is the boundary of the massif of the Gross Glockner.
Photograph by R. Carnovalini

126 bottom right The waterfalls of Krimml, broken into three different falls (this is the lower of the three) is the most spectacular in the Hohe Tauern; the volume of water can rise to 400,000 litres per minute. They can be reached quickly from Neukirchen.
Photograph by Stefano Ardito

127 top After climbing to the summit of the Gross Venediger, one climbs back down to the valley along this trail that leads to the Obersulzbach Tal, in the distinctive and harsh setting of the granite Hohe Tauern.
Photograph by Stefano Ardito

127 bottom Another phase in the easy and spectacular climb from the Kursinger hut to the Gross Venediger through the Obersulzbachkees and across the 3,413-metres elevation of the Venediger Scharte.
Photograph by Gianluca Boetti

THIRD DAY

from the Alte Prager hut
to the St. Poltener hut
distance climbed: 550 metres
distance descended: 600 metres
time: 5 hours

This is a relaxing stage, with very little gradient, although there is a great deal of climbing and descending, along a panoramic trail that offers an excellent vista of the massif of the Gross Venediger. One begins along the trail of the Venediger Hoheweg, the standard route leading to the hut, which traverses at length and obliquely along the slope and then runs down to a bridge (2,185 metres) across the Gschloss Bach. One climbs on from there, in sight of the Viltrangen Kees, and then one continues along the trail of the St. Poltener Westweg. After crossing through a number of wild hollows, and after climbing over the spurs of the Roter Kogel, the Dichten Kogel, and the Fechteben Kogel, one reaches the high pass of Felber Tauern (2,545 metres), beyond which lies the St. Poltener hut (2,481 metres).

FOURTH DAY

from the St. Poltener hut
to the Karl Furst hut
distance climbed: 700 metres
distance descended: 560 metres
time: 5 hours 30 minutes

This is a transfer stage, and a pretty long one, leading to the base of the massif of the Granatspitze, not as tall or as abounding in glaciers as the Gross Glockner or the Gross Venediger. A number of lakes freshen and enliven this stage. One begins on the trail of the St. Poltener Ostweg, running past one lake after another — the Grauer See, the Schwarzer See, and the Gruner See, and beyond them stands the Grunsee hut (2,235 metres). One sets off again uphill, climbing up to the foot of the rocks of the Daber Kogele, and then one continues with a long crossing as far as the Daber See (2,424 metres). Here the trail splits: the best choice is offered by the 02, which climbs up to the ridge of the Amertaler Hohe, passing over the Amertaler Scharte (2,760 metres), and then drops down to the

foot of the Grosses Landegg Kopf, finally reaching the Karl Furst hut (2,629 metres). One can also take the Venediger Hoheweg, which skirts southward around the Glocken Kogel, leading finally to the hut, passing close to the Schandla See.

FIFTH DAY
from the Karl Furst hut
to the Rudolfs hut
distance climbed: 450 metres
distance descended: 750 metres
time: 5 hours

This stage is dedicated to the massif of the Sonnblick and the Granatsspitze — both these peaks can be reached along short variant trails — and one crosses the main crest of this massif before climbing down onto the broad Sonnblick Kees and reaching the popular and modern Rudolfs hut, headquarters for an alpine climbing school run by the Austrian Alpine Club OEAV, which can be reached along the chairlift that runs up from Enzinger Boden. One begins along the trail that runs up to the crest of the Rabenstein (2,873 metres, although here too there is a lower variant trail), then one crosses the Prager Kees, continuing along to the Granat Scharte (2,974 metres), a point of departure for the brief and relatively easy climb up to the Sonnblick and the Granatsspitze. From the saddle, where one enters the National Park of the Hohe Tauern, a track along the glacier leads down across the broad Sonnblick Kees,

running to the ridge of the Roter Kogel. A final descent, within view of the charming Weiss See, leads to the Rudolfs hut (2,351 metres).

SIXTH DAY
from the Rudolfs hut
to the Oberwalder hut
distance climbed: 1,000 metres
distance descended: 350 metres
time: 6 hours 30 minutes

The handsome stage that takes to the massif of the Gross Glockner and to the spectacular basin of the Pasterze features a long and enchanting walk across a glacier, which can become quite problematic if there is fog or bad weather. One begins along the comfortable oblique trail along the slope, running over the meadows of

128 bottom left A walker is shown here making the last section of the easy climb up to Sonnblick (3,038 metres), an excellent vantage-point which can be reached from the Granatscharte with a brief variant on the walking route described in this book. Photograph by R. Carnovalini

128 bottom right Overlooking the icy expanse of the Oberster Pasterzenboden, the Oberwalder hut constitutes a splendid vantage-point over the Gross Glockner, as well as a classic destination for visitors to the National Park of the Hohe Tauern. Photograph by Ernst Höhne

the Enzinger Leitl, which runs up (2,300 metres) to the Odenwinkel Kees. A track climbs up the middle of the glacier, veering off it (approximately 2,500 metres) onto the hollow of the Hoher Sand. A steep, tiring, but none-too-daunting trail in unspoilt wilderness climbs up along a crest to the Obere Odenwinkel Scharte (3,233 metres). In a very short time, one can climb northward to the easy-access peak of the Hohe Riffl (3,346 metres), where stands a large and conspicuous cross. From the pass, a broad track traverses on a slight incline down across the broad basin of the Oberster Pasterzenboden, reaching the broad crest, where the Oberwalder hut (2,973 metres) stands, a splendid vantage-point over the Pasterze and the Gross Glockner.

SEVENTH DAY

*from the Oberwalder hut
to the Erzehog-Johann hut
distance climbed: 780 metres
distance descended: 1,240 metres
time: 6 hours 30 minutes*

This is a stage with two personalities: at the beginning it features the best panoramic view of the Gross Glockner and the mighty expanses of glacier — Himalayan in appearance — of the Pasterzen Kees, then comes the up-close contact with séracs and the steep rocky or grassy slopes of the mountainside. The parking area of the Franz-Josef Haus, where the "road of the Hohe Tauern" comes to an end is where one comes into direct contact with the frenzy and crowding of mass tourism. The last stretch is quite exhausting.
One begins by crossing the broad ridge directly across from the hut; from there a steep little trail on the left leads one up to the easy Südlisches Bockkar Kees, down which one climbs all the way to the base, where there is a small lake. A broad oblique trail along the slope takes one past incredible views to the Franz-Josef Haus (2,369 metres) and to the end of the road. Another steep trail (there is also a cable railway) takes one to the glacier (2,200 metres) up which one climbs, shifting leftward. Tracks across the moraine lead to a steep trail that climbs up along grassy and rocky slopes all the way to the Hofmanns Kees (2,800 metres). One climbs up the glacier, crossing one particularly crevice-ridden stretch, and then continuing to the right, heading for the hut, within sight here. After crossing a crevasse, one follows an easy ridge of snow or stone ridge all the way to the Erzehog-Johann hut (3,454 metres).

*129 top In this picture, one can admire the strip of the Pasterze glacier, the most extensive (twenty square kilometres) and spectacular glacier in the National Park of the Hohe Tauern. The level of the glacier has dropped by about eighty metres over the past fifty years.
Photograph by A. Gogna/K3*

*129 bottom
The Glocknerhaus, a venerable and comfortable mountain hotel owned by the Austrian Alpine Club, allows one to spend the night at an altitude of 2,137 metres, within sight of the peak of the Gross Glockner.
Photograph by Stefano Ardito*

EIGHTH DAY

*from the Erzehog-Johann hut to Kals
distance climbed: 340 metres
distance descended: 1,860 metres
time: 7 hours 30 minutes*

The final day is one long descent, pretty tough on the legs, toward Kals and the Kalsertal. Before starting this long descent, one may choose to climb to the peak of the Gross Glockner. At the end of this descent is a dirt road that runs down toward Kals; one can take a taxi down at this point. If one does choose to climb the Gross Glockner, one begins along an easy glacier, then reaches a steep gully filled with snow or ice, which leads up to the ridge. One climbs up along plates (second degree) all the way up to the Klein Glockner (3,783 metres).

After crossing a narrow and lofty saddle, one climbs to the peak of the Gross Glockner (3,798 metres). After returning to the hut, one climbs down a crest with a few equipped trails, and which one leaves in order to climb down onto the little glacier of the Kodnitz Kees. From the pass of the Schere (3,043 metres), one crosses the Teischnitz Kees, and then on down to the Studl hut (2,801 metres), an excellent vantage-point overlooking the southwestern slope of the Gross Glockner. A broad trail runs down through the Kodnitz Tal as far as the Luckner hut (2,241 metres), from where a little road runs down to the Neues Luckner Haus (1,918 metres). One can then reach Kals (1,325 metres) by taxi, by hitchhiking, or on foot.

FROM LAKE GARDA TO THE PASUBIO AND VERONA

A great circuit in the Prealps
between the Veneto and the
Trentino, along the *Sentiero della
Pace* and the European Trail E5

Rocky walls and remarkable
mountain flowers, woods of beech and
holm oaks and wild gullies, panoramic
views of the Po plains and the Alps.
Extremely popular with local walkers
and climbers, but only infrequently
visited by those coming from farther
afield, the Prealps between Veneto
and Trentino are extremely abundant
in attractions for the walker. The
same can be said, of course, of the
entire mountain chain that separates
the high Alps from the low-lying plains
of the Po, a chain that covers the
limestone spires of the Grigne, the
ridges and lakes of the Orobie, the
massifs of Concarena and Presolana,
the peaks overlooking the lakes of Iseo
and Garda. Further east the procession
extends with Mount Grappa, the
highlands of Asiago, and Alpago.
More than all others, however, attention
should be given to the peaks that
separate the town of Verona and Lake
Garda from Rovereto and the spurs of
the Dolomites. Among these peaks,
Monte Baldo, *Hortus Italiae*, the
"Garden of Italy," as it was known to
the herbalists of the sixteenth and
seventeenth centuries, is certainly the
gentlest. Rich in mountain blooms of
every sort, this mountain overlooks
Lake Garda, with an extremely steep
sheer slope, in which high limestone
walls stand out. Extending for more
than thirty kilometres, its crest
separates the lake itself from the
Adige Valley. Once the fogs of early
summer have dispersed with the
progressing season, this crest is also a
renowned vantage-point with a view of
the Venetian plains and the Alps.
Just a bit further to the north, Monte
Altissimo di Nago offers equally
spectacular views, especially of the
Dolomites of Brenta and the Sarca
valley; from up here, Lake Garda
appears as a giant fjord wedged in
among the mountains. Beyond the
valley of the River Adige — which is

130-131 A halting place along the lofty "Strada delle gallerie" built by Italian soldiers through the rocks of the Pasubio; this road includes no fewer than fifty-one tunnels. Through the fog of the valley tower the spires of the Little Dolomites.
Photograph by Stefano Ardito

131 top The steep massif of Mount Baldo, the Hortus Italiae *of the herbalists of the seventeenth century, serves as a backdrop to the waters of the lake and to the rocks crossed by* Gardesana Occidentale, *one of the most panoramic roads in the area .*
Photograph by Simeone Huber/SIE

here locked in the rocky embrace of Val Lagarina — the wooded uplands of the Lessinia slope gently downhill to the south, toward the high plateaus of the Valpolicella and the city of Verona. At their northwesternmost extremities, the limestone peaks of the Carega, the Baffelàn, the Cornetto, and the Sisilla have long been well known to climbers and walkers as the "Little Dolomites." Upon the walls and faces of these mountains, routes of high difficulty have been blazed by many of the great figures of Venetian mountaineering like Gino Soldà and Renato Casarotto. To the north, beyond the highway pass of Pian delle Fugazze, the procession of peaks ends with the Pasubio. An enormous limestone massif, defended by high, sheer faces and grooved by wild high valleys, this mountain became legendary during the World War I as one of the most contested and bloodiest battlefields in the war between Italy and the Austro-Hungarian Empire. Beginning on 15 May 1916, the *Strafexpedition*, the "punitive expedition," of the imperial troops caught Italy's generals completely off guard, forcing them to beat a hasty retreat. The Pasubio, overlooked during the early years of the war, became a fundamental key to the entire front. Bloody battles took place in the spring and summer of 1916, continuing through the following two years. At the foot of the Pasubio, on 10 July 1916, the two Irredentists Fabio Filzi and Cesare Battisti were captured by Austro-Hungarian troops; the two were Austro-Hungarian citizens who had volunteered as soldiers in the Italian army, and they were later executed in Trent for treason. The year 1917 witnessed great projects of military engineering at high elevations, such as the two roads built by the Italians along the southern slopes (the *Strada degli Eroi*, or Road of Heroes, and the *Strada*

Duration: 9 days.
Elevations: ranging from the 97 metres of Avesa to the 2,259 metres of Cima Carega.
Season: from May to late October. We recommend against the hottest weeks of the summer.
Signage: the white and red of the local trails and the trail E5, wooden

Trent, from Polsa to Rovereto, from Pian delle Fugazze to Rovereto and Recoaro, from Giazza, Croce, and Erbezzo to Verona.
Overnight Accommodations: huts of the CAI and private owners, hotels and bed-and-breakfasts in the low valleys.
Alpine Guides: Montrekking Rovereto (39) (464) 438430.

132 The Cima Telegrafo (2,200 metres) is the second-highest on the Baldo. Here we see its northern slope, marked by ancient glacial cirques and crowned by unimpressive rocky walls. Photograph by Riccardo Carnovalini

stakes with green trailmarkers for the *Sentiero della Pace* (Trail of Peace).
Degree of difficulty: short and easy equipped trails.
How demanding: average.
Equipment: normal walking gear.
Peaks: the highest and most interesting ones are all along the route. Among them are Mount Maggiore (2,199 metres), the Cima Valdritta (2,218 metres), the Mount Altissimo di Nago (2,070 metres), the Cima Palòn (2,235 metres), and the Cima Carega (2,259 metres).
How to get there: Prada can be reached by bus from Brenzone, Malcesine, Garda, or Verona. Verona is on the railroad lines Bologna-Brenner Pass and Milan-Venice.
How to get around: Rovereto is on the railroad line Bologna-Verona-Brenner; regularly scheduled buses run from Malcesine to Verona and

Mountain Rescue: for the entire area, dial 115 - centre CNSA of Trent-Matterello.
Information Offices: APT of Recoaro (39) (445) 75070, APT of Rovereto (39) (464) 430363, APT of Vicenza (39) (444) 544805, APT of Verona (39) (45) 8030086, Tourist Bureau of Giazza (39) (45) 7847030.
Useful phone numbers: chairlift Prada-Costabella (39) (45) 7285079, Telegrafo hut (39) (45) 7731797, Chiesa hut (39) (464) 433030, Lancia hut (39) (464) 919135, Generale Papa hut (39) (445) 630233, Therapeutic community Pecori-Giraldi Pian delle Fugazze (39) (445) 630005, hotel Streva Pian delle Fugazze (39) (464) 89243, Giuriolo hut (39) (445) 75030, Fraccaroli hut (39) (45) 7050033, Scalorbi hut (39) (45) 7847029, hotel Belvedere Giazza (39) (45) 7847020, bus lines

Atesina Rovereto (39) (464) 433777.
Maps: it is enough to have the Kompass 1:50,000 n. 102 *Lago di Garda-Monte Baldo* and n. 101 *Rovereto-Pasubio*, or else the n. 121 *Sentiero Europeo E 5.*

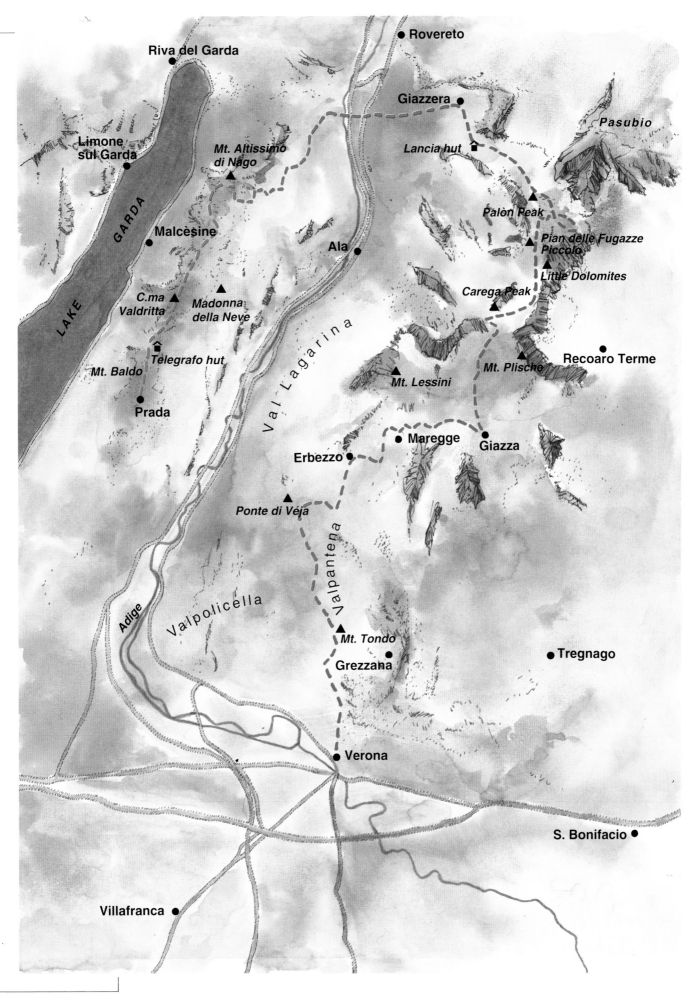

Rovereto

Riva del Garda

Giazzera

Pasubio

Limone
sul Garda

Mt. Altissimo
di Nago

Lancia hut

Palòn Peak

Malcèsine

Ala

Pian delle Fugazze
Piccolo

Little Dolomites

C.ma
Valdritta

Madonna
della Neve

Carega Peak

GARDA

Recoaro Terme

LAKE

Telegrafo hut

Mt. Plische

Mt. Baldo

Mt. Lessini

Prada

Val Lagarina

Maregge

Giazza

Erbezzo

Adige

Valpolicella

Valpantena

Ponte di Véja

Tregnago

Mt. Tondo

Grezzana

Verona

S. Bonifacio

Villafranca

133

delle Gallerie, or Road of Galleries), such as trenches carved into living rocks, such as tunnels for mines and countermines that honeycombed the base of the Cima Palòn and the peaks of the Dente Austriaco and the Dente Italiano. The most powerful mine of them all, tunnelled and set by the Austrians, destroyed most of the Dente Italiano, and contained fifty thousand kilograms of explosives. Traces of those bloody years can still be found everywhere along the old border, which now separates Lombardy and Veneto from Trentino Alto-Adige. More than the Marmolata, Adamello, and the Tre Cime, however, the Pasubio is the mountain that allows one to conceive of the madness of war, which took tens of thousands of young men to their deaths, in trench warfare under foul weather, in high rocky areas exposed to vicious

avalanches, deep in dark and twisting wormholes and galleries. One must certainly approve the decision of the government of the province of Trent, in 1985, to call the lengthy walking trail that runs along the old battle front the *Sentiero della Pace,* meaning the "Trail of Peace." Here fortresses, trenches, military roads, and artillery emplacements remind the walker at every point just how precious peace can be. This route makes use of only part of this full-fledged walking highway, and then turns south along the European Trail E5, among the limestone high valleys of Lessinia, which run down to the splendid city of Verona.

After the medicinal plants, the grade six routes, and the ancient trenches, the vineyards and the settings of Romeo and Juliet are a sweet and fitting conclusion to the trip.

FIRST DAY

From Prada to the Telegrafo hut
distance climbed: 350-1,250 metres
distance descended: 50 metres
time: 2-5 hours

A long stage, but varied and pleasant; it can be shortened considerably if the chairlift is in operation, running from Prada and the shores of Lake Garda all the way up to the comfortable Telegrafo hut, just a few metres from the second peak of the Baldo. From here, both sunrise and sunset are spectacular. The landscape is also quite interesting, featuring as it does huge glacial cirques interspersed with unassuming rocky walls, among which the old military mule-track winds and zigzags. From Prada Bassa (Osteria La Palazzina, 920 metres) one walks for a short distance along the road leading to Zignago; one then leaves that road, taking the marked trail that climbs up through the beautiful forest of beechwood and hazelnut trees in the Val di Sacco. After passing by the shepherds' huts of Ortigara (1,450 metres), and the little church of the Madonna della Neve (Our Lady of the Snows), one comes to the base of the Fort of Nàole, the old military road that runs along the crest of the range, leading off on the left to the point of arrival of the chairlift (1,815 metres) and to Chierego hut (1,911 metres). The trail climbs obliquely along the slope, runs past Bocchetta di Coàl Santo (2,074 metres) and Pass of the Cammino, skirts a rocky campanile, climbing on upward through an arid, sunny landscape to Telegrafo hut (2,150 metres), a short way beyond which stands the peak bearing the same name (2,199 metres).

SECOND DAY

from the Telegrafo hut to Chiesa hut
distance climbed: 850 metres
distance descended: 940 metres
time: 6 hours 30 minutes

This stage is one of the most spectacular panoramas of the Prealps and of all the mountains in Italy; it takes one across the peaks of Mount Baldo, allowing one to climb

134 top The Barana hut (2,110 metres), one of the most popular in the Venetian Prealps, is only a few minutes' walk from the Cima Telegrafo. We see it here in the light of sunset, with a backdrop of the main crest of Monte Baldo.
Photograph by R. Carnovalini

134 bottom A party of walkers moves across gentle meadows, which abound in splendid blooming springtime flowers, not far from the peak of Monte Altissimo di Nago (2,079 metres). In the background one can see the Colma di Malcesine (1,783 metres), the northernmost elevation of Baldo massif.
Photograph by R. Carnovalini

up Mount Altissimo di Nago, another renowned vantage-point. This area is particularly renowned for its mountain flowers, which long ago earned Mount Baldo the nickname of *Hortus Italiae*; it is partly protected by the Nature Reserve of Lastoni-Selva Pezzi, which extends over nine hundred seventy-eight hectares. We recommend setting out early in the morning in order to avoid thunderstorms and haze; from Tratto Spin it is possible to ride down to Malcesine by cable car. One begins on the crest, walking as far as Punta Pettorina (2,192 metres), from here one passes, on the right, the Cavallo di Novezza, and climbs up to the Cima Valdritta (2,218 metres), the highest peak on Mount Baldo. Then the trail runs by a number of other elevations, running over the Cima Pozzette (2,132 metres), and then descending gently among mountain meadows, with a splendid vista of the Dolomites. After passing the Bocca Tratto Spin (1,720 metres; the name is a distortion of *Tredes pin*, which is Venetian dialect for "thirteen pines"), one follows the cart-road downhill to the Bocca di Navene (1,425 metres). After a brief stretch on the asphalt, one continues to climb along a trail that crosses through an area undergoing reforestation, and then through a series of meadows. A cart-road takes one on to the Chiesa hut (2,060 metres), just under the summit of Mount Altissimo (2,078 metres).

THIRD DAY
from the Chiesa hut to Rovereto
distance descended: 1,850 metres
time: 6 hours

The descent from the crest of Mount Baldo toward the valley of the Adige and to Rovereto is not particularly long, and it can be considerably shortened if one takes a bus down from as high as S. Giacomo or Brentonico. The main attraction of this stage is certainly the Nature Reserve of Corna Piana, where in late spring one can admire splendid blooms of anemones, edelweiss, peonies, rhododendrons, and gentians, without a doubt deserving of a detour. There are also

a number of noteworthy old chalet along the route. Those who are in a hurry can save a day by taking a bus from S. Giacomo to Rovereto, continuing from there directly to the Lancia hut. One begins by descending along the cart-road that leads to the hut, which runs down along a series of switchbacks to the Bocca del Creer (or the Pass of Canaletta, 1617 metres), where the Graziani hut is located. One sets out again from there along a trail that runs down toward S. Giacomo, and from that trail another splits off, climbing southward toward the Corna Piana (1,735 metres): this detour (one hour, round trip) is especially interesting in the springtime, when the flowers are in bloom. The trail along the valley

continues through the deep Val de Vig, running by the houses of Maroc (1,213 metres), and finally fetches up on the paved road just prior to San Giacomo (1,194 metres). Marked trails that cross the paved road repeatedly allow one to descend to Brentonico (692 metres) and to Mori (204 metres), and from there it is definitely a good idea to take a bus to Rovereto (177 metres).

FOURTH DAY
from Rovereto to the Lancia hut
distance climbed: 740 metres
time: 2 hours 15 minutes

This very brief stage allows one to spend the morning touring Rovereto (one should especially pay a visit to the Castello, with the Museum of the History of the World War I, and the

135 top
The dolomitic walls of the Soglio dell'Incudine (2,114 metres) are some of the most impressive ones in the Pasubio. Practically level on its summit plateau, the massif drops away steeply toward the Vallarsa and the valley of the river Agno.
Photograph by Stefano Ardito

135 bottom
This picture shows the interior of the galleries of the Dente Italiano of the Pasubio. Inside the massif, both the Italian and the Austro-Hungarian armies dug dozens of kilometres of tunnels, which can be entered nowadays, though only with extreme caution.
Photograph by Stefano Ardito

handsome Palazzo del Municipio, or town hall); afterwards, one can climb up to the handsome Karst hollow of the Alpe Pozze and to the Lancia hut, in an area that is quite popular in winter, with downhill and cross-country skiers. One begins with a bus ride, via Toldo

136 On the summit plateau of the Pasubio one can see the easy trail that runs up from the Generale Papa hut to the 2,232-metre elevation of the Cima Palòn. In this area, Italian and Austro-Hungarian trenches ran only a few dozen metres from each other. Photograph by Stefano Ardito

SIXTH DAY
from the Papa hut to the Giuriolo hut
distance climbed: 1,000 metres
distance descended: 1,400 metres
time: 6 hours

This stage takes one from the massif of the Pasubio to that of the Little Dolomites, the wild spires that loom over Rovereto, invariably covered with alpinists and rock climbers from Vicenza and other nearby towns. Because this route is not particularly lengthy, it is a good idea to begin the day with a short round trip along the lofty and spectacular Road of Galleries, the most photographed site on the Pasubio. And so one follows the trail, which begins directly from the hut, leading quickly to a long and lofty horizontal traverse; from there one climbs off to the left to the Cima dell'Osservatorio (2,040 metres), and from there a mule-track leads back to the hut. Then one descends along the Road of Heroes, another incredible wartime trail, which descends through a series of tunnels across the Val Canale. After going through the Galleria Generale d'Havet (1,857 metres), one finds a series of shortcuts that take one to the Malga Fieno and to the Pian delle Fugazze (1,162 metres). One sets off again through the meadows and then through the woods until one reaches a little saddle (1,611 metres) on the ridge of the Cornetto, whereupon one descends steeply to the Malga Boffetal (1,435 metres), then one heads westward, skirting the elegant peaks of the Baffelàn and the Sisilla, and one fetches up at the pass of Campogrosso and the Giuriolo hut (1,457 metres).

(415 metres), Boccaldo (658 metres), and Pozza (696 metres), all the way up to Giazzèra (1,092 metres, 11 kilometres from Rovereto), the highest village in the region. On foot, one continues along the paved road, which turns into a dirt road that runs along an old war-time road built by troops of the Austro-Hungarian Empire. The road climbs with an occasional turn, entering the Val d'Orco, and leading up to Malga Chèserle (1,402 metres). After the *Sass scrit*, with its inscriptions, one crosses through the handsome hollows of the Sette Alpi and the Pozza Orionda, and then one climbs up to the Alpe Pozze and to the Lancia hut (1,805 metres).

FIFTH DAY
from the Lancia Hut to the Papa hut
distance climbed: 450 metres
distance descended: 380 metres time: 3 hours 30 minutes

This is a short but interesting stage, in a lovely Karst setting, with remarkable views of the Dolomites and the Prealps. The most interesting features here, however, are the incredible military constructions that still cluster around the highest peaks of the Pasubio massif.

Italian and Austrian trenches, dug just a few dozen metres apart, and above all, the tunnels for mines and countermines, give a clear picture of a harsh and brutal war. One must have a torch and a healthy sense of caution in order to tour the galleries: deep holes and collapsing rocks are everywhere. One begins along the well marked trail that climbs up along Karst terrain all the way up to the saddle of the Ròite (2,081 metres), then one crosses the northeast slope of the Piccolo Ròite, continuing along to the mouth of the Ellison tunnel, one of the most extensive in the entire Pasubio. Other narrow tunnels open out in the peaks of the Dente Austriaco and the Dente Italiano, separated by the Selletta dei Denti (2,166 metres). After descending to the Selletta Damaggio (2,200 metres), a last little climb upward takes one to the Cima Palòn (2,232 metres), the tallest peak on the massif. One descends, passing by other tunnels and a shelter in ruins. Then one passes the Rest point Granzotto-Marchi on the right, and one descends to the Gate of Pasubio and the Papa hut (1,928 metres).

SEVENTH DAY
from the Giuriolo hut to Giazza
distance climbed: 850 metres
distance descended: 1,550 metres
time: 7 hours

This is an interesting stage, as well as quite a long one — two huts along the route allow one to split it up into two days of walking — and it centres on the mountain group of the Carega, one of the massifs best beloved by the people of Verona; it then continues on through the lengthy and interesting Val d'Illasi. At the end of the day, one comes to Giazza (*Ljetzan* in the local dialect), one of the most intriguing and distinctive little villages in the entire mountainous zone surrounding Verona. The traditional Cimbrian

tongue, of Germanic stock, is kept alive. Traversing across the ridge of the Tre Croci massif is time-consuming and tiring (it takes at least two hours more) but worth the trouble.
One begins by following the trail that climbs to the foot of the Spires of the Fumante; from here, the trail climbs up to the Bocchetta dei Fondi (2,084 metres), and then continues along a steep climb to the Fraccaroli hut (2,230 metres) and to the Cima Carega (2,259 metres), an excellent and widely renowned vantage-point. From here, on a clear day, one can see the Adriatic Sea, Lake Garda, and the Dolomites. A steep descent takes one back to the Bocchetta Mosca and on to the Scalorbi hut (1,767 metres). One continues through the meadows of the Alpe Compobrun, skirting the rocks of Mount Plische, and passing quite close to the Revolto hut. There is a long stretch of trial that runs alongside a mountain stream, and then one walks along the road, with many shortcuts, to Giazza (759 metres).

EIGHTH DAY
from Giazza to Erbezzo
distance climbed: 1,150 metres
distance descended: 770 metres
time: 6 hours 30 minutes

This stage runs across limestone highlands that are dotted with villages and chalet, which form the head of the Squaranto Valley, with a great deal of climbing and descending. The stage begins by crossing the mountain stream called the Revolto, after which climbs up to the highly scenic Malga Parparo di Sopra (1,469 metres), where one runs into a paved road. On the way down, one reaches the very deep Vajo Squaranto, and one continues along past the Malga Teccele and the Contrada Merli all the way to Maregge (1,262 metres). With a great deal of climbing and descending, one reaches the Contrada Tinazzo, runs close to the houses of Zamberlini (1,227 metres), and continues upon a cart-road all the way to a little church and the Hotel Croce (1,147 metres). A dirt road that dwindles down to a path leads one to the enchanting Vajo dell'Anguilla (approximately 850 metres), which one follows southward until one reaches the track that climbs up to Erbezzo (1,118 metres).

NINTH DAY
from Erbezzo to Verona
distance climbed: 200 metres
distance descended: 1,210 metres
time: 6 hours 30 minutes

The final stage in this walk, which lies within sight of the plains, still runs through a surprising limestone setting, in which particular notice should be paid to the natural arch of the Ponte di Veja, to the rocky walls of Stallavena, which form the training place for climbers closest to the city of Verona, and to the amazing Val Borago, where one makes one's way across a short equipped road. At the end, one can reach the provincial capital by taking a bus from the vineyards of Avesa. One continues for a stretch along the provincial road to Verona, one passes the houses of Resti, Manar, and Portello, and then one descends steeply to the Ponte Basaginocchi (480 metres), then climbing back up to the Ponte di Veja (611 metres). A dirt road skirts the houses of Giare, leading to a paved road, which one then takes toward Fane, detouring from there onto the crest that leads to the Monte Comune (777 metres) and its little villas. Wending between fields and stands of chestnut trees, one continues to descend, once again reaching the road, and then uphill toward the Monte Tondo (704 metres) and the house of La Carbonara. After crossing another road, one reaches a religious institution, and beyond that one descends steeply into the unspoilt Val Borago. Ladders and metal cables help in climbing over the "Grande Salto," some twenty-five metres high, and then one follows the wild valley until one emerges onto the gentle hillsides of Avesa; from there one can reach Verona by bus or on foot. If the weather is bad, a marked detour allows one to skip the gorge of the Val Borago.

THE DOLOMITE HIGH ROUTE No 2

From Bressanone to Feltre across the
Sella, the Marmolata, the Pale di San
Martino, and the Vette Feltrine

140-141 This picture offers a remarkable view of the main chain of the Pale di San Martino from Baita Segantini, a famous hut at 2,291 metres. The spire towering off to the left is the Cimon della Pala (3,185 metres), one of the most spectacular in the entire massif. Photograph by A. Gogna/K3

The fairytale spires of the Odle and the huge massif of the Sella, the glacier and the great face of the Marmolata, the mighty towers of the Pale, and lastly the wilderness of the Vette Feltrine, overlooking the valley of the river Piave and the plains of the Veneto. If the High Route No 1 leads in terms of history and popularity, there can be no doubt that the High Route No 2 of the Dolomites can certainly hold its head up in terms of sweep, variety, and natural beauty. Just a short distance from valleys that are favourites of mass tourism — Val Gardena, Val Badia, Val di Fassa, Val Livinallongo, San Martino di Castrozza, and Agordo — this trail offers walkers a succession of splendid stages in spectacular, unspoilt settings. Like its sister to the east, this is High Route was the product of intelligent, enthusiastic cooperation between mountain climbers and writers from Italy, Austria, and Germany. Among them, we should single out for special mention Mario Brovelli and Sigi Lechner. "A devoted mountain climber, a man who deeply loved nature... He loved the romantic atmosphere of nights spent in alpine rest points... When he was walking his favourite High Routes, No 1 and 2, one could hear from far away his Tyrolean singing, and one could smell the aroma of his pipe long before he actually hove into view." With these words, in his book *Großen Buch der Dolomiten - Hohenwege*, Franz Hauleitner recalled his wanderings in the company of Lechner, who was fifty years Hauleitner's senior. And just like the first one, the High Route of the western Dolomites is a voyage through the fantastic natural heritage of the Dolomites, the threats facing that heritage and the steps that are being taken to protect it. The tour on foot begins in Alto-Adige's Park of the Puez-Odle, then continues on through Trentino's Park of Paneveggio-Pale di San Martino, ending in the new, wild, unspoilt, and spectacular National Park of the Bellunese Dolomites. Along the way, one passes through territory where the monoculture of tourism and skiing, combined with the neglect and carelessness of a few, have done serious damage. Among these areas is the Sella, and the Marmolata, former queen of the Dolomites, now badly defaced. In 1988, two months of surveying and cleaning the slopes, done by

Mountain Wilderness, resulted in a truly saddening picture, showing a grim landscape of crevasses and even a rocky gully two hundred metres in depth filling up with garbage, kerosene stains on the splendid south face, kilometres and kilometres of metal cable abandoned at high altitudes. The mountains, however, are not made up of rocks, mugo pines, eagles, and chamois along. Around the group of the Sella, three ethnic groups have lived for the past several centuries: Germans, Ladinos, and Italians, making the Dolomites a sort of bridge, spanning and linking different peoples and cultures. There is no shortage of myths, as the nickname of "High Route of Legends" indicates, a name given to the trail by Brovelli and Lechner. In more concrete terms, the remains of Romanian roads and medieval tracks show the degree to which the high passes of the Dolomites have been important points in human history ever since the distant past. Like its neighbour to the east, this High Route is a summary of the history of mountain climbing on the Pale Mounts. The spires of the Odle have been the setting for the great feats of Giambattista Vinatzer — the great climber of the Thirties — and later for those of the brothers Messner, natives of the nearby town of Funes. The faces of the Sella have all been the most popular and most frequently climbed in the entire range of the Dolomites, with hundred of routes, of all degrees of difficulty. Only grazingly, one can admire the face of the Marmolata, a true university of difficult climbs, thanks to the routes opened by Vinatzer, Soldà, Gogna, Messner, and later by Mariacher and Giordani. From a closer vantage-point, as one zigzags among the saddles and spires, one can admire the most magnificent faces of the Pale, including in particular the Cimone, the Pala di San Martino, the Cima Canali, and the elegant spires rising around the Treviso hut. A bit higher, a bit more alpinistic than the first one, this High Route of the western Dolomites allows a walker greater freedom in choosing the challenges, and poses less problems with planning and advance reservations, offers a wide array of variant routes up to the most spectacular peaks. Few trails or routes in all the Alps offer a greater degree of satisfaction.

Bressanone

Cima Plose

FANES-SENNES-
BRAIES NATURAL
PARK

PUEZ ODLE
NATURAL PARK

Ortisei

Val Gardena

Sella

SCILIAR
NATURAL PARK

Canazei

M. PELMO
NATURAL
RESERVE

Fedaia

Marmolada

Fuchiade hut

Moena

Valles Pass

Predazzo

Cima di
Focobon

PANEVEGGIO
NATURAL PARK

Agordo

San Martino
di Castrozza

Croda Grande

Pale di San Martino

BELLUNESE
DOLOMITES
NATURAL PARK

Cima d'Asta

Sass de
Mura

Le Vette

Fonzaso

Feltre

USEFUL INFORMATION

Duration: 12 days.
Elevations: ranging from the 1,015 metres of the pass of Croce d'Aune and the 3,152 metres of the Piz Boè (or the 3,343 metres of the Marmolata di Penia).
Season: from July to September.
Signage: infrequent triangles with a "2" inset, white and red signage of the local Alpine Club trails.
Degree of difficulty: this route includes a number of equipped trails first degree rock climbing passages. Steep gullies full of snow may be present all the way up to July. One should not underestimate the challenge presented by the though easy glacier of the Marmolata.
How demanding: average. The stages are fairly short and the climbs and descents are not disproportionate. Like on the High Route No 1, the trail becomes increasingly demanding as one gets further and further south.
Equipment: normal walking gear. Useful to have body shape harness, short rope, screwgate karabiners and an abseil device for the equipped trails, ice axe and crampons for the glacier of the Marmolata. It is also a good idea to bring a length of climbing rope to secure the less experienced.
Peaks: the Piz Boè (3,152 metres) and the Marmolata di Penia (3,343 metres) can be reached with short detours, and we highly recommend the side trips. There is a wide array of other optional destinations, such as for instance the Sass de Putia (2,874 metres), the Cimon della Pala (3,184 metres), the easier Monte Mulaz (2,906 metres), and other peaks in the Vette Feltrine area.
How to get there: Bressanone can be reached via the railroad line Verona-Bolzano-Brenner-Innsbruck, the A22 across the Brenner Pass, or the State road 12 of the Brenner Pass. From Feltre, one can take a train to Bassano or Padova, and regularly scheduled buses leave for Belluno, Trent, and Vicenza.
How to get around: regularly scheduled buses to the Gardena Pass, the Pordoi Pass, the Lake of Fedaia, the San Pellegrino Pass and the Cereda Pass, the cable car from Rosetta to San Martino di Castrozza.
Overnight accommodations: huts of the CAI and private owners.
If you want to camp out: you have a problem. Free outdoor camping is forbidden almost everywhere, and the terrain at high elevations is rocky and uncomfortable.
Alpine Guides: (39) (471) 794133; this number operates only in the summer, otherwise contact the Local Bureau of Tourism Selva of Val Gardena.
Weather Forecasts: Centro Informazioni Valanghe Arabba (39) (436) 79227.
Mountain Rescue: dial 115 or 118 or else, only in the province of Belluno, call the headquarters of the CNSA in Pieve di Cadore (39) (435) 33118.
Information Offices: Tourist Bureau of Bressanone (39) (472) 836401, Tourist Bureau of Funes (39) (472) 844522, Tourist Bureau of Selva Val Gardena (39) (471) 795122, Tourist Bureau of Canazei (39) (462) 61113, Tourist Bureau of San Martino di Castrozza (39) (439) 768867, APT of the Feltrino (39) (439) 2540, APT of Moena (39) (462) 573122.
Useful phone numbers: Bressanone hut (39) (474) 57131, Genova hut (39) (472) 840132, Cavazza hut (39) (471) 836292, Boè hut (39) (471) 847303, hut and hotel Savoia Passo Pordoi (39) (462) 61279, Hut/Casa del Turista of the Pass of Pordoi (39) (462) 61205, Castigliona hut (39) (462) 61117, Contrin hut (39) (462) 61101, Fior di Roccia hut of the Pass of San Pellegrino (39) (437) 599120, Passo Valles hut (39) (437) 599136, Volpi hut (39) (437) 599420, Pedrotti hut (39) (439) 68308, Pradidali hut (39) (439) 64180, Treviso hut (39) (439) 62311, Boz hut (39) (439) 64448, Dal Piaz hut (39) (439) 9065.
Guide Books: *Alta Via 1 & 2 high level walks in the Dolomites* by Martin Collins (Cicerone Press) Walking in the Dolomites by Gillian price (Cicerone Press).
Maps: Kompass 1:50,000, n. 56, n. 59 *Sella-Marmolata*, and n. 76 *Pale di San Martino*, Tabacco 1:50,000, n. 9, 3, and 7, and 1:25,000, n. 05, 06 *Val di Fassa e Dolomiti Fassane*, 022 *Pale di San Martino*, and 023 *Alpi Feltrine*, Geo Grafica 1:50,000 n. 5, 6, and 10. The IGM maps cover *Lusòn*, *S. Maddalena*, *S. Cristina Val Gardena*, *Corvara in Badia*, *Marmolata*, *Passo di Valles*, *S. Martino di Castrozza*, *Garès*, *Fiera di Primiero*, *Le Vette*, and *Feltre*.

143 A lovely little church stands out among the verdant meadows of Santa Maddalena di Funes. In the background are the peaks of the Furchetta (3,025 metres) and the Sass de l'Ega (2,915 metres) and the broad saddle of the pass of San Zenon (Kreuzjoch, 2,294 metres), traversed by the High Route.
Photograph by Stefano Ardito

FIRST DAY
from Bressanone to the Genova hut
distance climbed: 500 metres
distance descended: 630 metres
time: 4 hours

This is a brief stage, an introduction to the High Route, in no way tiring thanks to the cable car and lifts that run from Bressanone to the Plose. Very popular with the inhabitants of the South Tyrol, but not well known to tourists, the massif of the Putia is one of the most spectacular and impressive mountains in the Dolomites.
One begins by riding up in a cable car to the Plose hut (2,447 metres): if the cable cars should happen to be shut down, then one should take a bus up

to the hotel of Valcroce (Kreuztal, 2040 metres) and continue on foot from there. In any case, one continues along the ridge of Mount Fana Grande (Pfannsspitze), enjoying the spectacular vistas, and from there one climbs down among ski lifts and ski slopes all the way to the Pass of Eores (Kofeljoch, 1,845 metres). There is a short walk along a paved road, then a dramatic gully takes to the Forcella de Putia (Peitlerscharte, 2,361 metres), within sight of the Val Badia and the Val Sella. A panoramic and lofty traverse, running obliquely along the slope, takes one to the Pass of Poma (Kreuzkofeljoch, 2,340 metres) and to the Genova hut (Schluter hut, 2,297 metres).

SECOND DAY
from the Genova hut to the Puez hut
distance climbed: 800 metres
distance descended: 600 metres
time: 5 hours

Another stage that is not particularly long, featuring the spectacular presence of the Odle, the jagged chain that separates the Val di Funes from the Val Gardena, leading on to the uplands of the Puez, within a short distance of the Sella. A splendid and interesting variant route can be followed, by taking the Trail of the Odle, which runs north and west of the mountain chain, then returning to the main route running to the Firenze hut: this means

144 top The Genova hut (2,297 metres) stands a few minutes' walk from the crest that separates the valleys of Lusòn and Funes, offering a comfortable halting *place among the massifs of the Odle and the Putia. The panorama includes the mountains of the Val Badia, as well. Photograph by Stefano Ardito*

144 bottom From the high Valle di Funes, one can admire a complete vista of the massif of the Odle. The peak at the centre of the photograph is the Furchetta (3,025 metres). The north *face of the Furchetta, which was first scaled by Hans Vinatzer in 1935, remains one of the most dramatic and difficult in all the Dolomites. Photograph by Marco Milani/K3*

145 top A party of walkers is shown walking along the trail that leads from the Cavazza hut to the Pisciadù hut (2,585 metres), in the heart of the northern slope of the Sella, climbing up toward the high plateau and the Piz Boè. Rock faces and snow-filled gullies — even in late summer — make this natural amphitheatre one of the most alluring places in the Dolomites. Photograph by A. Gogna/K3

145 bottom The broad grassy saddle of the pass of Gardena and the massif of the Sella are shown in this picture, taken from the Cir Pass (2,466 metres). It is possible to make out the faces of the Sass de la Luesa (2,615 metres), the Mesules (2,994 metres), and of the Torri del Murfreid (2,631 and 2,724 metres). Photograph by Franz Hauleitner

FOURTH DAY
from the Cavazza hut
to the Castiglioni hut
distance climbed: 560 metres
distance descended: 1120 metres
time: 7 hours

A two-fold stage, which is unfailingly interesting, allows one to round out one's familiarity of the Sella, and to get close to the glacier of the Marmolata. The first part of this walk runs through a grim and majestic landscape; one should finish it off with a climb to the vantage-point of the Piz Boè, if the weather is good; this is the highest point on the Sella. It is possible to spend the night at the Pordoi Pass, thus reducing the length of the stage: it would be wise, however, to venture onto the glacier and up to the high elevations of the Marmolata fairly early in the morning; on the other hand the Viel del Pan, the trail running between the Pordoi Pass and the lake of Fedaia, renowned for its incredible vistas, is a fairly easy walk. One passes near the little lake of the Pisciadù, and then climbs back up the wild Val di Tita

lengthening the walk by about three hours. One begins by crossing slightly treacherous rocky ground until one reaches the Furcia de Medalges (Kreuzjoch, Forcella San Zenon, 2,294 metres).
Then one enters a steep gully, which is blanketed with snow until quite late in the season, and which leads to the Forcella de la Roa (2,616 metres). Beyond this is the Forcella Forces de Sielles (2,505 metres); one works one's way pretty easily through equipped trails, reaching the Puez hut (2,475 metres), on the Puez plateau; this hut is a classical destination of excursions setting out from the Val Gardena.

THIRD DAY
from the Puez hut to the Cavazza hut
distance climbed: 630 metres
distance descended: 420 metres
time: 4 hours 30 minutes

Thi is a very spectacular stage.
One enters one of the most popular and crowded areas of all the Alps.
The impressive faces, the free-standing towers, the snow-filled gullies even in full summer, the dramatic plateau at the summit — all these features make the Sella one of the loveliest places on the Pale Mounts. One follows the trail that runs gently down to Forcella Ciampai (Ciampaijoch, 2,366 metres), one crosses the uplands of Crespeina, where one can find the lake of the same name (2,529 metres). After crossing the Pass of Crespeina (Crespeinajoch, 2,529 metres) and the Pass of Cir (Cirjoch, 2,469 metres), one climbs down into spectacular landscapes, within sight of the Sella, to the Pass of Gardena (2,121 metres). Beyond this pass, a gentle trail leads one to the mouth of the Val Setùs, which climbs all the way up to the Cavazza hut (2,583 metres), set on the boulders of the Pisciadù.

(equipped trails), finally emerging onto the highland of the Sella. After climbing the Antersass (2,907 metres), one descends to the Boè hut (2,871 metres). Here, one can choose between the trail that climbs up to the left, to the Piz Boè (3,152 metres) and the trail that skips it, running off to the right. From the Forcella Pordoi hut (2,809 metres), a trail leads among scree to the Pordoi Pass (2,239 metres). A gentle climb up through meadows and ski lifts leads to the Viel del Pan hut (2,432 metres), and from here one descends obliquely along the slope, with a splendid view of the Marmolata, to the lake of Fedaia and the Castiglioni hut (2,054 metres).

FIFTH DAY
*from the Castiglioni hut
to the Contrin hut
distance climbed: 270-650 metres
distance descended: 870-1,110 metres
time: 3 - 6 hours 30 minutes*

This stage, dedicated to the Marmolata, features the most enchanting and spectacular glacial and high-mountain settings in all the Dolomite range. Given the shortness of the trip, we would definitely recommend beginning it with the

handsome and quite easy climb (alpine walk glacier) from the Fiacconi Pass to the Marmolata di Penia, which could be further rounded out with a descent along the hobniled road of the western ridge.
One begins by riding up, in the chairlift, to the Pian dei Fiacconi (2,676 metres); from here, a track runs off to the right across the glacier, leading to the Forcella Marmolata (2,910 metres) along gentle slopes. As an alternative, one can climb the glacier, which is

followed by easy small rocks and the lofty ridge of the Schiena del Mul, until one reaches the Marmolata di Penia (3,343 metres). This round-trip walk takes about three hours, while the descent along the hobnailed road of the western ridge is strictly for experts. There is most likely enough time to return to the Pian dei Fiacconi and to pass the saddle. From here, a steep partly equipped gully, followed by an easy and comfortable trail, leads down to the Contrin hut (2,016 metres).

SIXTH DAY
*from the Contrin hut
to San Pellegrino Pass
distance climbed: 660 metres
distance descended: 760 metres
time: 4 hours*

This is a relaxing stage, in a less dramatic and grim setting than that of the Marmolata del Sella, though still quite interesting and enjoyable. One leaves the more popular areas of the Dolomites. Around Forca Rossa, one crosses a particularly unspoilt area, that is threatened by new ski lift facilities. Given the shortness and ease of the trip, it might be a good idea to continue as far as Passo

Valles, so that the next morning one can have all the time one needs to make the crossing of the Pale di San Martino. The trail climbs up a step of the valley, and then crosses a hollow, running up to the Cirelle Pass (2,683 metres), beyond which a rapid descent through pastures brings one to the Fuchiade hut (1,874 metres). Towards the right (south-west) the marked trail continues obliquely along the slope until the broad and verdant saddle of the Passo San Pellegrino (1,919 metres).

SEVENTH DAY
from San Pellegrino Pass to the Volpi hut
distance climbed: 1,050 metres
distance descended: 400 metres
time 5 hours 30 minutes

Another day with a two-fold personality, the first half extending across the solitary Altopiano degli Zingari — one should be particularly careful here if there is fog — and the second half lying on the wild northern slope of the Pale of San Martino, where steep gullies and lofty saddles offer the walker a fitting introduction to one of the most spectacular

massifs anywhere in the Dolomites. The trail climbs through a series of meadows, crossing a ski lift area, and then overlooks the Altopiano degli Zingari, which one crosses, finally reaching the Forcella di Pradazzo (2,220 metres). A quick descent, with a remarkable panoramic view of the Pale, leads one to the pass of Valles (2,031 metres). One sets out again obliquely, until one reaches the Forcella di Venegia (2,217 metres),

one skirts the Cima Venegiotta, and then one climbs to the pass of the same name (2,303 metres).
A handsome route with a great deal of climbing and descending through the large summit hollow of the Val Focobòn leads the walker to the Arduini Pass and on to the Volpi hut (2,571 metres). It is possible to climb up to the summit of Mount Mulaz (2,906 metres, two hours, round trip), high above the hut, with its remarkable vistas.

EIGHTH DAY
from the Volpi hut to the Pradidali hut
distance climbed: 680 metres
distance descended: 970 metres
time: 6 hours

One of the most demanding stages of the High Route leads one, along the Trail of the Farangole, to the heart of the Pale di San Martino. Equipped sections, rock climbing of first and second degree and snowfields make the trail quite interesting, rich as it is with spectacular views of all the peaks of the Pale. After climbing up to the Mulaz Pass, one continues uphill until one reaches the Pass of the Farangole (2,932 metres); from here, one can see the Val Grande and the central chain of the Pale. One continues along with a steep descent into a hollow full of gravel and snow, over which looms the Campanile of Focobòn, and then, with a descending trail, on to the mouth of the Val Strut. One continues to descend across steep grassy slopes (be particularly careful when there is snow on the ground or when it is raining) until reaching the Pian dei Cantoni. One quickly reaches the Pedrotti alla Rosetta hut (2,581

147 top The summit ridge of the Marmolata separates the gentle slopes of the glacier from the daunting south face. This photograph was taken from the Marmolata di Penia, at 3,343 metres the tallest peak in the
Dolomites. Atop the peak of the Marmolata di Rocca (3,309 metres) one can see the upper terminus of the cable car which runs up from Malga Ciapela.
Photograph by Marco Milani/K3

147 bottom In this classic vista of the Marmolata, seen from the north, it is easy to pick out the glacier along which the High Route runs up, following the route that was used in 1864 by the climbing party of Paul Grohmann and his guides, on their way up to climb to the peak for the first time.
Photograph by Gianluca Boetti

147

metres), which tends to be fairly crowded because of the nearby cable car, but which is in any case a splendid vantage-point. A long and spectacular traverse at the base of the Pale di San Martino and the Cima Immink, followed by a long and fairly easy equipped stretch, bring one to the Passo di Ball (2,443 metres), and from here one can get down quite quickly to the Pradidali hut (2,278 metres).

and emerges onto the dirt road along the valley of the Val Canali (1,350 metres).
A final, not particularly demanding, steep uphill climb leads to the Treviso hut (1,631 metres), in a pleasant and relaxing setting.

reaching the ruins of the Casera Regade (1,683 metres). A descent through the woods and a dirt road take one to the Cereda Pass (1,361 metres), along the road that links Fiera di Primiero with Agordo.

ELEVENTH DAY
from Cereda Pass to the Boz hut
distance climbed: 1,200 metres
distance descended: 830 metres
time: 7 hours 30 minutes

Solitary and exhausting, this stage takes one into the authentic wilderness of the Vette Feltrine, which are part of the National Park of the Bellunese Dolomites. This is a walk with no major obstacles or difficulties, but which features stretches on steep ground in the long crossing of the slopes of the Cimonega group, and with brief equipped trails and snow fields. Anyone who wishes to spend more time on this stretch of the High Route may choose to split this stage in half, spending the night at the comfortable and capacious (it sleeps twenty-three) but often crowded rest point Feltre. One follows the road all the way to the houses of Mattiuzzi (1,201 metres), and from there, the handsome gully of Intaiada leads, with a lengthy and exhausting climb, to the Forcella Comedon (2,067 metres), beyond which lies the rest point Feltre-Bodo (1,930 metres). After passing the Val Canzoi on the left, one crosses the large saddle of Col dei Bechi (1,960 metres), where the lofty trail of the Caserin begins, at the foot of the Cimonega and the Sass de Mura. After reaching the Pass de Mura (1,867 metres), one descends quickly to the Boz hut (1,718 metres).

NINTH DAY
from the Pradidali hut
to the Treviso hut
distance climbed: 600 metres
distance descended: 1,300 metres
time: 4 hours

After leaving the central area of the Pale, one ventures on into the southern chain of the same, among elegant dolomite towers that bound the Val Canali and along alluringly surprising highlands and plateaus. After leaving the hut, one climbs up with an alluring view upon the face of the Cima Canali all the way to the pass of Lede (2,698 metres), beyond which one descends along a gully and then across scree and meadows to the rest point Minazio (2,250 metres).
One continues along the left slope of the high valley of the Lede, and then reaches the end of that valley,

TENTH DAY
from the Treviso hut to Cereda Pass
distance climbed: 620 metres
distance descended: 800 metres
time: 4 hours

After leaving the Pale di San Martino definitively behind one, one looks out onto the Valle del Mis and the chain of the Vette Feltrine, where one will spend the last two days of the High Route. On this day, there are fairly limited climbs and descents, and not a very tiring trail: this is not true for the two spectacular stages that will follow. One begins with a climb up obliquely along the slope, and then continues through the Vallon d'Oltro, all the way to the Forcella d'Oltro (2,229 metres). One descends along a brief, steep stretch, and then continues at some length on difficult terrain at the base of Cima Feltraio and the Campanile di Regade, until

148 This picture gives us a spectacular winter view of the Cimon della Pala (3,185 metres). The symbol of the massif of the Pale, this peak is often nicknamed "the Matterhorn of the Dolomites," and *has a relatively easy standard route (the final stretch is of second degree), which is accessible to experienced walkers or to those with a guide.* Photograph by L. Ramires/ White Star

TWELFTH DAY
from the Boz hut
to Passo di Croce d'Aune
distance climbed: 750 metres
distance descended: 1,180 metres
time: 7 hours

The last stage of the High Route
No 2 allows the walker to become
better acquainted with the Vette
Feltrine, which in some areas are
gentle and grassy — as is the case
in the Piazza del Diavolo — while in
other stretches they are dramatic
and rocky, and in all cases are
remarkably Mediterranean in nature.
The final climb down from the Dal
Piaz hut is tiring and hard on the
legs. It may be a good idea to spend
the night in the hut, climbing up at
nightfall or at sunrise toward the
Vette Grandi or the Pavione.
After quickly reaching the Passo di
Finestra (1,766 metres), one climbs
along a lofty ridge toward the Upper
Mount Zoccar and the Sasso di
Scarnia. With a few equipped
passages, one crosses the Passo di
Ramezza (2,038 metres) and one
enters the spectacular Karst hollow
of the Piazza del Diavolo, one of the
most solitary and remarkable places
in the Vette Feltrine. After climbing
up to the Passo di Pietena (2,094
metres), one descends into the next
hollow of the Busa delle Vette,
beyond which one will encounter the
Pass of the Vette Grandi (1,994
metres) and the Dal Piaz hut (1,990
metres). Here the view extends out
toward Mount Grappa and the
upland of the Seven Districts. A very
steep descent along an old military
road and then along a winding mule-
track lead to the Passo di Croce
d'Aune (1,015 metres), and from
there one can take a bus to Feltre.
It is also possible to continue on foot
toward the Colle del Melone and the
Belvedere hut, in the direction of
Pedavena and Feltre (760 metres of
distance, requiring an extra two
hours of walking).

149 top The chain of the Pale di San Martino looms above Paneveggio Forest. The daunting Dolomitic massif and the vast woods of fir trees form part of the park covering 15.800 hectares, established in 1967 by the provincial government of Trent. Photograph by Luciano Ramires/ White Star

149 bottom A path runs obliquely along the slope, winding along an extended walk across the Rocchette. This is near the pass of Regade, just before the steep descent in the direction of the pass of Cereda. Photograph by Franz Hauleitner

THE DOLOMITE HIGH ROUTE No 1

From Lake Braies to Belluno
through the Fanes, the Tofane, the
Pelmo, the Civetta and the Moiazza,
the Bosconero, and the Bellunese
Dolomites

"There are valleys where I come from that I have seen nowhere else on earth. Just like the landscape shown in certain old prints from the Romantic period, one takes a rapid look at the vista and immediately thinks: this can't be real, there can't be places like this on the planet. And yet they exist: with the same solitude, the same improbable crags half hidden by trees and shrubbery tottering at the edge of the void, and the same stunning waterfalls. They are perhaps less splendid, one must confess, than the triumphant high valleys of the Dolomites, girt round by glittering white crags. Nonetheless, they are more enigmatic, more intimate, more secret." With these words, in the 1950s, the great Italian writer and climber Dino Buzzati described the Bellunese Dolomites. Born in Belluno himself, Buzzati was especially aware of the remarkable allure of the southernmost chain of the Dolomites, which links the massifs of the Vette Feltrine with the great wall of the Schiara, across solitary summits with names that often sound arcane and odd: Sass de Mura, Pizzocco, Sagròn, Feruch. For the walker that undertakes the High Route No 1, the first High Route through the Dolomites to have been conceived and marked out, the wild massifs of Belluno — which have enjoyed for decades the protection of numerous state nature reserves established back in the Sixties, and which were named part of a national park in 1991 — are only part of the route. Along this High Route, for a good solid week before reaching the area in question, walkers can cross through and admire many of the most spectacular and best known places in the Pale Mounts. Lake Braies, over which looms the wall of the Croda del Becco. The solitary

uplands of Fanes. The splendid valleys that lies in the shadow of the Tofana di Rozes.
The enchanted castle of the Pelmo. The great wall of the Civetta, the "wall of walls" in the history of Alpine climbing. The wild valleys at the foot of the Moiazza and of the Tamer. The thread of this remarkable skein of walking, however, ineluctably leads toward Belluno and the "deep South" of the Dolomites. The concept of this trail was the brainchild, in the early Sixties, of a remarkable mixed team of Italians and Germans. Piero Rossi, a Bellunese author and climber, was the first to dream of the trail.
From 1963 onward, he was assisted greatly by Toni Hiebeler, a renowned Bavarian climber and the editor-in-chief of the magazine *Alpinismus*, which in 1966 published the first article to discuss the High Route. A decisive contribution came as well

150 The northern slope of the Pelmo looms over the green meadows of Malga Durona, where the Città di Fiume hut stands at an altitude of 1,917 metres. The north face of the mountain was climbed for the first time in 1924 by Roland Rossi and Felix Simon.
Photograph by Stefano Ardito

151 The walls of the Pelmo (3,168 metres) are seen at dawn from the Lagazuoi hut, one of the finest vantage-points in the Dolomites, where one rests along the High Route, after a lengthy and lonely crossing of the massifs of Conturines and Fanes.
Photograph by Gianluca Boetti

from Mario Brovelli, a clerk with the *Ente del Turismo* (or Chamber of Tourism) of Belluno, as well as the man who conceived a master plan that included four High Routes, along with Venetian climbers Giovanni Angelini and Armando Da Roit, as well as Sigi Lechner, an alpine guide from Garmisch. And this splendid cooperation and harmonious teamwork among mountaineers from different nations appears even a hint more noble when one remembers the enormity in those years of the painful question of South Tyrolean irredentism. This route is splendid and walkers of every degree of stamina and skill can venture confidently upon it, as every bit of the route is quite easy, with the possible exception of the last descents across the great wall of the Schiara, which is a stretch that can be skipped in favour of an alternative route down. The High Route No 1 of

the Dolomites has a further symbolic meaning, representing as it does a high bridge between two worlds and two civilizations: the Germans and the Italians. These two cultures have often come into contact and at times friction just around the Pale Mounts. The stories that walkers bring back from this walk are often tinged with wonder and deep feeling. "Every single kilometre of the one hundred fifty kilometres of the trail will charm and deeply impress anyone who loves the mountains," wrote Toni Hiebeler in 1966. "The High Route runs through a true land of enchantment, where enormous mountain massifs and uncanny huge rocky bastions veer sharply up, looming over forsaken pastureland, while spires tilt and lean, all askew, near walls that loft heavenward above marvelous, eye-gladdening stands of larch."

And, writing twenty-four years later, the Austrian alpinist and author Franz Hauleitner struck much the same note. For mountain climbers, or for those who have simply a keen interest in mountain climbing, the walls of the Cima Scotoni and the Tofane, of the Civetta and the Pelmo, and of dozens of less well known summits and peaks, they all remind us of remarkable adventures and achievements of the past. It is not an easy task, given these illustrious forebears and these illustrious chapters of history, to add much more to an introduction to the most renowned High Route of the Dolomites, quite likely the most celebrated trail of the Alps as a whole, standing head-and-shoulder with the Tour of Mont Blanc. It is probably useful here to set forth a bit of practical advice however: the presence of snow in the gullies and on the high passes means that it is wise to carry an ice axe through the month of July; it is necessary to reserve one's berth in every hut from the middle of July until the end of August; in a number of stretches of the trail (especially between the Tofane and Civetta) it is possible to pick and choose among the many variant trails. We venture to hope that it is even more useful to point out that walking a walking trail means experiencing sights, challenges, feelings, and thrills that change constantly, never the same two days in a row or even two hours in a row, always different for each different walker. The author has thrilled to the

152 bottom The cross on the Cima Col Becchei (2,794 metres), panoramic spot in the Park of Fanes-Sennes-Braies, stands stark against the sky. The standard route from the Limo Pass runs along a path through the meadows and then across easy rocks, through which runs an Austro-Hungarian trail dating from the First World War I.
Photograph by
F. Raiser/K3

sight — among these same peaks — of such classic spectacles as the walls of the Civetta, Tofana, and Pelmo, the sunsets and dawns over the Lagazuoi and the Nuvolau, the glittering blue of the Adriatic and the Venetian lagoon from high atop the peaks of the Bellunese Dolomites. Equally sweeping feelings have affected this author in the woods around Lake Braies, in the sunny Mediterranean splendor of the mountain meadows of Fanes, at the foot of the walls of Cima Scotoni and the other peaks nearby. Or further along, among the eerily shaped rocks of the Moiazza and the Tamer, or in the endless Ardo Valley — so long, intricate, and unspoiled — that links the Settimo Alpini hut and the foot of the Schiara with the outskirts of Belluno, a true sign of the end of the walk. The Alps are far away: here the atmosphere is truly prealpine, though let that be in no way considered a slight on the trail.

At times, it is among the lesser ranges that one can most easily find wilderness and solitude. It is well to say, in conclusion, that the importance of the Bellunese Dolomites should be understood not only by walkers and mountain climbers. Eagles, chamois, and the lynx live among these mountains, making them that much more precious and worthy of our protection. "The Park of the Dolomites is the greatest gift that Belluno can give to Europe," wrote Piero Rossi in 1966 . Later came the Park of Fanes-Sennes-Braies in Alto-Adige and the Park of the Dolomites d'Ampezzo in the Venetia region. In 1991 the National Park of the Bellunese Dolomites became reality: let all our readers walk its trails with the utmost understanding and respect.

152-153
The entrancing light of sunset illuminates the Lagazuoi hut (2,752 metres), which stands on the ridge of the Lagazuoi Piccolo, a peak that was harshly fought over by Italians and Austro-Hungarians during the First World War. In the distance, one sees the Croda da Lago and the Pelmo.
Photograph by Claudio Chiaretta

153 bottom
The head of the wild Val Travenanzes and the western face of the Tofana di Rozes (3,225 metres), seen from the Lagazuoi ridge . At bottom right, one can make out the rubble of the Castelletto, where the Italian army set off a mine in July of 1916.
Photograph by Stefano Ardito

153

Duration: 10 days.

Elevations: ranging from the 540 metres, of Bolzano Bellunese and the 2,750 metres of the Monte Lagazuoi.

Season: from July to September.

Signage: dark-blue triangle with an inset "1," while the trailmarkers of the CAI are white and red.

Degree of difficulty: this is not only the most classic, but the easiest High Route in the Dolomites, presenting an absolutely minimum degree of difficulty if one sticks to the basic trail. The exception, however, is to climb down the steep southern slope of the Schiara, along a demanding hobnailed trail, which is exceedingly lofty in stretches, with climbing passages that range up to the second degree. This section of the route can be skipped by climbing down from the Bianchet hut toward La Muda and the state road No 203.

How demanding: average. Like on the High Route No 2, the trail becomes increasingly demanding as one gets further and further south.

Equipment: normal walking gear. Equipment for a scrambling trail (slings, short rope, a screw gate karabiner, an abseil device) is needed only during the last stage.

Peaks: there are a great many interesting peaks that can be reached via slight detours from the High Route. Among the easier of these, we should mention the Croda del Becco (2,810 metres), from the Biella hut, the Tofana di Rozes (3,225 metres), from the Giussani and Cantore huts, the Schiara (2,563 metres). The next peaks are quite demanding, and it might be wise to be accompanied by a guide: the Pelmo (3,168 metres), the Civetta (3,220 metres), and the Moiazza (2,865 metres).

How to get there: Braies can be reached by regularly scheduled buses from the railroad stations of

Monguelfo and Villabassa, on the line Bressanone-Dobbiaco-Lienz. From Belluno one can take a train back toward Treviso and Venice, or else a bus toward Feltre, Trent, Cortina, and Auronzo.

How to get around: regularly scheduled buses to the pass of Falzarego, the pass of Giau, the Forcella Staulanza, and the pass of Duran.

Overnight accommodations: huts of the CAI and private operators, hotels and bed-and-breakfasts in the towns of the low valleys.

If you want to camp out: you have a problem. Free outdoor camping is forbidden almost everywhere, and the terrain at high elevations is rocky and uncomfortable.

Alpine Guides: Alpine guide group of Cortina (39) (436) 868505.

Weather Forecasts: contact the tourist bureaus.

Mountain Rescue: dial 118, or else, in the province of Belluno, call the headquarters of the CNSA in Pieve di Cadore (39) (435) 33118, and at Cortina (39) (436) 2943.

Information Offices: Tourist Bureau of Braies (39) (474) 78660, APT (Local Bureau of Tourism) of Cortina (39) (436) 3231, APT of the Valzoldana (39) (437) 787349, APT of Belluno (39) (437) 940083, APT of Agordo (39) (437) 62105, APT of Auronzo (39) (435) 9359.

Useful phone Nos: Regional Park of the Dolomites of Ampezzo (39) (436) 867707, Administrative Office of the former -ASFD Belluno (39) (437) 944830, Biella hut (39) (474) 866991, Sennes hut (39) (474) 501092, Munt de Sennes hut (39) (474) 501311, Fodara Vedla hut (39) (474) 501093, Pederu hut (39) (474) 501086, La Varella hut (39) (474) 501079, Fanes hut (39) (474) 501097, Lagazuoi hut (39) (436) 867303, Dibona hut (39)

(436) 860294, Giussani hut (39) (436) 5740, Nuvolau hut (39) (436) 867938, Palmieri hut (39) (436) 862085, Città di Fiume hut (39) (437) 720268, Venezia hut (39) (436) 9684, Tissi hut (39) (437) 721644, Sonino hut (39) (437) 789160, Vazzoler hut (39) (437) 660008, Carestiato hut (39) (437) 62949, Bianchet hut (39) (437) 87294, San Sebastiano hut (39) (437) 62360, Sommariva hut (39) (337) 528403, Settimo Alpini hut (39) (437) 941631.

Maps: Kompass 1:50,000 n. 57 *Brunico-Dobbiaco*, n. 55 *Cortina d'Ampezzo* and n. 77 *Alpi Bellunesi*. Tabacco 1:50,000 n. 6, 2, and 4 *Belluno-Feltre-San Martino di Castrozza* and 1:25,000 n. 03 *Cortina d'Ampezzo-Dolomiti Ampezzane*, n. 015 *Marmolata-Pelmo-Civetta-Moiazza* and n. 024 *Prealpi and Dolomiti Bellunesi*. Geo Grafica 1:25,000 n. 1 and 3 *Monte Pelmo-Monte Civetta*. The IGM maps 1:25,000 area cover Villabassa, *Alpe Fanes, Cortina d'Ampezzo, Tofane, Monte Pelmo, Forno di Zoldo, Cencenighe Agordino, Cime di San Sebastiano*, and *Monte Pelf*.

Guide Books: *Alta Via n. 1 & n. 2 high level walks in the Dolomites* by Martin Collins (Cicerone Press); *Walking in the Dolomites* by Gillian price (Cicerone Press).

155

FIRST DAY

From Braies Lake to the Pederu hut
Distance climbed: 900 metres
Distance descended: 770 metres
Time: 6 hours

Lengthy and charming, the first stage of the High Route sets out from the enchanting Lake of Braies — one of the jewels of the Val Pusteria — and then winds its way up along a difficult high valley toward the Porta Sora 'l Forn and the Biella hut.

The subsequent stretch of trail, which crosses the uplands of Sennes and Fanes, is less exhausting. If one reaches the Val Pusteria in the morning, one can spend the night at the Biella hut, and then climb up to the nearby Croda del Becco, the first in a series of exceptional vantage-points. From the hotels (1,495 metres) which line the banks of the Lake of Braies, one can follow the trail that skirts the lake to the right, crossing the mouth of the Val Foresta (Grunwaldtal), and beginning the steep climb up to the foot of the face of the Croda del Becco (Seekofel, 2810 metres). A succession of steep, gravelly slopes and hollows

(in one of these hollows lies the Lake of the Giovo, or the Jaufensee, 2,026 metres) leads up to the Porta Sora 'l Forn (Ofenkarscharte, 2,388 metres), a vantage-point overlooking the Tre Cime, the Croda Rossa, the Sella, and the Odle. Immediately beyond this point is the Biella hut (Seekofel Hutte, 2,327 metres), from which a partly equipped trail runs out on the right toward the Croda del Becco. One continues southward along a cart-road all the way to the Sennes hut (2,122 metres), in the middle of a lovely, verdant hollow. One continues along the dirt road that slopes gently down to the Pian di Lasta, and then runs more steeply down to the Pederu hut (1,545 metres), at the head of the Val Tamores.

SECOND DAY

from the Pederu hut
to the Monte Lagazuoi hut
distance climbed: 1,550 metres
distance descended: 350 metres
time: 7 hours

This is quite a lengthy stage, running from the beautiful uplands of the Fanes and on into the spectacular high valley of Lagazuoi, in the shadow of the dramatic walls of the Cime Fanis and the Cima Scotoni, one of the most celebrated, difficult, and rich in alpinistic history in the Dolomites. The Lake of Lagazuoi is particularly idyllic, and on a sunny day the temptation to take a swim here is great. The monotonous dirt road of the first portion of this stage can be travelled by jeep: the man who runs the Pederu hut will gladly take passengers in his jeep. One can end the stage at the comfortable Scotoni hut. One begins with the dirt-road described above, though the trail splits off from it, running through extensive pastureland. From the Fanes hut (2,042 metres), one can admire the splendid pastureland of Pices Fanes and the limestone large slabs of Cima Nove, and then one crosses the pass of the Ju de Limo (Limojoch, 2,172 metres); one then descends to the Malga Fanes Grande (2,104 metres) and one climbs up to the Pass of Tadega (in Ladin, the Rhaeto-Romanic language as spoken in Trentino-Alto Adige, it is called the Ju de l'Ega, 2,157 metres), at the foot of a colossal avalanche of huge boulders. One continues along the meadowlands of the Plan de Ciaulunch and the Plan des Sumorones, and the Marmolata rises into view. A bit further on, the path splits at a fork. The left-hand trail rises sharply and steeply to the Forcella del Lago (2,480 metres), then dropping down to the Lake of Lagazuoi; the right-hand trail then continues along the slope all the way to the Scotoni hut (1,985 metres), from there continuing along the valley floor. One continues climbing up the Lagazuoi Valley among desolate scree. At last, walking along ski slopes, one reaches the Monte Lagazuoi hut (2,710 metres), a renowned vantage-point.

THIRD DAY

from the Monte Lagazuoi hut
to the Nuvolau hut
distance climbed: 920 metres
distance descended: 1,090 metres
time: 5 hours 45 minutes

This is a stage of reasonable length, devoted to the Castelletto, with its disquieting tunnels, at the base of the walls of the Tofana. Those who are in a hurry can descend on foot or by cable car to the Pass of Falzarego, climbing up to the Averau hut, and continuing along with the following stage. From the Cinque Torri hut, actually, there are two different routes. Those who are in search of great vantage-points should climb up to the Nuvolau. Those who prefer the woodlands atmospheres may choose to head to the Palmieri hut, at the foot of the Croda da Lago: if this is the case, it might be a good idea to spend the night at the Cinque Torri hut. After descending back down to the Forcella Lagazuoi (2,571 metres), one reaches the Forcella Travenanzes (2,507 metres), and then the Forcella Bos (2,330 metres); a little way past this last Forcella is the entrance to the tunnels of the Castelletto (torch required), and beyond the tunnels an equipped trail takes one back to the main trail. At the foot of the wall of the Tofana di Rozes, one traverses downhill as far as the Dibona hut (2,000 metres). A dirt road leads to the state road from Cortina to the pass of Falzarego (1,742 metres), and one follows that highway for a short distance. A mule-track leads up to the Cinque Torri hut (2,130 metres), and from there one climbs up to the Scoiattoli hut (2,230 metres), the Forcella Nuvolau (2,416 metres), and the Nuvolau hut (2,575 metres), on the summit of the same name.

FOURTH DAY

from the Nuvolau hut
to the Città di Fiume hut
distance climbed: 400 metres
distance descended: 1,010 metres
time: 6 hours 15 minutes

This is a long stage, one of the most exciting to be found along the High Route due to the panoramas stretching out in all directions. The equipped trails of the first part do not pose excessive problems, and they can be avoided in any case by passing over the Forcella Nuvolau. Leaving behind one the frenzied confusion of the areas around Cortina, one finds oneself in a more natural and authentic atmosphere: the battle to preserve the area around the Pelmo from a system of ski facilities has been carried on for decades by environmentalist of Venetia and of the world at large. One begins by descending from the summit with a few equipped passages. A gully and a trail running over the meadows bring one to the pass of Giau (2,236 metres). A quick uphill climb brings one to

Forcella Giau (2,360 metres), and from there one descends to the Lake of the Baste (2,281 metres) and to Malga Mondeval (2,155 metres), climbing back up to Forcella Ambrizzola (2,277 metres), where the trail intersects with the path from the Palmieri hut. In increasingly solitary settings, one reaches the Forcella Col Duro (2,293 metres), dropping down sharply to the Malga Prendèra (2,073 metres), and continuing from there with further short bouts of climbing and descending until one comes to the stupendous hollow of Malga Durona, alongside which is the Città di Fiume hut (1,917 metres).

158 top The light of dawn creeps over the walls of the Pelmo.
Photograph by Luciano Ramires/ White Star

158 bottom The unassuming yet distinctive massif of the Cinque Torri, which is actually formed by about twenty spires, is one of the classic destinations for walkers and climbers in the area surrounding Cortina. This is the Torre Grande (2,361 metres), the tallest of the lot.
Photograph by Ernst Höhne

FIFTH DAY
from the Città di Fiume hut
to the Tissi hut
distance climbed: 700 metres
distance descended: 370 metres
time: 5 hours 45 minutes

This is one of the most spectacular stages in the High Route, taking one from the Pelmo massif to the massif of the Civetta, and one reaches the best vantage-point overlooking the great north face of the Civetta. As a variant trail, one can cross the Pelmo along the lofty but not particularly difficult Flaibani Trail, passing by the Venezia-De Luca hut, the classic destination of excursions setting out from Borca di Cadore and San Vito: in this case, we would recommend that another stage be added to the High Route. One begins along the trail that runs in the shadow of the north faces of the Pelmetto and the Pelmo, then one descends to Forcella Staulanza (1,766 metres), and one follows for a short while the road toward Zoldo Alto. A dirt road leads on to Casera Vescovà (1,722 metres), and from there one continues among ski lifts as far as Forcella d'Alleghe, to the Casera di Pioda (1,816 metres) and to the mule-track that runs up to the Sonino al Coldai hut (2,132 metres). After passing the Forcella of the Lake of Coldai (2,190 metres) and walking around the lovely Lake of Coldai, one begins to skirt the remarkable north face of the Civetta, which here is actually looking northwest, and is therefore lit up at sunset. From the Forcella di Col Negro one climbs down of the terrace to the Val Civetta, directly at the base of the wall. From the Forcella di Col Reàn one climbs to the right up to the Tissi hut (2,250 metres).

SIXTH DAY

from the Tissi hut to the Carestiato hut
distance climbed: 350 metres
distance descended: 760 metres
time: 4 hours 45 minutes

Another stage of remarkable beauty, at the foot of the wall of the Civetta, the place where the sixth degree was for the first time climbed in 1925, and along the base of other equally spectacular walls such as the Busazza, the Cantoni di Pelsa, the Torre Venezia, and the Torre Trieste. During the latter part of the stage, one will be deeply stirred by the walls of the group of the Moiazza, beginning with the Castello delle Nevere. From the fork in the Val Corpassa, one enters a world that is quite different from the better known parts of the Dolomites. The scree, the mugo pines, the not-always well-marked trails — everything announces that one is nearing the Bellunese Dolomites. From the hut, one climbs back down to the saddle, and then continuing along so as to complete the traverse of the Val Civetta. After crossing the Col di Pelsa (1,954 metres), one continues on to the base of the Cantoni di Pelsa and of the Torre Venezia. Encountering a dirt road (nearby is the Casa Favretti), one follows it into the woods and climbs briefly as far as the Vazzolèr hut (1,714 metres), another vantage-point that is considered to rank among the finest in the Dolomites. Aside from the Torre Venezia and the Torre Trieste, one will surely be astounded at the wall of the Busazza. One sets out again along the access cart-road that leads to the hut, then descending and leading to a fork (1,420 metres). One climbs up among larches, mugo pines and scree to the base of the Castello delle Nevere. After crossing over the Forcella di Col Palanzin (1,700 metres) and the Forcella di Col de l'Ors (1,800 metres), one crosses a ledge, passing by the Casera del Camp (now in ruins) and climbing up to the Forcella del Camp (1,933 metres), from which one can see the main wall of the Moiazza. The trail runs down into the Val Framònt, climbing up among the scree and continuing on to the Carestiato hut (1,834 metres).

SEVENTH DAY

from the Carestiato hut
to the Sommariva hut
distance climbed: 570 metres
distance descended: 550 metres
time: 4 hours 30 minutes

This is a stage of transition, in which one leaves behind the best known mountain groups and enters the Bellunese Dolomites, skirting the spectacular chain of the Tamer and the Castello di Moschesin: places that were virtually unknown until the Sixties, but which have been rendered classic and very popular by the High Route. One begins with a quick descent to the pass of Duran (1,601 metres), then one drops down for a short distance to the road for Agordo, and one detours uphill toward Forcella Dagarei (1,620 metres): near the fork a plaque commemorates Rossi and Hiebeler, two of the devisers of the High Route No 1. The trail cuts high over thepastures of the Val Missaglia,

160 Just behind the comfortable Vazzolèr hut (1,725 metres) one can see the powerful, 1,100 metres high walls of the Busazza, which. The first ascent to its peak, by Renzo Videsott and Domenico Rudatis in 1929, was one of the great adventures of mountain climbing in the Dolomites.
Photograph by Stefano Ardito

161 top When looking northward from the pass of Duran, the spurs of the Tàmer and of the cime di San Sebastiano block one's view of the Val Zoldana. On the left is the massif of the Moiazza, a mighty peak towering 2,865 metres.
Photograph by A. Gogna K/3

161 bottom The VII Alpini hut stands at an altitude of 1,490 metres, in the enchanting hollow of the Schiara (2,563 metres). On high, against the sky, one can just glimpse the spire of the Gusèla del Vescovà.
Photograph by Stefano Ardito

then it crosses a scree and it continues on to the base of the handsome pieces of architecture in rock of the Tamer on all the way to the Forcella Pan d'Orso (1,775 metres). After passing by the Casera Moschesin (1,800 metres) and the Forcella Moschesin (1,940 metres) one climbs down for a short way, continuing along the nearly level Balanzole Trail until reaching the Sommariva hut (1,857 metres), among splendid meadows.

EIGHTH DAY

*from the Sommariva hut
to the Bianchet hut
distance climbed: 610 metres
distance descended: 1,210 metres
time: 6 hours 30 minutes*

This is a lengthy stage, over the magnificent massifs of the Pramper and the Talvena, in settings that are both spectacular and truly little known. Here the usual route of the High Route is still slightly different from what our experience recommends. It is possible, in fact, to stay overnight at the Rest point Dal Mas, and to continue the next day at elevation, thus avoiding the descent to the Bianchet hut, with the subsequent climb back up.
It is necessary to have a campstove and cooking equipment. Each walker can choose. One begins by climbing up to the Portella Piazedel (2,097 metres), from which one continues with a great deal of climbing and descending until reaching the Forcella Sud del Van de Zittà ("Città" on the maps, 2,395 metres), and from there one can see the Schiara. A steep climb down takes one to the Van de Zittà de Fora, a desolate Karst hollow beyond which a trail with switchbacks leads to the Rest point Dal Mas (1,632 metres), where we would highly recommend camping out to those who wish to spend a night in the wild. Otherwise, one climbs easily up to the Forcella Lavaretta (1,704 metres), from which once again one has an excellent view of the Schiara.
After climbing down to a fork — the ridge trail continues toward the Rest

point of the Màrmol and the Schiara — one climbs down on the right, among the mugo pines and then on into the beech grove, and on to the comfortable Bianchet hut (1,245 metres).

NINTH DAY

*from the Bianchet hut
to the Settimo Alpini hut
distance climbed: 1150 metres
distance descended: 950 metres
time: 7 hours*

This is the stage of the Schiara: a splendid route, abounding in sensational panoramic vistas, but which demands experience in making one's way over lengthy and lofty equipped trails (as much as seven hundred metres of vertical distance!), with climbing passages. Otherwise, an alternative route — which we recommend to everyone, no matter how experienced, if the weather turns foul — involves a descent from the hut to the paved road, which requires one-and-a-half hours. Walkers with a very sure foot are encouraged to climb up to the peak of the Schiara. One begins by climbing back up to the main trail, and to the nearby mountain summer meadow of Casonèt de Nerville (1,641 metres), from which one climbs steeply toward the Forcella di Nerville. Stopping short of it, one crosses a hollow, and climbs over small rocks, still snow-covered in early summer, to the Forcella del Marmòl (2,262 metres) which separates the Schiara from the Pèlf. From the pass, a remarkable and deeply moving vantage-point, one climbs up to the right over small rocks all the way to the fork for the peak of the Schiara (2,565 metres, two hours, round trip, an easy and lovely route, but very lofty). In short order, one reaches the campground of the Màrmol (2,280 metres). One begins to climb down over lesser walls and gullies; one climbs a chimney 70 metres tall, and climbs down at length over easy but treacherous terrain, entering the gully that climbs up to the Ferrata Zacchi. Along this latter feature, with very lofty but well equipped trails, one climbs down again as far as the scree that are reached (1,870 metres) in the area around the grotto of the Portòn. A trail leads to the Settimo Alpini hut (1,498 metres).

TENTH DAY
from the Settimo Alpini hut
to Bolzano Bellunese
distance climbed: 50 metres
distance descended: 1000 metres
time: 3 hours

The final descent down to Bolzano Bellunese and the provincial capital is an enchanting voyage through the typical landscape of the Bellunese Dolomites, which have been under the protection of a National Park since 1991. One walks through a limestone ravine, down which the trail runs, switching back and forth from one wall to the other. It is possible to begin the day with a climb up to Mount Pelf (2,502 metres, four hours, round trip) to a vantage-point which can be reached from the hut via marked trails. The main trail runs down through a

series of switchbacks (known to those who climb it as "Mount Calvary"), then reaches the valley floor of the river Ardo, continuing for a great distance along this river, which abounds in little falls and rapids. A sharper descent brings one down to village Mariano

(681 metres), where the ruins of a building stand. One continues through the woods to the Case Bortot (694 metres), and from there four kilometres of paved road running downhill brings one to Bolzano Bellunese (520 metres), which is in turn linked to the provincial capital by regularly scheduled buses.

THE DOLOMITE HIGH ROUTE No 4

Along the High Route of Grohmann
from the Sesto Dolomites to the
great massifs of Cadore and
to Pieve

162 top The lake of Sorapiss, at an altitude of 1,923 metres, offers one of the most relaxing experiences to be had along the High Route. Nearby is the Vandelli hut; overhead loom the Dito di Dio and the glaciers of the north slope of the Sorapiss. Photograph by Marco Milani K/3

162 bottom Seen from the Sasso di Sesto, the Tre Cime di Lavaredo (Cima Piccola 2857 metres, Cima Grande 2999 metres, Cima Ovest 2973 metres) seem to float upon an ocean of fog. To the left is thr ridge of the Paterno (2,744 metres). Photograph by L. Collinet/ Agence Freestyle

164 The historical central area of San Candido stands at an elevation of 1,174 metres and is one of the most enchanting in all of Alto Adige. This picture was taken near the source of the river Drava, and therefore within the watershed of the Danube. Photograph by Stefano Ardito

The crowding and the views of the easy trails around the Tre Cime, the authentic wilderness and the demanding trails of the route that zigzags among the "giants of the Cadore," the massifs of the Sorapiss and the Antelao that form — together with the Marmarole — one of the most pristine areas in all the Dolomites. If the High Routes, No 1 and 2 require that the walker spend a week or more to move from the celebrated, classical areas on to the truly wild peaks of the Schiara, the Tamer, and the Vette Feltrine, here — in contrast — the transition is exceedingly rapid. In the middle of it all, the group of the Cadini di Misurina is one of the most

astonishing sights in the Dolomites: abounding in spires, great towers, spectacular, wild high valleys that demand a day set aside just for them, perhaps with a rest in the pleasant Fonda-Savio and Città di Carpi huts. In technical terms, this High Route is more difficult than many others. The ledges and the slabs that one will encounter in any walk around the Sorapiss and the Antelao demand to be sure-footed and experienced in mountain walking and scrambling on rock. Should one encounter bad weather, especially in the area around the rest point Comici, the routes down are lengthy and anything but easy. On the plus side, the environment is truly pristine, impressive, and wild, with the cirques and glaciers of the Sorapiss and the Antelao, creating a blend of the vertical beauty of the Dolomites with the glaciers and deep snowy gullies that remind those of the Western Alps. Like the nearby High Route No 5, which traverses the Marmarole, the High Route No 4 ends at Pieve di Cadore, the little town where the great Renaissance artist Titian was born. This trail was conceived in 1966 by Mario Brovelli and was marked out on-site by Brovelli himself, with the assistance of Toni Hiebeler, Sigi Lechner, Piero Rossi, and, especially, by Antonio Sanmarchi and Franz Pangerls. It was dedicated to Paul Grohmann, one of the leading figures in the mountaineering exploration of the Dolomites, a remarkable character who has, unfortunately, been widely ignored by Italian mountain climbers. Born in Vienna in 1838, Grohmann first began to visit the Dolomites in 1862, after first catching sight of their "enchanting silhouettes" from high atop the distant ridges of the Hohe Tauern. In 1862, Grohmann made the second ascent of the Marmolata, while in the following year he was the first to climb the Antelao and the Tofana di Rozes, as well as being the first to follow the route established by John Ball up the Pelmo. In 1864, the Viennese climber conquered Cristallino di Misurina, one of the loveliest peaks

of the massif of the Cristallo, and then went on to climb the summit of the Sorapiss. On the descent from the Sorapiss, in the brief sheer vertical chimney which constitutes the most difficult passage of the route, the guides Lacedelli and Dimai executed the first rappel descent climbing history. In the years that followed, Grohmann added to the list of his achievements the main peak of the Cristallo, the Tre Scarperi, the Sassolungo, and the Cima Grande di Lavaredo. He was, in short, the most important figure in the era of great mountain conquests, the Dolomites' equivalent of the great English climber, Edward Whymper. In 1875 Grohmann bade farewell to the Dolomites. Two years later, at the foot of the Antelao and the Sorapiss, climbing in the Dolomites entered a new phase. Luigi Cesaletti, a guide from San Vito di Cadore, made a solo climb up the Torre dei Sabbioni — widely known as the "Corno del Doge" — the first to be conquered of the lesser, particularly jagged peaks. This marked the beginning of the phase during which the Campanile Basso di Brenta, the Torri del Vajolet, the Campanile di Val Montanaia, and the other great monoliths in the region became the true problems set to be solved by a new generation of adventurers. The history here, however, is only in part that of the allure of these mountains.
A considerable portion of the walkers, walkers, and climbers — among them, the author of this book — encountered for the first time the Pale Mounts in their most famous peaks: the Brenta, the Tre Cime, the massifs of the Catinaccio, the Sella, the Marmolata, and the Pale. Even for mountaineers that have worked through hundreds of days on the faces and trails of the Dolomites, a visit to the great and savage massifs of the Antelao, the Marmarole, and the Sorapiss is always an opportunity to discover something new. And for that reason, the ongoing battle of the Comitato, which has been demanding for years that a Regional Park be established, deserves to be crowned with success.

Sillian

AUSTRIA

Dobbiaco

S. Candido

Western Alps

Mt. Elmo

Val Pusteria

Carnic Alps

Dobbiaco

DOLOMITES
OF SESTO
NATURAL
PARK

Sesto

BRAIES
NATURAL PARK

Tre Scarperi Peak

Croda Rossa

Dolomites

Tre Cime
di Lavaredo

Cadini di Misurina

Cristallo

Misurina

Misurina

Auronzo

Tre Croci Pass

Val di Ansiei

S. Caterina

Cortina d'Ampezzo

Sorapiss

Cadore

Sorapiss

Group of the Marmarole

MT. PELMO-
MONDEVAL-
GIAU PASS
NATURAL RESERVE

Mt. Tranego

Pieve
di Cadore

Antelao

Pieve di Cadore

ITALY

Valley of Boite

USEFUL INFORMATION

Duration: 6 days.

Elevations: ranging from the 880 metres of Pieve di Cadore to the 2,624 metres of the Forcella del Nevaio.

Season: from July to September.

Signage: local trailmarkers are white and red, and very infrequently one sees the triangles of the High Route.

Degree of difficulty: the High Route No 4 is one of the shortest and at the same time one of the most technically demanding routes in the Dolomites, with difficult equipped stretches and climbing up rocks (both climbing and descending) that range up to the second degree.

How demanding: average. The stages, though they do run over treacherous ground, are not particularly lengthy.

Equipment: normal walking gear, with harness, short rope, screw gate karabiner and abseil device for the equipped stretches, as well as a length of rope to secure the less experienced. Ice axe useful year round.

Peaks: experienced walkers can climb the Paterno (2,746 metres), a splendid vantage-point over the Tre Cime. In order to reach the Cima Grande di Lavaredo (2,999 metres), the Sorapiss (3,205 metres), and the Antelao (3,263 metres) it would be wise to be accompanied by a guide.

How to get there: San Candido can be reached by train (the railroad line Bressanone-Brunico-Dobbiaco-Lienz) or by bus from Bolzano, Cortina d'Ampezzo, or from Austria, or else by car from Bressanone, Cortina d'Ampezzo, or from Austria (Lienz) along the border at Prato alla Drava or from Cadore via the pass of M. Croce Comelico. From Pieve di Cadore one can take a train (line for Belluno and Venice), or else a bus toward Cortina d'Ampezzo, Belluno, or Venice.

How to get around: bus from the Auronzo hut to Misurina and from Misurina and from the pass of Tre Croci to Auronzo and Cortina.

Overnight Accommodations: huts of the CAI, AVS or private operators, hotels and bed-and-breakfasts at the beginning and the end.

If you want to camp out: camping is forbidden on the valley and in the Park of the Dolomites of Sesto, and made more difficult at high elevations by the rocky terrain. We recommend against it.

Alpine Guides: Alpine guide group at Cortina (39) (436) 868505.

Weather Forecasts: contact the tourist bureaus.

Mountain Rescue: dial 118, in the province of Belluno, call the headquarters of the CNSA in Pieve di Cadore (39) (435) 33118.

Information Offices: Tourist Bureau of San Candido (39) (474) 73149, Tourist Bureau of Misurina (39) (436) 39016, Tourist Bureau of S. Vito di Cadore (39) (436) 9119, Tourist Bureau of Pieve di Cadore (39) (435) 31644

Useful phone numbers: Tre Scarperi hut (39) (474) 966610, Locatelli hut (39) (474) 72002, Lavaredo hut (39) (436) 39135, Auronzo hut (39) (436) 39002, Fonda-Savio hut (39) (436) 39036, Città di Carpi hut (39) (436) 39139, Vandelli hut (39) (436) 39015, San Marco hut (39) (436) 9444, Galassi hut (39) (436) 9685, Antelao hut (39) (435) 75333.

Guide Books: *Klettersteig, Scrambles in the Northern Limestone Alps* by Paul Werner - equipped ways in the limestone alps of Austria /Germany; *Via Ferrata, Scrambles in the Dolomites* by Hofler & Paul Werner (Cicerone Press).

Maps: Kompass 1:50,000 n. 58 *Dolomiti di Sesto*, n. 55 *Cortina d'Ampezzo* and n. 77 *Dolomiti Bellunesi*; Tabacco 1:50,000 n. 1 and 4, Tabacco 1:25,000 n. 010 *Dolomiti di Sesto*, 03 *Cortina d'Ampezzo e Dolomiti Ampezzane* and n. 016 *Dolomiti del Centro Cadore*; Geo Grafica 1:25,000 n. 2 and 4, IGM 1:25,000 Dobbiaco, *Tre Cime di Lavaredo, Lago di Misurina, Monte Antelao*, and *Pieve di Cadore*.

.

FIRST DAY

From San Candido to the Locatelli hut
Distance climbed: 1,080 metres
Distance descended: 50 metres
Time: 4 hours

A lovely place in which to become acquainted with the Dolomites of Sesto, the Val Campodidentro is one of the most pleasant valleys in this section of the Pale Mounts, and offers an excellent walk in the shadow of the frowning Cima dei Tre Scarperi.
The steep final climb leads up to the Locatelli hut, a renowned observation point viewing the Tre Cime, but also one of the most crowded sites in the entire range of the Dolomites.
This climb can be completed quite easily in the course of a day, even if one begins from the foot of San Candido. If one reaches the area in the evening,

one can simply stay overnight in the pleasant Tre Scarperi hut, operated by the AVS of Bolzano. From the town of San Candido (Innichen, 1,174 metres) one follows the road leading to Sesto-Sexten for a distance of three-and-a-half kilometres: this distance can also be covered by bus. Either on foot, in a taxi, or by hitchhiking, one then continues along the dirt road of the Val Campodidentro (Innerfeldtal) all the way up to where this dirt road is sealed off with a crossbar (1,500 metres). A short climb takes one up to the handsome plateau of the Tre Scarperi hut (Dreischusterhutte, 1,626 metres). One continues along the plateau, and then one climbs up into the high valley of the Rio di San Candido (Innichbach). The trail climbs to the

166 top left At an altitude of 2405 metres, the Locatelli hut is a remarkable vantage-point over the northern walls of the Tre Cime. The High Route crosses

it after a steep climb to the foot of the Tre Scarperi and of the other peaks of the Sesto Dolomites. Photograph by F. Raiser/K3

166 top right The crowded trail that leads from the Lavaredo hut and the Auronzo hut, at the foot of the Spigolo

Giallo and the southern walls of the Tre Cime, is one of the best known in the Dolomites, as well as being an

excellent vantage-point over the entire chain of the Cadini di Misurina. Photograph by Franz Hauleitner

right, along steep scree, and then it crosses a mountain stream and climbs sharply up to the Pass of the Alpe Mattina (Gwengalpenjoch, 2,446 metres), where one can see the Tre Cime. With a great deal of climbing and descending one can reach the Locatelli hut (Dreizinnenhutte, 2,405 metres), a handsome point of observation for the north face. The day is completed with a walk to the foot of the faces or an exploration of the relics of the First World War, around the Torre di Toblin.

SECOND DAY

*from the Locatelli hut
to the Fonda-Savio hut
distance climbed: 490 metres
distance descended: 560 metres
time: 4 hours 30 minutes*

This is a stage with two differing personalities, ranging from the crowded trails and huts that surround the Tre Cime to the solitary and rock-

of the Cima Ovest. From the Forcella Col di Mezzo (2,315 metres) one quickly reaches the chaotic parking area of the Auronzo hut (2,320 metres). As an alternative to that route, one can walk obliquely along the slope to Forcella Lavaredo (2,457 metres), and then climb down to the hut of the same name (2,344 metres), then continuing onward to the Auronzo hut along a dirt road. Still more interesting is a tour of the wartime tunnels that cross the Paterno. In any case, one continues onward through the meadows of Forcella Longères, and then one follows the Bonacossa trail; this trail follows a war ledge with equipped stretches. Then comes a descent (ropes and ladders), followed by a high equipped ledge, which leads to the Forcella di Rinbianco. A final climb takes one to the Tocci Pass and to the Fonda-Savio hut (2,367 metres), nicely located in the heart of the Cadini.

THIRD DAY

*from the Fonda-Savio hut
to the Vandelli hut
distance climbed: 900 metres
distance descended: 1,270 metres
time: 7 hours*

This is a long stage, which the more contemplative walkers may choose to split up into two parts, in order to enjoy at their leisure the view of the massif of the Cadini. If one does so, one may choose to sleep either at the Città di Carpi hut or at the Cristallo hut, on the state road 48. Also handsome is the Cirque of the Sorapiss, which one reaches at day's end. One begins by climbing (over snowfields or scree) the broad hollow of the Cadin del Nevaio, and at the far end of that, one climbs (using metal cables) up to the high Forcella del Nevaio (2,624 metres). One descends over small rocks to the Forcella Verzi (2,550 metres), and then proceeds

girt massif of the Cadini di Misurina, one of the most astonishing areas in the Dolomites. At the beginning of this stage, it is possible to choose between the trail that runs around the Tre Cime from the north and the west and the other trail, to Forcella Lavaredo, which allows the walker to view the wartime tunnels of Paterno. From the hut, the "official" route of the High Route skips the trails to Forcella Lavaredo entirely, and sticks to a trail that runs down into a deep valley, emerging on the uplands of Grava Longa (Lange Alpe), in the shadow

166 bottom
The Cadini massif overlooks Città di Carpi hut (2,110 metres).
Behind it, one can make out the Cima Eotvos (2,825 metres), the Cima Cadin San Lucano (2,839 metres), and the Cima Cadin di nord-est (2,788 metres).
Photograph by Franz Hauleitner

along a daunting — but actually fairly easy — gully, partly equipped, all the way to the scree of the Ciadin delle Pere. In short order, one reaches the Città di Carpi hut (2,110 metres). An easy trail leads to two forks in the paths (the trails that run off to the right lead to Col de Varda and Misurina) and then one descends to the state road 48, not far from the hotel Cristallo (1,368 metres). A little track runs among the woods of Valbona and then reaches a handsome uphill trail that leads to the Vandelli hut (1,928 metres) and to the Lake of Sorapiss. As an alternative, one can climb down to Misurina, taking a bus to the Pass of Tre Croci, and then following the classic trail to the hut.

FOURTH DAY

from the Vandelli hut
to the San Marco hut
distance climbed: 880 metres
distance descended: 830 metres
time: 7 hours

This is a lengthy stage, which completes the tour around the Sorapiss from the east. This trip can be broken up by an overnight stay at the Comici camping area. The route includes some of the loftiest and most treacherous passages of the High Route, over ledges and not always equipped lofty walls. The environment is truly untouched and is already a foreshadowing of that of the "giants of the Cadore," while around Forcella Grande it is possible to sight ibex. There is a lovely view of the Torre dei Sabbioni, one of the first Dolomitic spires to be climbed by a human. One begins by climbing up toward the moraines of the eastern glacier of the Sorapiss; then one traverses a treacherous gully, and then continues along the Ferrata Vandelli. One continues along not equipped small rocks all the way to the crest of the Croda del Fogo (2,200 metres). A ledge leads one to the Comici camping area (2,000 metres), whence one continues along the Minazio trail, which is less exposed but also not equipped. After crossing the Busa del Banco, one climbs up to the Forcella Alta del Banco (2,260 metres), continuing along a ledge to the Valle San Vito (2,000 metres). This valley can then be climbed all the way up to the Forcella Grande (2,255 metres), where one can look out over the Antelao. One then climbs down a steep, difficult valley to the San Marco hut (1,823 metres).

FIFTH DAY

from the San Marco hut
to the Antelao hut
distance climbed: 1,070 metres
distance descended: 1,090 metres
time: 6 hours

Another demanding stage, which features the crossing of the Forcella del Ghiacciaio, on boulders that are quite slick and require great care. As a variant, it is pleasurable, advisable, and anything but trivial to take the standard route of the Antelao (3,264 metres, 6-7 hours round trip), with long stretches of first and second degree climbing up. The environment of the north slope of the Antelao is quite unusual. One begins with the trail that runs down into the woods, traverses under the Cima Bel Pra and Cima Scotter, and then climbs up to Forcella Piccola (2,120 metres). From here, one climbs down to the Galassi hut (2,010 metres). One begins to climb up again along a trail that leads to the moraine of the western glacier of the Antelao, and then one reaches the Lastrone del Plan dei Arboi, a smooth equipped wall with fixed ropes and second degree stretches. After reaching the Forcella del Ghiacciaio (2,524 metres), one climbs down along ramps and small ledges to the high valley of the Antelao. Another uphill stretch takes one to the Forcella Piria (2,096 metres), and from here one travels with a great deal of climbing and descending to the Antelao hut (1,796 metres), an excellent vantage point on the Marmarole.

SIXTH DAY

from the Antelao hut
to the Pieve di Cadore
distance climbed: 50 metres
distance descended: 970 metres
time: 2 hours 30 minutes

The final descent toward Pieve di Cadore, birthplace of the Renaissance artist Titian follows a long and quite pleasant dirt road, running largely through the woods. One should follow this road all the way to Forcella Antracisa (1,693 metres) and to the Pancera hut. From here one can remain on the road that runs around Mount Tranego, descending through Pozzale (1,054 metres), and on to Pieve di Cadore (880 metres), or else one can follow the marked trail, which is shorter but less well-marked, along the Val Marilongo and the Costa Nuda.

167 top The San Marco hut, standing at an elevation of 1,823 metres, at the base of the Sorapiss, opens its doors to the walkers who have just made the exhausting descent from the Forcella Grande. This place is known as the "Col da chi da os," which means in Venetian the "Col of those who live behind".
Photograph by
Stefano Ardito

167 bottom The dramatic northern slope of the Antelao (3,263 metres) is shown in a photograph taken from the Galassi hut, the base-camp for the climb up to the peak. Here begins one of the most demanding stretches of the High Route, which runs eastward around the Antelao, with passages of considerable exposure.
Photograph by
Franz Hauleitner

THROUGH THE CARNIC ALPS

From the source of the river Piave to the great forests of the Tarvisio, and the foot of the majestic peaks of the Carnic Alps

168 The impressive southern faces of the Gamspitz (1,847 metres), an elegant peak that stands just south of the border chain, looms over Timau and the valley of the But. In the foreground stands a group of distinctive wooden shepherds' huts, at the foot of the Gamspitz.
Photograph by Marco Milani/K3

"The Carnic Alps would be a softer version of the Julian Alps, if it were not for the fact that so great a rocky peak as the Cianevate (also known as the Kellerwand, 2,775 metres); if this mountain were located near a tourist resort, it would be as well known and as frequently climbed as the better known peaks of Sesto or Cortina... More than any other peaks, I have always been attracted by the Creta Grauzaria, which looms over the Aupa valley, and that great hulk of the Sernio, both peaks raising their white boulders high into the blue sky. The Carnic waters splash away, and the valleys lie green and verdant. The edelweiss blooms on the mountain meadows, and in my heart, full and solemn, ring the bells of Paularo."
It is not easy, in the literature of the Alps and Alpinism, to find pages devoted to the savage crests, the green valleys, and the rocky faces of the Carnic Alps that mark the boundary between Italy's Friuli and Austria's

Carinthia. The words that we have quoted are taken from *From a Mountain Climber's Life*, the best known work by Julius Kugy. Only rarely, however, did the mountain climber and author, born in Gorizia and a long-time resident of Trieste, a great lover and explorer of the Julian Alps, venture up among the Carnic peaks that lie so close to "his" mountains. Later, too, and on both faces, very little has been written about these mountains. The Carnic Alps are overshadowed by the nearby Dolomites, to the west, and by the Julian Alps, to the south-east. And yet, this border-straddling range is absolutely spectacular, and is worth a tour by walkers and mountain climbers alike. Boulders, watercourses, little glaciers, glaciers, forests, all make it a destination of considerable interest. To the west, around the source of the river Piave, rise the limestone peaks of the Peralba and the Avanza, joined to the south by the massifs of the Terze, the Creta Forata, and Tudaio. Here, the long chain of the southern Carnic Alps extends southward (these are also known as the Dolomiti d'Oltre Piave), stretching all the way to the forests and high plateaus of the Cansiglio, including surprising and spectacular peaks such as the Campanile di Val Montanaia. To the east of the Peralba, the powerful mass of the Coglians, rising to an elevation of 2,780 metres is the tallest and the most spectacular of them all. Thousands of walkers and climbers come here every summer along the easy standard route from the south, and along the more difficult route, from Austria, or via one or another of the many rock climbing routes. At the foot of the peak, which was scaled for the first time in 1865 by Paul Grohmann with two Friulian guides, lies Volaia Lake, one of the most handsome lakes in the limestone Alps. To the south, other solitary massifs stand alongside the Coglians. To the east, beyond the pass of Monte Croce Carnico, as the Italians call it (the Austrians call it the

168-169 From the pass of Monte Croce Carnico, through which passes the road that runs from Tolmezzo to Lienz, one can admire the mighty bulk of the Cogliàns, which is the highest mountain in all the Carnic Alps, at 2,780 metres.
Photograph by Marco Milani/K3

Plockenpass), stand the splendid and little-known massifs of the Creta di Timau, the Avostanis, the Pal Grande, and the Pal Piccolo. Grassy on many of the faces, these mountains have walls of solid, sheer rocks, the goal of some of the finest climbing exploits to grace this mountain chain. It is harsh and sunny on the Italian faces, while the Austrian faces are gentler and are mantled with beautiful woods, as is the valley of the Gail; from here the chain continues to other major peaks — in particular, the Creta d'Aip and the Cavallo di Pontebba — all the way to the pass of Pramollo. And here things change. Gentler, grassier, or woodier, almost all the way up to the summits, the Sinauz and the Poludnig, the Oisternig and the Sagràn promise no great adventures to climbers. Here a walker with classic tastes will find splendid routes and vast vistas

while climbing up to the peaks, while those who prefer excitement can explore — on the Italian faces — the full-fledged wilderness of the high valleys of Malborghetto and Rio Bianco, protected by small but important State nature reserves. The fauna here, which includes eagles, chamois, and bears which returned on their own from the Slovenian Triglav park, is another major attraction in this area. Respectively to the north and the south of the crest of the Carnic Alps run two of the most interesting and least well known of the great Alpine trails. The Karnischer Hohenweg, on the Austrian face of the chain, was the brainchild of Walther Schaumann, and created during the Sixties with the assistance of the Austrian Alpine Club, the Austrian army, and a few industrial groups. At that time, many huts were either renovated or built

brand new. Faced with a lack of funds, work on the Italian faces led in 1975 and 1976 to the completion of the Traversata Carnica by Ettore Tomasi, Sergio De Infanti, and other mountain climbers in the region. The routes converge in many points, and have a number of resting points in common; they allow walkers to mix and match their routes, passing from one trail to the other, and taking advantage of the many detours. The route that we describe here makes use freely of both parallel trails, and also coincides, between the lake of Volaia and the Casera Pramosio, with the Carnia Walking, created in the Eighties by the local chapter of the Italian Alpine Club, with help from the Carnic Mountain Community. We believe that it is the finest possible introduction to one of the most entrancing and least well known corners of the Alps.

USEFUL INFORMATION

Duration: 10 days.
Elevations: ranging from the 750 metres of Tarvisio to the 2,780 metres of the Monte Coglians.
Season: from July to the first weeks of October.
Signage: white and red for the Karnischer Hohenweg, the Carnic Crossing, the Carnia Walking, and local trails.
Degree of difficulty: brief and easy equipped trails on the climbs (it is possible to avoid them) up to the Peralba and the Coglians; the principal route is quite easy.
How demanding: average.
Equipment: for walking, with an ice axe in the early season.
Peaks: the peaks of the Peralba (2,694 metres) and the Coglians (2,780 metres) lie along the base-trail, and can be reached along easy standard routes with short equipped passages. The same is true of the Monte Lodin (2,015 metres) and the Oisternig (2,052 metres). Among the many peaks that can be reached via

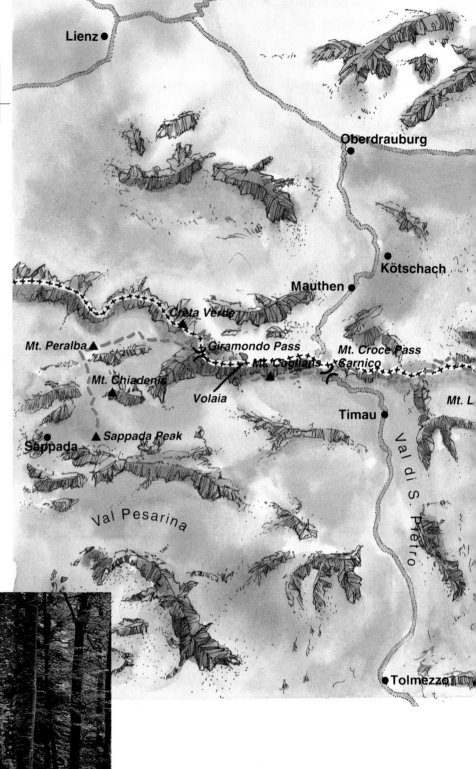

slight detours, we should mention the Avanza (2,489 metres), the Pal Piccolo (1,866 metres), the Creta di Timau (2,217 metres), and the Poludnig (1,999 metres).
How to get there: Sappada can be reached by bus from the railroad stations of Calalzo di Cadore (where the line that runs from Venice terminates) and San Candido (railroad line Bressanone-Lienz). Tarvisio is on the railroad line Udine-Villach-Vienna.

How to get around: regularly scheduled buses to the pass of Monte Croce Carnico (via Mauthen and Tolmezzo) and to the pass of Pramollo in the direction of Pontebba and Hermagor. There are many other possibilities for those who choose to descend to the valley and leave the route.
Overnight accommodations: huts of the CAI, the OEAV, and private owners, bed-and-breakfasts and little mountain hotels.

If you want to camp out: the relatively gentle climbs and descents and the absence of any restrictions make it possible to backpack.
Alpine Guides: (43) 4715-8358.
Weather Forecasts: Guardia forestale (39) (428) 2471 or tourist bureaus.
Mountain Rescue: in Venetia call the headquarters of the Mountain Rescue of Pieve di Cadore (39) (435) 33118, in Friuli all the stations of Forni Avoltri (39) (433) 72022, Moggio Udinese

170 As one
proceeds eastward,
the forests of Carnia
become thicker and
more spectacular.
In this picture, two
walkers are seen
walking in the
enchanting forests of
the Tarvisiano.
Photograph by
Gianluca Boetti

171 The towering
Pic Chiadenis, seen
here from the
verdant Val Fleons,
rises directly facing
the better known
peaks of the Avanza
and the Peralba,
and can be reached
from the Calvi hut
via a lofty and
spectacular trail.
Photograph by
Ulderica Da Pozzo

(39) (433) 51599 e Cave del Predil (39) (428) 68055; for the Austrian side call Kotschach-Mauthen (43) (4715) 8243, Hermagor (43) (4282) 5385, and mountain rescue in Tarvisio (39) (428) 2013.

Information Offices: Tourist Bureau of Sappada (39) (435) 469131, ATP (Local Bureau of Tourism) Chamber of Carnia (39) (433) 929290, Tourist Bureau of Tarvisio (39) (428) 2135, Tourist Bureau of Kotschach-Mauthen (43)(4715) 8516, Tourist Bureau of Hermagor (43) (4282) 2043.

Useful phone numbers: Calvi hut (39) (435) 469232, Eduard-Pichl hut (43) (4719) 244, Lambertenghi-Romanin hut (39) (433) 72017, Marinelli hut (39) (433) 779177, Steinewender hut, for

information contact the APT (43) (4715) 590, Egger Alm (43)(4284) 287, Dellacher Alm, contact the Tourist Bureau of Dellach (43)(4282) 270516, Whirthaus Starhand, Whirthaus Oisternig, there is no telephone, Nordio hut (39) (428) 60045, Goriacher Alm, there is no telephone.

Guide Books: *The Kalkalpen Traverse* by Alan Proctor (Cicerone Press) - the limestone alps bordering Austria and Germany.

Maps: Tabacco 1:25,000 n. 01 *Sappada-Forni Avoltri*, n. 02 *Forni di Sopra e Forni di Sotto*, n. 08 *Carnic Alps and Western Julian Alps*. Likewise Tabacco is the *Carta dei Sentieri della Carnia*, edited by Attilio De Rovere.

FIRST DAY

*From Sappada to the Calvi hut
distance climbed: 870 metres
distance descended: 500 metres
time: 4 hours*

The first day of this walking route is devoted to climbing the Peralba, a splendid limestone peak that looks out over the source of the river Piave. If one is not interested in reaching the summit, and if one reaches Sappada reasonably early, it is possible to continue directly on toward the lake of Volaia, part of the subsequent stage. One begins at Sappada (1,217 metres), climbing by taxi or by hitchiking to the hut of the source of the river Piave (1,830 metres). A trail and then a dirt road lead up to the Calvi hut (2,167 metres). One continues to the nearby Pass of Sesis (2,312 metres), where the fairly easy standard route begins, climbing up (short equipped passages) along the north ridge of the Peralba all the way to the peak (2,694 metres). Here, the view is interesting both toward the Dolomites of Sesto and the Carnic massif. Along the same route, one can climb back down to the pass and to the hut.

SECOND DAY

*From the Calvi hut to Volaia Lake
distance climbed: 900 metres
distance descended: 710 metres
time: 6 hours*

This stage brings one to the foot of the massif of the Coglians, the destination for the following day. The evergreen woods are magnificent, as are the views from the Pass of Giramondo and the nearby lake of Bordaglia, and there is a splendid atmosphere in the cirque that surrounds the Volaia Lake. The Eduard-Pichl hut and the Lambertenghi-Romanin hut are just a few minutes' walk away from each other. One begins by returning to the pass of Sesis (2,312 metres), and from here one descends into the Val Fleons, until one reaches the Upper Casera Fleons (1,864 metres). At a fork, one leaves the dirt road toward Pierabec, and one continues along among woods, passing the Lower Casera Fleons (1,500 metres). One passes by the Lake of Bordaglia, and then one climbs up to the Giramondo Pass (2,005 metres), coming down onto the Austrian faces. Back in the woods again, one crosses to the Obere Volayer Alp (1,709 metres). From here, one climbs up to the Eduard-Pichl hut (1,959 metres), overlooking the lake of Volaia and the dramatic north face of the Coglians. After walking around the lake, one can easily reach the Lambertenghi-Romanin hut (1,970 metres).

THIRD DAY

*from Volaia Lake to the Marinelli hut
distance climbed: 950 metres
distance descended: 780 metres
time: 6 hours*

With panoramic vistas, the summit of the Coglians should have a day all to itself. We advise climbing up along the easy standard route from the south, following the route established in 1865 by Paul Grohmann, with his guides Sottocorona and Hofer: experienced walkers may also choose to climb up the scrambling trail on the north side, which includes long stretches of second degree, and requires ice axes and crampons at the beginning of the season. From the Lambertenghi-Romanin hut, one follows for a short distance the mule-track leading to Collina, and then one proceeds along the face down the Sentiero Spinotti (short equipped passages), which crosses a grassy shoulder (2,200 metres) and then drops down into the broad high valley of Ploto, which cuts across the southern face of the Coglians. One can climb this valley all the way up to the easy rocks of the summit (2,780 metres), where one can gaze out across the Dolomites and the Gross Glockner, the Julian Alps, and the plains of Friuli. After climbing back down the gully, one finds a trail running along the face that leads to the ridge of the Pic Chiadin and on to the Marinelli hut (2,111 metres).

172 A view of Sappada, the friendly little village at an elevation of 1,217 metres, which lies in the northeastern corner of Venetia. This is the starting point for the Traversata Carnica and for our route.
Photograph by Ulderica Da Pozzo

173 top Today
criss-crossed by a
dozen routes and
by a classic via
ferrata, the north
face of Cogliàns
was first scaled in
1895, by Hans
Kofler.
Photograph by
Attilio De Rovere

173 bottom At an
elevation of 1,959
metres, the Eduard
Pichl hut overlooks
the dark waters of
the Volaia lake.
Here, at the base of
the imposing north
face of Cogliàns,
about sixty people
can spend the
night.
Photograph by
Stefano Ardito

FOURTH DAY

*from the Marinelli hut
to Casera Pramosio
distance climbed: 1,150 metres
distance descended: 1,750 metres
time: 6 hours 30 minutes*

A long and interesting stage, that allows one to leave behind the massif of Cogliàns, to cross the pass of Mount Croce Carnico, and to proceed to the foot of the handsome peaks of the Pal Piccolo and Grande, Avostanis, and the Creta di Timau. There is a very nice grassy hollow, in the middle of which stands the Casera Pramosio. One descends to the little lake of Plotta and on to the Casera Monumentz, crossing through the distinctive landscape of the "Scaletta," and then one descends to the pass of Mount Croce Carnico (1,360 metres, hotel), which is crossed by a road that links Tolmezzo with Mauthen and Kotschach. A short descent on the paved road on the Italian face leads to an intersection, from which a long and handsome mule-track leads obliquely along the face to the foot of the summits of the Pal Piccolo, the Cuelat, and the Pal Grande. After crossing the pass of the Pal Grande (1,760 metres), one returns to Austria, crossing over the saddle of Avostanis as well (2,093 metres); from here, it is a short trip, along the grassy crest, to the summit of the Avostanis (2,193 metres, half-an-hour, round-trip), and then one descends to the little lake of Avostanis (1,936 metres), to the Casera Malpasso, and to the Casera Pramosio Bassa (1,521 metres).

FIFTH DAY

*from Casera Pramosio to Straniger Alp
distance climbed: 650 metres
distance descended: 620 metres
time: 5 hours*

While the peaks of the Carnic Alps become gentler and easier, the further eastward one goes, one can return to the Austrian face, which here abounds in forests and pastures, many of which offer lodgings or sleeping quarters. One begins along the route that was followed the previous day, and then one turns to the right and one climbs along the trail that leads to the pass of Pramosio (1,788 metres); beyond that, one descends to the Zollner See and to the Steinewender hut (1,720 metres). One sets off again, crossing Mount Lodin (2,015 metres), a variant trail allows one to circle around it, to the north, and descending from there to the Straniger Alp (1,492 metres), in the midst of a splendid array of meadows.

SIXTH DAY

*from Straniger Alp to Pass of Pramollo
distance climbed: 950 metres
distance descended: 900 metres
time: 6 hours*

This is a fairly long stage, with a great deal of climbing and descending, remaining always quite close to the mountain crest, with a view toward the end of the day of the rocky Mount Cavallo of Pontebba. One begins by climbing up to the edge of the woods, until one reaches a fork in the way (1,752 metres), followed by a saddle (2,017 metres) linking the Hochwipfel — one can quickly reach the summit (2,186 metres) with a slight detour — and the Creta di Lanza. A descent here takes one to the Zankl hut (1,606 metres) and on down to the Rattendorfer Alp (1,531 metres). Another climb running obliquely along the face takes one around the

Zweikofel and on to the ski area surrounding the Rudnig Alp (1,622 metres). From here, the classic route along the *Karnischer Hohenweg* along a dirt road and then on a trail continues obliquely along the face toward the Nassfeld hut and the Pass of Pramollo. We would definitely advise one to climb up along a well-marked trail to the Saddle of Aip (1,942 metres) and to the nearby rest point of Lomasti. A steep descent — on the right, the standard route of Mount Cavallo di Pontebba, cuts away — leads to the meadows of the Pass of Pramollo (1,552 metres), the centre for a ski area.

SEVENTH DAY

from Pass of Pramollo to Egger Alm
distance climbed: 450 metres
distance descended: 570 metres
time: 4 hours 30 minutes

This is a short and pleasant stage, which leads from the ski area that lies in the shadow of the Gartnerkofel, on to the lovely grassy expanses around the Egger Alm, again set in an enchanting and unspoilt landscape. One begins by climbing up to the Gartner Sattel (or Guggajoch, 1,863 metres), beyond which one climbs down to the Garnitzer Alm (1,624 metres). One continues along through a splendid fir tree wood, then one

EIGHTH DAY

from Egger Alm
to the Nordio-Deffar hut
distance climbed: 560 metres
distance descended: 670 metres
time: 5 hours 30 minutes

A pleasant and relaxed stage, deep in the forest vastness which blankets the northern faces of the mountains of Poludnig, Sagran, and Oisternig. For those who collect peaks, so to say, one can begin the day by climbing to the summit of Mount Poludnig (1,999 metres, 2 hours 30 minutes extra, round trip). One begins among the lovely meadows that lead on to the Dellacher Alp (1,365 metres) and

174 This picture shows the broad summit crest of Monte Cròstis, a solitary peak 1,894 metres tall that looms just to the south of the dramatic Zuc dal Boor, overlooking Chiusaforte and the deep Valley of the Fella.
Photograph by Marco Milani/K3

175 top The rocks of the Pal Piccolo (1,866 metres) are criss-crossed by climbing routes; the Traversata Carnica runs around the base. In the background. beyond the pass of Monte Croce Carnico, stands the Creta Collina (2,689 metres).
Photograph by Ulderica Da Pozzo

175 centre The Creta di Aip (2,279 metres), one of the most interesting peaks in the Carnic Alps, can be seen in this photograph taken at Sella Valdolce. It was scaled for the first time in 1886, and can be climbed nowadays by about thirty different routes.
Photograph by Ulderica Da Pozzo

175 bottom Camporosso in Val Canale (835 metres), is one of the most enchanting little villages in the area around Tarvisio, toward the end of the route. The village is located on the watershed between the rivers Tagliamento and Gail, which is to say, between the Adriatic Sea and the river Danube.
Photograph by Marco Milani/K3

reaches the border at the saddle of Spalla (1,432 metres), and then on, obliquely along the Italian faces, in the high valley of the Rio Bianco, which narrows, further downhill, into a splendid ravine that is protected by a State Nature Reserve. After crossing the saddle of Rio Bianco (Zillensattel, 1,497 metres), one continues to the saddle of Chersenizza and to the Egger Alm (1,415 metre), winding up in the heart of a splendid hollow of pastureland.

the Gortschacher Alp (1,649 metres). One then climbs sharply upward toward the saddle (1,886 metres) that separates the peaks of the Sagran and the Starhand. A quick climb down leads to the Whirthaus Starhand (1,459 metres), a comfortable hut that can be reached via a road that runs up from the valley of the Gail. From here, a good trail runs up to the narrow saddle of Lom (1,499 metres) descending further along to the Nordio-Deffar hut (1,210 metres), at the edge of a dark and dense evergreen forest.

NINTH DAY
*from the Nordio-Deffar hut
to Goriacher Alm
distance climbed: 1,360 metres
distance descended: 920 metres
time: 6 hours*

This stage is chiefly devoted to the Oisternig to stand higher than 2,000 metres, and it offers the umpteenth spectacular view of the crossing. This stage features, in particular, the giants of the Julian Alps, from the Jof Fuart to the Mangart, from the Triglav to the Jof of Montasio. Reaching Tarvisio before nightfall is certainly not out of the question. One begins by climbing back up the trail that one has already

TENTH DAY
*from Goriacher Alm to Tarvisio
distance descended: 960 metres
time: 3 hours*

The final day of walking consists of a quick descent, with the Julian Alps unfailingly in sight, along with the great forest that spreads out at their feet; this trail leads rapidly to Coccau, close to the border and just a few kilometres from Tarvisio. The trail runs back into Italy, and then descends among forest clearings to the edge of the forest of the Inferno Couloir. One walks through the heart of the forest to Coccau (672 metres). On foot or by bus, one quickly covers the four kilometres from here to Tarvisio.

covered, and then turning to one's right, at the foot of the southern face of the mountain, all the way to the Sella Bistrizza and the Wirthaus Oisternig (1,722 metres). A trail leading through the meadows takes one right up to the peak of the Oisternig (2,052 metres) and the spectacular view from up there. After returning to the hotel, one continues south along the broad grassy ridge line that leads to the Schonwipfel hut (1,712 metres), and from there one can quickly climb up to the nearby Mount Acomizza (1,813 metres). A good trail runs down its eastern ridge all the way down to the Sella di Bartolo (1,175 metres), and from there a dirt road runs down to Camporosso. One then climbs onward and upward along the crest that runs around the gully of Canale of Strabuzza, one passes by a shoulder (1,489 metres), skirting to the left of the Mount Capin di Ponente, and then one continues along the crest all the way to the Mount Goriane (1,693 metres) and the Goriacher Alm (1,644 metres).

176 The light of sunset transforms the dizzying faces of Monte Rosa into a spectacular symphony of colours.
Photograph by Marcello Bertinetti/ White Star